"In this fascinating and readable book, Jane Duffus gives us a real taste of the amazing women who built Bristol and links it superbly to women's achievements and women's oppression worldwide."
Julie Bindel, journalist and feminist activist

"Jane's amazing book will have you captivated with insights about the awesome women who shaped Bristol and leave you feeling inspired to go out and make your own mark on the world."
Kate Smurthwaite, comedian and feminist activist

"Jane Duffus has done a brilliant job of restoring these 'forgotten' women to their rightful place in history. Important and colourful stories, passionately researched and beautifully told. I love this project."
Viv Groskop, journalist and broadcaster

"Our ability to understand the present day is hampered when the circumstances of women in the past remain unrecorded. Jane Duffus continues to redress this imbalance by illuminating women whose legacy, whether for good or bad, helped form Bristol."
Lord-Lieutenant Peaches Golding OBE, feminist and entrepreneur

"The reading of these tales is as compelling as a good detective story. Jane Duffus is bringing us part of the missing record of who and what makes Bristol. This book includes the shining exceptions, the pioneers and the trailblazers as well as the women who played their part in making Bristol but were never celebrated in their time."
Thangam Debbonaire, politician

"A fascinating and engaging glimpse into the quietly (and not so quietly) heroic lives of the many women whose contributions to Bristol's history have been forgotten or unfairly sidelined over the years, or even simply barely known about – [Jane's] research is as exhaustive as it is impeccable."
Matthew, reader review via email

"Was given this and the other volume as a present and have really loved them. Really bringing Bristol to life for me, and how terrible these amazing stories of these women had not been shared before. Very readable and so important to hear these stories. Great book."
Elaine, Reader review on Amazon

"This is a great idea and a great book that celebrates the history of women and women's activism in Bristol. You can dip into it and find someone immediately interesting and it has something for everyone - whether you are interested in women's history, local history, or political history. I love the cover image too!"
PMT, reader review on Amazon

"The Women Who Built Bristol is an exciting compendium of women who have pushed boundaries, and pioneered social and scientific breakthroughs ... This is a thought-provoking, inspiring and fierce book, giving much-deserved prominence to a lot of courageous women, many of whom would otherwise have lacked it. It's a considerable undertaking to pull together such a book, too, which makes it all the more commendable. This is definitely a book to buy and to keep going back to over the years."
Tom Nash, The Heroine Collective review

◆Tangent Books

The Women Who Built Bristol: Volume Three
First published 2025 by Tangent Books

Tangent Books
www.tangentbooks.co.uk
richard@tangentbooks.co.uk

ISBN 9781914345388

By Jane Duffus

Cover illustration: Tina Altwegg
Cover design: Joe Burt
Typesetting: Joe Burt (www.wildsparkdesign.com)

A CIP record of this book is available at the British Library.

Printed by Short Run Press, Exeter using paper from a sustainable source.

This book is dedicated to the wonderful
women in my life who have propped
me up through a tricky few years.
Thank you x

FOREWORD

By Helen Holland MBE

Many years ago, I attended a training session on media and communications and one of the statements made by the trainers has stayed with me all this time. It was that the press are interested in "ordinary people doing extraordinary things and extraordinary people doing ordinary things".

Reading the third volume of *The Women Who Built Bristol*, this thought kept coming back to me, over and over again.

Here we have another book full of wonderful women, some very ordinary on the face of it, and others with extraordinary lives but their backgrounds, experiences, influences and stories, whatever their 'station' in life, have contributed to the Bristol we know and love today. Bringing their stories to life, Jane paints pictures that make you say: "There are women I wish we knew more about". Knowing the streets where these women lived and worked means that, after reading this volume, you will always remember those connections in future, or want to go and find those locations and discover more of their herstory.

Walking down Chessel Street in Bedminster, as I often do, I always look up to the blue plaque reminding us that Jessie Stephen (who is profiled in Volume One of *The Women Who Built Bristol*) lived there. Incidentally, a few years ago, when a telegraph pole was erected obliterating the view of Jessie's plaque, we complained, the story was picked up by the *Bristol Post*, and the pole was removed soon after. I feel a real connection to Jessie because, in 1982, when I was elected as Secretary of the (then) Bristol Labour Women's Council, there was a group of older women activists and trade unionists who were regular attendees of our monthly meetings (held in the upstairs room at The

Rummer in St Nicholas Market) and who were contemporaries of Jessie's. The archive of Bristol Labour Women's Council was full of minutes of meetings, articles from local newspapers and photographs, and I wish I still had those records. Ellen Malos, one of the socialist feminist women included in this volume, was also a member of the Women's Council and it is impossible to quantify the combined impact locally, nationally and internationally of that membership on legislation, policy and culture.

The first two volumes of *The Women Who Built Bristol* have included women who were Bristol city councillors (including Jessie) from the earliest days of the franchise and, over my 33 years as an elected member on Bristol City Council, I would frequently show people around the wonderful Council House (now called City Hall) and pause in the Conference Hall (now called the Queen Elizabeth II Conference Hall). Every Mayor and Lord Mayor since 1216 is listed, carved into the stone in perpetuity. You might start looking for a woman's name on the right hand wall as you walk in, but let me save you time by saying you won't find one there. Indeed, even on the left hand wall, you will be three-quarters of the way down before you find Florence Brown's name, the first woman to become Bristol's First Citizen in 1963. It only took 740 years! (Florence is profiled in Volume One of *The Women Who Built Bristol*.)

One woman who I knew very well and worked with on the City Council was Joan McLaren, who I was so pleased to see is an entry in this volume, and she is also one of those illustrious names on the wall. When the Labour Group of councillors elected Joan as our nomination for Lord Mayor for the succeeding year, and a male councillor was put up to stand against her, Joan, looking at those walls with those names, just said: "All those men...". She won the nomination!

This volume of *The Women Who Built Bristol* will, as the two earlier ones did, leave you wanting to know more, to go and look at homes, workplaces, churches, shops and see where these women lived their lives. It will strike chords that remind us that the Bristol we share today is the product of hundreds of ordinary and extraordinary women, and it will remind us to remember and recognise those sisters as we carry their banner forward.

When Labour's **Helen Holland** stepped down from Bristol City Council in 2024, she did so as the city's longest-serving Councillor in recent times having been a member for 33 years. Between 2007 and 2009, Helen was the Leader of Bristol City Council, and was also the Leader of the Labour Group in Bristol for ten years. Initially a special needs teacher, Helen moved from Nottingham to Bristol in 1975 and went on to represent Hartcliffe and Withywood for three decades (she was re-elected eight times) as well as to take up several cabinet positions including Planning, Transport & Development, Partnerships & Regeneration and, from 2017- 2024, Adult Social Care. During her time with Bristol City Council, Helen helped to deliver several major projects including the Cabot Circus Shopping Centre and the restoration of Queen Square. Alongside her council work, Helen held roles on the boards of numerous charity and community organisations and gave her time generously to support Bristol and its citizens. Helen has championed women's issues and representation through her Labour Party membership, serving on the South West Regional Labour Women's Committee, National Labour Women's Committee, and as a Bristol City Councillor from the then-Women's Committee when first elected, through to the Bristol Women's Commission as the Mayor's representative. She has also served on regional, national and European forums, and worked with the Local Government Association, supporting councils and councillors across the country.

INTRODUCTION

By Jane Duffus

As I sit here looking at another 250 women from the past whose stories have been written down in the hope that their names will live on, it dawns on me that *The Women Who Built Bristol* books are really a reflection on grief.

We will all grieve, it's an inevitable part of loving someone. But when, in January 2024, I started pulling this book together from all the notes I had amassed in the previous few years, I was doing so having recently lost my own mother.

Initially I couldn't face the idea of trawling through the lives of all these impressive dead women. And when I did start writing, I found myself feeling irrationally bitter about the many women whose lives had been longer than my mother's had been. Where was the fairness in that? But when you start reading about these women's stories, where is the fairness in any of it? It's not fair that women have been written out of history for so long, nor that their lives have been so much harder than those of the men who occupied the same spaces but did so more noticeably.

Having always affectionately, and informally, referred to the women I write about as 'my old dead women', I began to wonder if maybe this was too flippant. After all, the women I am writing about are not just names, they are also somebody's relative. These women might be dead, but (hopefully) they once had people who loved them. However, I decided that most of these women seemed like they had a good sense of humour and would probably take 'my old dead women' in the warm spirit with which it is intended. I've always tried to be respectful when telling the stories of these women. And while not all of the 750 women in the three volumes of *The Women Who Built Bristol* are what we might consider sheroes, I firmly believe that each of them has a story that needs to be shared and a name that needs to be heard. And names are important. I bang on about names a lot.

There is a lot of weight to be felt in a woman's name because, unlike a man's name, a woman's name is likely to change throughout her life yet at no point is it ever really her own. Historically, babies were often given first names that had belonged to deceased members of the family. And the surname that a child of a married couple would be given would be her father's name. While the surname of a child born to an unmarried couple is also typically the father's, meaning the child has a level of separation from its mother in official records. If a daughter marries, her surname often changes to that of her husband's family. There's the practical fact that this change makes it difficult for historians to follow this woman through resources such as census reports and family trees. But there's also the abstract fact that a woman rarely keeps her own name during her life, meaning she has to work doubly hard to forge her own identity.

That's essentially all I want to do with these books: keep these women's names in the conversation. This is the third volume of *The Women Who Built Bristol*, which means we now have the stories of 750 women collected across the series so far. But it's not a lot. Considering that the books span roughly 1,000 years, that's not even one woman a year. I already have more than 100 women in my notes for a potential Volume Four and that list keeps on growing. Just as a handful of examples, Bristolian women I'd love to find out more about include the tightrope walker Mary Aherne, sweet shop owner Edna Huddlestone, bus conductor Daisy Marshall and workhouse matron Sarah Player.

Across all *The Women Who Built Bristol* books, diversity is important. Obviously, the reason for these books was the lack of diversity in most existing history resources which largely favoured men's history but don't have the courage to label themselves as books about men's history. Personally, I think it's much more effective to own your discrimination! Between 2012 and 2018, I ran the all-female What The Frock! Comedy project, exclusively championing the talents of women in the comedy circuit: an environment that was (and is) disproportionately male-heavy and where many comedy clubs would (and do) host all-male line-ups but don't have the balls to identify themselves as men's comedy clubs.

I actively want to profile less privileged voices, which are often overlooked in history books, whether female or male. And race is also something I am very aware of. Clearly, Bristol has a difficult history here due to its involvement in the trading of enslaved people but the race issue extends beyond this. As a white woman, I do not feel best placed to be speaking up but equally I should not be making excuses for why there are so few ethnically diverse women represented here. This is certainly not for the want of trying to find stories about these women's experiences and I would warmly welcome suggestions to include in any further books. You are invited to get in touch with me via the 'contact' page of my website, janeduffus.com

Thank you so much for your continued support of *The Women Who Built Bristol* series. So much has happened with this project since 2017, when work on Volume One began, and it has been humbling to see how the extraordinary women within the pages have been embraced and celebrated by readers. Wherever you live, please never stop looking for stories about women and please never stop saying their names. The problem of women having been erased from history is certainly not exclusive to Bristol and sadly applies to every single corner of the globe. So please keep on searching and sharing the stories of all the wonderful women you hear about.

A NOTE ABOUT THE COVER OF THIS BOOK

The Bristol-based artist Tina Altwegg was commissioned to design the cover of this book after I was blown away by her interior illustrations for Volume Two back in 2019. I also worked with Tina on a separate book project in 2021.

Tina and I sat down over tea and cake in Bedminster one morning to discuss which women from Volume Three would be the most suitable to represent the 250 sheroes within these pages. And because this volume has a strong theme of working women, Tina decided to lean into the many varied industries that Bristol's women worked in… and, in many cases, which today's Bristolian women continue to work in.

I made it very clear that I felt we absolutely definitely needed a woman in a big hat, because I had come across so many grainy newspaper photographs of redoubtable and fine women in big hats while researching all three volumes of *The Women Who Built Bristol* - although none have struck a chord in my heart more than Miss FM Townsend. Therefore, at the bottom of the front cover, carrying the weight of all Bristol's women and girls, is Miss FM Townsend and her extraordinarily large hat. I have come to adore the Philanthropist Fanny Townsend and invite you to also fall in love with her. What a woman!

Swimming across the brim of Miss Townsend's massive hat is a woman representing Pat Charles or Jenny James, who both achieved astonishing feats in the water. They are joined on the hat by Ice Cream Vendor Maria Policella, Builder Isabel Hatherley (who owned a building company, although wasn't literally a builder but, you know…) For bonus points, Isabel is wielding her chisel beside the Bristol Cenotaph, which was designed by the Architect Eveline Blacker, who you can find in Volume One.

Keeping Miss Townsend's hat balanced on the right hand side we have a hard-working Midwife (we have several midwives in this volume, but I'd like to particularly draw your attention to Margaret Jaycock and Lizzie Walker).

Winding their way up one of the steep Bristolian roads that we all know so well we find Mycologist Lilian Hawker examining some spores; then we have one of the seven Doctors profiled in this book; who is standing beside Photographer Gladys 'Brownie' Brownlee (honestly, you'll just love her far-reaching story); and Brownie is taking the graduation photograph for one of our academics, most likely Dina Dobson-Hinton who was obliged to travel to Dublin in order to receive her graduation certificate; and to mark that achievement she is enjoying a drink poured by one of the three pub Landladies celebrated in this book.

Finally, on the top layer of this illustration, winding their way up towards Pilot Constance Leathart in her World War Two plane, we first meet Musician Mabel Downing playing her mandolin. To Mabel's left is the Astronomer Irene Toye Warner-Staples, gazing up at the night sky as well as Bristol's famous hot air balloons; and last, but by no means least, we have a young woman working hard at the Great Western Cotton Factory loom who represents the many women included in these pages who shed blood, sweat and tears in the various factories that Bristol has housed over the centuries. And if you think that the loom bears a passing resemblance to a famous bridge in Clifton, well, that's up to you and your imagination.

Tina has done the 250 women in these pages proud with her wonderful illustration and I'm so appreciative of all of her talent and efforts. If you'd like to see more of Tina's work, you can find her on Instagram: @winged_fox

A-Z OF THE WOMEN WHO BUILT BRISTOL

HILDA ADAMS
1890–1972, DOCTOR

In 1909, Hilda Ewins (as she was born) was one of the first women to be admitted to Bristol University's Medical School, following hot on the heels of Kathleen Cole[1], who was the very first woman admitted in 1907. However, the school was distinctly unenthusiastic about having either Hilda or Kathleen in its fold because, urgh, who would ever want or trust a lady doctor so, really, what was the point?

While begrudgingly allowing the two women to attend lectures, the School steadfastly refused to admit them to the residents' dining room with the rest of the student doctors (aka the male students). Instead the women had to eat their meals with the nurses, despite those meal times being completely unsuitable for the erratic hours kept by a student doctor. Hilda later said: "I became terribly thin because I could not get enough to eat." To make matters worse, she also struggled to get enough rest because she was told it was "not nice" for young women to sleep at the hospital where all the male medical students rested, yet no alternative sleeping facilities were provided for the women. There weren't many women so they didn't need much space. But still, not one tiny little room could be found for them. Sigh.[2]

Hilda had been born in Bedminster and was one of four children. Her mother Paulina had died when Hilda was just nine, and her father worked as a clerk. With this childhood, it is even more impressive that she went on to break ground as a woman in the male-dominated field of medicine.

Hilda worked in a number of hospitals in Bristol before moving to Guildford where she became the lone woman doctor

1   Kathleen Cole has her own entry in this volume.
2   'Obituary: Dr Hilda Adams', *Bristol Evening Post*, 10 July 1972.

at a GP surgery. She married Arthur Adams in 1918 when she was 28. They moved to Cambridge and had one son, who became paralysed after contracting polio. However, with Hilda's help and medical knowledge, her son went on to complete a degree and find work to support himself.

SARAH ASHMEAD
1796-1876, ABOLITIONIST

When Sarah Merrick married land surveyor and map maker George Ashmead in 1823 she became an ardent supporter of his campaign to abolish slavery. Sarah and George became abolitionists early in the 1830s, regularly attending meetings about the rights of dissenters and on the topic of anti-slavery. George was also the Secretary of the Bristol Anti-Slavery Association and, in a letter to the *Bristol Mercury*, he asserted that slavery was: "The foulest stigma which has ever stained the nation".[3] Slavery was abolished in the UK in 1833 but continued in the US until 1865, and the Ashmeads remained steadfast in their abolitionist views and actions.

ARABELLA ASTRY
1694–1722, HEIRESS

The story of slavery in Bristol and the surrounding area is well known but there is always a great deal more to be learned. And this is why Arabella Astry[4] is included here. She was the privileged daughter of Sir Samuel and Elizabeth Astry. After her

3   arnosvale.org.uk/george-culley-ashmead
4   Although sometimes the name is spelled 'Astrey', 'Astry' seems more common.

1715 marriage to Charles Howard, she set up home at Henbury House, also known as The Great House, a few miles north-west of Bristol. This was an impressive house with large gardens and a formal avenue leading up to the property. Arabella had inherited the home after her father's death in 1712.

In the grounds of the property is a colourful gravestone for Scipio Africanus, an enslaved man who is thought to have lived from 1702 to 1720. The story of how Scipio came to the house is not recorded. Some reports suggest he was born there as the son of an enslaved West African woman. However, Charles' father had been President of the Board of Trade and Plantations between 1715 and 1718, during which time approximately 54,000 enslaved Africans were taken to the Americas and, given Scipio's age, it could be that the Howard family received him during this time.[5] It is also believed that Scipio had been freed before his death at the age of 18. The elaborate grave he was given, which is out of character with most in the graveyard, suggests Scipio was held in high esteem by the family.

Both Arabella and Scipio's stories highlight the need to record these largely unwritten lives.

ETHEL BAKER
1884–1941, WRITER

Born in Clifton on 11 January 1884, Ethel Winifred Baker is possibly better known (in relative terms, admittedly) for the character of Ann Green.

Inspired by a simple gravestone for the real Ann Green in a Clifton churchyard, Ethel decided to write a romantic novel

5   Dr Laurence Brown, 2010, *The Slavery Connections of Marble Hill House*, University of Manchester.

called *Ann Green of Clifton*, which was published in 1936. Ethel was possibly aided by the fact that her father James had been a Bookseller and Bookbinder on The Mall in Clifton. The Baker family was deeply religious so it is perhaps not surprising that young Ethel was drawn to graveyards.

Miss Ann Green of Clifton, republished in 1974, draws heavily on the local environment, encompassing the history and botany of Bristol, and giving mention to various local places and characters such as the former gallows on Pembroke Road and the artist Rolinda Sharples[6]. The fictional Ann is the daughter of a Bristol merchant living at Clifton Court (now the Nuffield Hospital). She falls in love with an Oxford don who is keen for economic and social reform. But, of course, their romance is tested and the would-be-lovers have all sorts of romantic hurdles to clamber over on the path to happiness.

The real Ann Green, according to research done by William Evans, was born around 1810 and, by 1839, was running a lodging house at 13 Buckingham Place in Clifton. By 1863, she was running another lodging house in Lower Harley Place in Clifton, off Canynge Road. She died in the mid-1860s of cancer.[7] By 1939, Ethel was living in the same area as fictional Ann, with Ethel's home being 34 Canynge Square.

In addition to *Miss Ann Green of Clifton*, Ethel's writing veered between poetry, prose, plays and fiction. Her other works include *Rose of the Spirit: Unison Song* (1931), *Dowry Square* (1936) and *Penelope* (1939). Ethel's manuscripts from 1915-1939 are stored at the University of Bristol. However, writing wasn't Ethel's only accomplishment. After attending Clifton High School from 1897 to 1904, she trained as a social worker in Bristol. There are also suggestions she may have worked as a gardener. She never

6   Rolinda Sharples is profiled in Volume One of *The Women Who Built Bristol*.
7   uwe.ac.uk/faculties/CAHE/Documents/Research/Regional-history/RH4Evans.pdf

married or had children. Ethel is buried at St Andrew's Church in Clifton and her gravestone is in what is now known as Birdcage Walk.[8] At her funeral in 1941, a verse of *Rose of the Spirit* was performed to music.

ADA BALLS
1875–1967, TITANIC SURVIVOR

London-born Ada Elizabeth Hall had a humble beginning as the youngest of seven siblings to a family in Hackney. Ada's first job involved working in a coffee house. Her 1896 marriage to Martin Balls saw her become Ada Balls, a name that would become embedded in maritime history.

Living in Essex, Ada and Martin had two sons but Martin died in 1902. To support the family, Ada began to take in laundry alongside her work as a live-in parlourmaid in London, while her sons went to live with one of Ada's brothers. Meanwhile, one of Ada's sisters, Emily, had married a Bristolian man called the Rev James Bateman with whom she had emigrated to Florida.

Recognising that Ada would have a much better quality of life if she joined her in the US, Emily persuaded her sister to sail to the US with James, who had been in Bristol visiting his family in Staple Hill. The plan was for Ada's sons to sail over and join her at a later date. So Ada travelled to Bristol to join John, and therefore Staple Hill became her last British address before they set sail.

Ada and James boarded the Titanic in Southampton on 10 April 1912 as second-class passengers. Ada had ticket number 28851 which had cost £13. She had attended a prayer meeting in

---

8   The Helen Dunmore historical novel *Birdcage Walk* (2017) is, as the name suggests, inspired by this beautiful area of Bristol and is well worth a read. Helen Dunmore is profiled in Volume One of *The Women Who Built Bristol*.

the second-class dining-room on the night of 12 April, and she went to bed around 10.30pm. Therefore she was fast asleep when the Titanic fatefully struck an iceberg.

Her room mate, Marie Jerwan, woke Ada exclaiming: "We've had an accident!" But a weary Ada took no notice and returned to sleep. She was only roused to wake properly when her brother-in-law James came to the cabin and insisted that Ada get dressed and come on deck immediately. Once outside, James helped Ada into one of the lifeboats and, as her boat was lowered to the water, he called out: "If I don't meet you again in this world, I will in the next." James was one of the 1,517 people who drowned that night.

Although one of the very last people to leave the ship, Ada survived the sinking of the Titanic and made it to the US, settling in Baltimore, where her sons joined her the following year. In 1925, she married an American man named William Perrine. Ada's story was written up as a poem by her friend Lottie Hasler under the title 'Lessons from the Loss of the Titanic', which was published in a 1920 book called *Poems of Progress*.

RHODA BARNES
1901-1993, TOBACCO FACTORY WORKER

Strange as it might seem to younger readers, in the past it was not uncommon for people to live in the same house for their entire life. And Rhoda Barnes lived at 88 Parson Street for at least 84 of her 92 years. Back when Rhoda was a child, her home at the very end of Parson Street was at the edge of what was the boundary of Bristol: of course, in the intervening years, Bristol's boundary has eked itself further and further out.[9]

---

9   The house is still there although, with a modern addition at No 90, it is no longer the house at the end of street.

Rhoda was one of seven children born to Florence and Stephen Barnes. Stephen worked in a nail factory, and the household also included Florence's brother and his wife. So we can assume that life at 88 Parson Street (which was not a particularly big property) was pretty cosy.

Recalling what life was like in Southville at the start of the last century, Rhoda remembered three farmers' barns along Parson Street (1: Withers on the Bridge, 2: Sawrells and 3: Hoopers), and farmers walking their 50 cows up and down Parson Street every day to take them to graze in the fields. Rhoda also remembers sitting on the doorstep of No 88 with her sister and listening to the call of the plovers in the field opposite: a bird that is now all but extinct. Nightingales could be heard singing in the fields, and peacocks were kept in the garden of a mansion house that used to stand nearby.

Animals and nature featured heavily in Rhoda's childhood, and when she was 12 she had a donkey who grazed with the horses on the Novers Slopes before being stabled nearby overnight. Driving the donkey and cart, Rhoda would take her friends for outings to Bishopsworth Common, Whitchurch Lane and Headley Lane before coming back to the Novers.

Other timely reminders of the past that Rhoda remembers from her childhood include the lamplighter who would come daily and the woman selling cockles from a basket on her head, as well as the fact there seemed to be no crime so nobody locked their doors. She even had a touch of affection for the old privy at the end of the garden, despite the constant swarm of flies which lived in it.

When Parson Street School opened in 1908, Rhoda was there on the first day, attending with the girl who lived next door. Rhoda stayed at school until she turned 14 in 1915 at which point she began work at the Wills Tobacco Factory on Raleigh Road, earning five shillings a week and getting just one week of holiday a year. "I used to love going to work, mind," said Rhoda. "There was a lovely bunch of us, we used to play the forewoman up. I was always the last to get there and just as I got to the door the forewoman would just lock it."[10]

In June 1922, Rhoda married John Smith with whom she had one son, Vernon, who was killed during World War Two when he was just 21.

FREDA BARON
1885–1975, LAND ARMY LEADER

The daughter of the Lord Mayor of Bristol, Freda Baron took an active role in the Women's Land Army during World War One. Prior to the war, she had been living a comfortable life with her family at 18 Whiteladies Road while working as a schoolteacher. Freda was the eldest of three daughters and one son to Barclay, a doctor at the Bristol General Hospital, and his wife Jane. Barclay was also a City Councillor and served as Lord Mayor of Bristol from 1915–1917. He was given a knighthood in the 1918 New Year's Honours. His death, only 18 months later, was so notable that his funeral was held at Bristol Cathedral.

As Lord Mayor, Barclay took a keen interest in the recruitment campaign for soldiers and, as a doctor, he paid close attention to the welfare of wounded soldiers who were returning to Bristol: he would often meet the ambulance trains at Temple Meads. To support her father's war work, Freda became active in the Women's Land Army, which began in 1916 as a small scheme to replace the work done by male farmers and farmworkers who

10   Rhoda Barnes, 1988, 'Letter from Parson Street' in *More Bristol Lives*, Bristol Broadsides, p146-147.

had gone to fight in the war. By the time the war ended, there were 23,000 women in the Land Army. On 7 February 1918, Freda attended a procession of 500 Bristolian women who marched to the Colston Hall[11] for a meeting that called for increased food production and a greater enrolment in the Land Army. A photo survives of a uniformed Freda striding out while leading a group of recruits on a training exercise in Devon.

In 1965, Freda wrote a booklet called *The Lighter Side of Life of a Lord Mayor's Daughter*, which covered the years 1915–1917. One of the accounts it detailed covered a lunch held at the Mansion House in 1917, in which a group of Indian cavalry officers was entertained. She noted: "I was sitting next to a Sikh, rather fearsome, with his hair tucked up under his turban and his black beard. We could not, unfortunately, speak each other's language, but by dint of smiling at each other constantly, I felt we were friends by the time lunch ended."[12]

After the war, Freda took up a post at the Bristol Employment Exchange, where she led the Women's and Juvenile Department. One issue that her team was concerned with was the difficulty that wealthy households had with obtaining and retaining good servants. At a national inquiry into the problem, which was held in London, Freda explained that going into service had something of a PR problem: "[Freda] believed that domestic work was still looked upon by many workers in other occupations as the lowest and most menial kind of work. Girls were thus prejudiced about service without knowing anything about it."[13]

In the 1939 Register, Freda, who remained single throughout her life, was helping to run a women's boarding house at

---

11   While I acknowledge the Colston Hall has now rightly been renamed and is now called the Bristol Beacon, I am referring to it by its original name in this book because that is the name it was known by when the events in the book happened.
12   Clive Burlton, 'Sikh the Truth on the Role of Men From India Who Fought in World Wars', *Bristol Evening Post*, 26 March 2019.
13   'Why servants are scarce', *Western Daily Press*, 15 May 1923.

Cheltenham Ladies' College. By the time of her death in 1974, she was back in Bristol, living on Pembroke Road, Clifton.

LUCY BEAUMONT
1869–1937, ACTOR

In 1919, aged 50, Lucy Beaumont achieved something that would be almost impossible for a woman to do in 2025: she acted in her first movie. Not only that, but she would go on to appear in almost 60 films, acting right up until her death.

However, it is a little misleading of me to imply that when she moved into movies at the age of 50 Lucy was a newcomer to performing, because for 27 years previous to that she had been a much respected theatre actor. Lucy cut her theatrical teeth in Bristol where she was no stranger to the stage, whether being cast in pantomimes at the Prince's Theatre on Park Row or performing in comedies elsewhere in the city.

Lucy Emily Pinkstone may have been born in London but she was educated at Clifton High School after her family returned to Bristol when she was a toddler; her parents were originally from Bedminster. Her first marriage was to fellow actor William Beaumont in 1889 when Lucy was 20. They divorced in 1899 due to Lucy's relationship with another actor, Douglas Harris, whom she married as soon as her divorce came through. This second marriage lasted until Lucy's death. She had no children with either man.

Movie casting directors made the most of Lucy's petite stature of 5ft and regularly put her in the role of women who were older than her actual age, meaning that Lucy built an impressive résumé of matrons and mothers among her 60 films. This trend began with her first role, as Widow Mackey in *Sandy Burke of the*

U-Bar-U (1919), and continued to her final role in 1937 as Nurse Rebecca in *Maid of Salem*.

Although 21st century Bristolians have forgotten Lucy, back in the 1930s things were very different. For example, during the Equity strike of 1919, Lucy was noted for being the first female actor to walk out on strike. And in 1934, there was a radio documentary celebrating her achievements called 'Lucy Beaumont: Bristol's Hollywood Film Mother'.

Writing about her death in New York City, the *Chicago Daily Tribune* noted: "Lucy Beaumont ... known to many as the mother of the screen, died tonight. Miss Beaumont, who had been in the United States 20 years, portrayed mother parts on the screen with some of the leading actors during the past generation."[14]

ANNA BEDDOES
1773-1824, POET

Anna Maria Edgeworth (as she was born) had a great gift for writing romantic poetry.[15] And while her sister Maria Edgeworth[16] is already appreciated for her writing about education and her many moral novels, the talents of her sister Anna have largely been overlooked until fairly recently. Five years younger than Maria, Anna wrote passionate and melancholic poems to colleagues of her husband during a period of deep unhappiness and frustration.[17]

In April 1794, Anna married Experimental Physician Dr Thomas Beddoes, moving from her family home in Edgeworthstown, Ireland, to join him in Bristol. Significantly,

14 'Obituary', Chicago Daily Tribune, 25 April 1937.
15 Wahida Amin, 2013, 'The Poetry and Science of Humphry Davy', University of Salford.
16 Maria Edgeworth is profiled in Volume One of *The Women Who Built Bristol*.
17 beddoes.dmu.ac.uk/annabeddoes

Thomas was trying to find a cure for consumption, which had caused the death of some of Anna's siblings as well as her two stepmothers. Thomas felt the cure lay with inhaling a variety of gases. From 1799 to 1801, he employed chemist Humphry Davy as his Apprentice and Superintendent at the Medical Pneumatic Institute, and their laboratory in Dowry Square, Hotwells, was a lively and exciting place.

Records show that Thomas and Humphry had many volunteers, including members of Anna's family, and others from the fields of science and engineering. Their experiments with nitrous oxide and its effects (Humphry called it 'laughing gas') attracted the Romantic poets Samuel Taylor Coleridge and Robert Southey. We know that Anna had volunteered at the Institute because Thomas recorded in 1799 how Anna, when walking up Clifton Hill, "frequently seemed to be ascending like a balloon"[18].

It quickly became obvious that the detailed experimentation with gases had failed to find a cure for consumption and Humphry left in 1801. Anna maintained contact with him, and her private letters and poems tell us that an intense relationship existed between the two.[19] Anna's poems from 1803 to 1806, found in letters to Humphry, have more recently been recognised for their content and style. Her poetry showed an elegance in the way she wrote about her loneliness and frustration. It is significant that Humphry copied some of Anna's poems alongside his own poetry to her and placed them beside his scientific experiments. Humphry's notebooks typify the time when the arts and sciences were not seen as separate entities.[20]

Anna's poems of loneliness and passion were also found in the private letters of another colleague of her husband, Davies Giddy,

18   Thomas Beddoes, 1799, *Notice of Some Observations Made at the Medical Pneumatic Institute*, Biggs & Cottle, p10.

19   digitalcollections-staging.lancaster.ac.uk/collections/davy/1

20   Richard Holmes, 2008, 'Davy on the Gas' in *The Age of Wonder*, Harper Press, p235-304.

an engineer and consumption patient. Anna turned to Davies for moral support, particularly when she was widowed in 1808 aged just 35. Her loneliness was exacerbated when Davies had married earlier that year, and Humphry went on to marry in 1812.

Davies continued to support Anna as she spent the rest of her days ensuring her four children received a good education. The Beddoes children were born between 1801 and 1808 during the only time we know that she wrote such emotional poetry. It is possible, although it's pure speculation, that an increasingly unwell Thomas may not have fathered all of Anna's children.[21]

Anna died in Florence, Italy, during a trip with her daughters. Two years after her death, and with great poignancy, Humphry penned a significant poem. Unhappy in his marriage, the poem is most likely about Anna and strongly hints at his love for her. In Greek, he refers to Anna as "above mortality".[22]

MARY BENGOUGH
1841–1917, SUFFRAGIST

One of the 13 Bristolian women who signed the 1866 mass women's suffrage petition was Mary Bengough. That only 13 women from Bristol were among the 1,500 signatories is unusual, but what's less unusual is that Mary signed as simply 'M T Bengough' to obscure her identity. Nor is it unusual that she gave her address as being in an area of Bristol that wasn't where she actually lived. Mary states she lived in Stapleton when all the evidence suggests she lived in Clifton: the 1881 census shows widowed Mary living there with a daughter and step–daughter. By 1901, the family had

21 Rachel Hewitt, 2017, *A Revolution of Feeling: The Decade that Forged the Modern Mind*, Granta, p380.
22 beddoes.dmu.ac.uk/annabeddoes. With enormous thanks to Carrie Dunne and John Beddoes for all of their help with this entry.

relocated to London. Unfortunately, we don't know more about Mary or what prompted her to be one of the 13 bold Bristolian women to sign this historical petition. But the fact she did makes her worth remembering, however briefly.

PAT BENNETT, BEATRICE HARRIS & KATHLEEN SPACEY
FAMILY OF ST PAULS WOMEN

Author's note: In 1983, Pat Bennett, a school cleaner, was interviewed by children from St Barnabas School for a Bristol Broadsides book. She was interviewed with her mother Kathleen Spacey (born Kathleen Harris) and her aunt Beatrice Harris, and the three women talked about their extraordinary ordinary lives. Because this entry covers three related women and their lives, it is presented differently to most others in this book.

Kathleen Broderick (1914–1999) was born at Francis Place in St James Barton. With her labourer husband David Spacey she had six children, although two died in infancy. One of her surviving daughters was Pat Bennett, who we will meet later in this entry. One of Kathleen's younger sisters was Beatrice Broderick (1919–2006) and by the time Beatrice was born the family was living at 3 Walter Street, St Pauls. Their mother, Rose Broderick, gave birth to all of her babies at home, with either Sister Harper from the Bristol Royal Infirmary or "a good neighbour" helping: "They didn't have babies in the BRI in them days," said Kathleen.

Kathleen and Beatrice's father, John Broderick, worked in the building trade and served in World War One. As the eldest sibling, Kathleen was expected to help her mother raise the younger children. "They used to look upon me as their mother," she recalled, adding a memory from when she was 13: "I did all the washing. We used to buy sheets of pins. We had to pin all the washing to them. We had to scrub, wash, turn a great big mangle. We worked hard, really. My mother's mangle was tied to the ashbin because she couldn't afford a stand, and it was one of those you turn with the big wooden rollers to squeeze the water out." Kathleen recalls that, although she attended Castle Green School in Old Market, she had to miss a lot of classes because of having to stay home to help her mother, which was a shame as she particularly enjoyed geography and art lessons.

Kathleen's sister Beatrice went to the same school but, with their parents not being able to afford school dinners, the girls went with other working–class children to the nearby tabernacle[23] for a free midday meal: and at Christmas, they got an orange from the tabernacle as a treat!

The children who interviewed the sisters in 1983 asked them what they had done for entertainment in the 1920s: "Walking, mostly, we went on a lot of walks," said Beatrice, adding that Blaise Castle and Blaise Woods were popular destinations. With their father often drinking to excess, it was perhaps preferable to keep out of his way: "We had very hard times. Father was always drunk, wasn't he? We had a new set of china every week," says Kathleen. Their father John was often out of work so family items would sometimes need to be pawned to buy essentials.

After school, Kathleen's first job was at the Ridingberry's factory on Gloucester Lane, St Phillips, where she helped make wooden toys such as wheelbarrows, horses and prams. "I used to upholster little horses, you know, the wooden ones, the seats. Then I went paper sorting at the same place. They'd buy all the waste paper and you'd sort all the different kinds: newspaper,

23   A tabernacle is a place of worship that is usually built of materials such as wood or tin, rather than the stone which is typically used for churches.

craft paper, brown papers, writing papers. They'd bale up and sell them away." Beatrice also worked there: "I loved paper sorting, very interesting, that is if we found anything. If we had bank work, we used to find sixpennies and pennies and ha'pennies. They used to pay for our bit of dinner. I was also in service, doing the housework up in Redland for a rich family."

Thinking about how St Pauls has changed over the years, Kathleen's daughter Pat Bennett said: "People have bathrooms now, which we didn't have when I was a little girl. We used to have a tin bath out the backyard. We used to come in once a week on a Sunday for everybody to bathe. Now you've only got to turn a tap and you've got a nice hot bath, haven't you? ... There was a fish shop. You could only get fish and chips in those days, not like you can today, sausage and chicken." The introduction of heating was also to be celebrated, as was the range of furniture that became available to make the home more comfortable.

After the slum clearance of St Pauls, the families who had lived there were rehoused to Knowle West and they lamented the lack of community in the new estate: "It's very rare you see anyone you know," said Beatrice. "I've got a next door neighbour, well, I never see her, not friendly at all." Thinking back to the community they had enjoyed in St Pauls, she said sadly: "It was very nice, better than what it is now. It used to be really lovely. Everybody was friendly. You could call on your friends, neighbours and all was different then. If you were ill, you could call on them, or if anybody had a baby or anything like that you could call on them, it was quite different." Kathleen added: "Posh people used to live in City Road [St Pauls]. They used to have servants, they all had maids and things like that. We used to live next door to people that was well off but we all played together and mixed with everyone."

Kathleen met her husband David Spacey at the Venture Inn at Knowle West, when he approached her and asked for a chip from the fish and chip wrapper that she was enjoying. They went to church together the next day and, while it wasn't love at first sight, David finally won her heart and they married at St Peter's Registry Office on Castle Street in April 1934. Meanwhile, Beatrice met her husband George at the Crown & Dove pub on Bridewell Street and they married in 1938.

One of Kathleen's daughters was Dorothy Patricia Bennett (1939–2000), known as Pat, who was a young child during World War Two. She attended an infant school on North Street and remembers growing up when food and clothing were still rationed. Later on, Pat was a pupil at the Portway Girls' School in Shirehampton, which was a large school for 800 girls: "I cried the day it was time for leaving, but the times were very hard in those days and your mothers couldn't afford for you to stay on at school like they can today, so I had to leave and get a job." However, Pat had to miss a whole year of school when she spent a year in hospital with partial paralysis and suspected polio: "There was a lot of polio around in those days, especially if you ate ice-cream – it seemed to bring a lot of it on, a certain make of ice-cream.[24] But today you have your sugar lumps[25] at the doctor's and the clinics, which prevent you from having anything like this."

After school, Pat's first job was in a cleaning shop called Brooks in Shirehampton. She also made men's suits for Bedford Tailoring in St Pauls, waited tables in a restaurant in Bath, worked as a 'lollipop lady' for the old St Barnabas School and, by 1983, was a cleaner for the new school. She met her husband in 1958 on a blind date and said: "He must have thought I was all right, he asked to see me again!" Pat acknowledged that she had enjoyed a

24   There was a myth that eating too much ice-cream could cause polio. This myth began because polio cases tended to rise in summer, which was also a time when people ate more ice–cream. However, it is not true. You can eat all the ice-cream you want and you won't get polio. NB: I am not a medical professional.

25   From the early 1950s until 2000, the polio vaccine was typically given on a sugar lump, with the sugar intended to disguise the bitter taste. It is now usually given as an injection.

much more comfortable homelife than her mother or aunt had due to the increase in wages and the developments in modern conveniences: "It [used to be] gas lighting in the houses and gas lighting outside, where you've got your electric lights now in the road. And there wasn't any gadgets like you've got today: electric kettles, irons. There were no Hoovers, you used to brush all your carpets, or put them on the line and beat them."[26]

REENA BHAVNANI
1949–2008, ACTIVIST

In 1958, 11-year-old Reena Bhavnanai and her family emigrated from Delhi, India, to Willesden, London. Reena's parents worked as a teacher and a lawyer and, between them, they instilled a strong sense of right and wrong in their daughter, who came to Bristol to attend university in 1970. Reena's subsequent imprint on our city should never be forgotten.

In the 1970s, Reena helped to set up Bristol Black Sisters and she was a member of the Organisation of Women of African and Asian Descent, which was founded in 1978 and had a branch in Bristol. During her professional career, Reena was committed to researching race, gender and class divides and she demonstrated a relentless commitment to tackling racial and gender inequality. She worked as an Educational Psychologist for schools and clinics and, between 1979 and 1984, she was a Continuing Education Policy Adviser for the BBC. In 1985, Reena became the Education Officer for Racial Equality at Bristol Council, while also lecturing at universities including Oxford.

Despite her cancer diagnosis in the early 2000s, Reena

---

26   Pat Bennett, 1983, in *St Pauls People Talking*, Bristol Broadsides, p38–52.

pushed ahead with her PhD at London's City University, which she completed in 2004. Her subsequent book, *Tackling the Roots of Racism: Lessons for Success,* was published in 2005. Alongside her activism and professional career, Reena was a devoted wife and a mother to two children.

In her obituary, *The Guardian* said: "Reena was down-to-earth, enormous fun and a wise and witty conversationalist. She was also a stylish dresser, a great gossip and a cook whose home was a haven of music, hospitality and conviviality, where friends spent happy hours of banter and drunken political debate ... Reena strove to make ours a better society – and in the process helped to make all who knew her into better people."[27]

EDITH BIRKHEAD
1889-1951, WRITER, ACADEMIC

Hailing from Yorkshire, Edith Birkhead was the youngest of seven children and went on to earn a degree from the University of Liverpool. She immediately threw herself into writing and her first published book was *The Tale of Terror: A Study of the Gothic Romance* in 1921: one of the first books to explore the public fascination with supernatural stories. The reviews for this book were impressive and, in *The Times Literary Supplement,* Virginia Woolf gave a whole page to it. By the time the book was published, Edith had been in post at the University of Bristol for a year as a Lecturer in English Literature and, by 1930, she had been promoted to Senior Lecturer. Edith published two further books in her career, which were also studies of gothic writing.[28]

27   theguardian.com/theguardian/2008/sep/09/1?CMP=gu_com
28   With thanks to Lucy Whitfield for the nomination of Edith Birkhead to this book.

KATE BISHOP
1849-1923, ACTOR

Although born in Lambeth, London, actor Kate Alice Bishop was brought up in Bristol. She began treading the boards at the tender age of 14, when she started appearing in Shakespearean productions: her first ever professional performance was at the Theatre Royal (now the Bristol Old Vic) in 1863. The Bishops were a performative dynasty: her mother Charlotte Bishop, a professor of music, also hailed from Bristol. Kate's father Thomas was an actor as was her brother Alfred, and Kate's daughter Marie Löhr would eventually become an actor, too. This family tradition stretched back to Kate's maternal grandfather William Woulds, who had co-run a theatre in Bath with William Macready (a name familiar to anyone with a passing interest in the Bristol Old Vic[29]).

As a teenager growing up in Bristol, Kate first performed alongside future stars including Helen Terry[30] and Henrietta Hodson as a member of James Chute's theatre company. It didn't take long before her talents were recognised and she was signed up for productions further afield, for example in Manchester and London. Kate's performance as Violet Melrose in *Our Boys* at the Vaudeville Theatre in London was so acclaimed that she stayed in the role for the entire four years and four months of the show's run. By the time *Our Boys* closed in 1879, it had become the longest running theatre show of all time.[31]

In the early 1880s, perhaps prompted by the death of her mother in 1883 and feeling the need for a change, Kate followed

29   Sarah Macready is profiled in Volume One of *The Women Who Built Bristol*, and Mazzarina Macready-Chute is profiled in this volume.
30   Helen Terry is profiled in Volume One of *The Women Who Built Bristol*.
31   Of course, anyone with half an interest in theatre knows that *Our Boys* has since been trumped by Agatha Christie's *The Mousetrap*, which has been running continuously since 1952. For more about Agatha, take a look at her entry in Volume Two because yes, pretty much every woman has a connection to Bristol and, my word, I've made it my job to find it.

a role to Australia where she married Lewis Löhr in 1885, who worked at the Melbourne Opera House. Their daughter Marie was born in 1890 and Kate temporarily retired from acting, although she gave elocution lessons to bolster the family's income. Kate returned to England in 1898 and, by 1900, she was back where she belonged on the West End stage where she remained a much-in-demand performer until her retirement in 1915.

In an interesting turn of events, by the time of Kate's death in 1923, the press broke the news under the headline]Marie Löhr's Mother Is Dead'[32]: which made a refreshing change from all the other newspaper stories about women which typically 'honour' the deceased woman by listing the achievements of the men who raised and/or married her. At least, in Kate's case, it was her daughter who saw the acclaim.

MAY BOLT
dates unknown, SOCIAL WORKER

This is a bit of an oddity but it's an interesting one from a social history perspective. Miss M E Bolt was the live-in proprietor of the Cottage Corner Club in Knowle, which was established in 1935. The Club was opened in October 1936 at a ceremony where the Lady Mayoress, Kathleen Moon, cut the ribbon at 54 Leinster Avenue: a 'cottage' that had been rented out to the Club for use as a social club and learning centre for girls and young women from underprivileged backgrounds. By 1937, the Club was also being used by the Bristol League of Civic Service to coordinate various forms of relief for the poor.

Cottage Corner Club, which was run by a committee linked

---

32 'Foreign news', *New York Clipper,* 4 July 1923.

to the Barton Hill University Settlement and the Juvenile Organisations Committee, offered a range of activities. These included a weekly women's meeting, sports for girls and boys in the field opposite, and a regular visit from a 'poor man's lawyer' (presumably offering affordable legal advice). The cottage quickly became too small for the number of people who wished to attend and so a hut was built next door to accommodate more people.

Caroline Dallimore, who grew up in Knowle, recalled attending the Cottage Corner Club as a child: "There was a high school working girls' club. I started there when I was about 10 ... We would sew, play games and learn about other countries and, later on, when I left school, we would save with the club to go on holidays. I went to Paignton and Teignmouth with the club."[33]

Not an awful lot is known about May Bolt, although she was clearly a pillar of the community because, as well as being the live-in Caretaker and part-time Worker at the Cottage Corner Club, she was also the Honorary Secretary of the nearby Knowle West Community Association, which represented 32 organisations working on the estate. In 1943, a similar Corner Cottage Club was established in Southmead and May helped to set this up. The final mention of May that I can find is from 1949 when she is listed as giving a talk to a local Women's Institute group which was reported as being "a real laugh"[34]. I'll bet it was.

ELIZABETH BOSLEY
1874-1956, BAKER

When her husband Walter Bosley died of cancer in 1908, Elizabeth Ann Bosley and their son William continued the family bakery

---

33 Caroline Dallimore,1977, 'A Wills Lady', in Up Knowle West, Bristol Broadsides, p16-22.
34 'Women's Institutes in the West', Western Daily Press, 24 December 1949.

business at 43 Bedminster Down Road. Born Elizabeth Cook, she married Walter in 1896. In addition to William, there were also four younger children to be provided for, so Elizabeth needed to work hard to keep a roof over all of their heads.

Things were made even harder when William was called up to serve during World War One, leaving home in 1914 when he was just 18. To help with the bakery, Elizabeth employed a number of 'C3 men': people who were considered unfit to fight.[35] However, this also meant they were largely unfit to work, certainly in the hard manual work that Elizabeth needed their help with, leaving her having to do much of the heavy lifting herself, quite literally. And this frequently involved lifting 112 lb sacks of flour unaided. Inevitably, such manual work took its toll on Elizabeth and, by the end of the war, she was described as a wreck.

Elizabeth remarried in 1920, becoming Mrs Donaldson. At that time, she retired from the bakery which William ran after the war with his wife. Elizabeth instead kept home for her new husband, whose job was as a yeast deliverer. We don't need to use too much imagination to guess how they might have met.

MARY BREILLAT
1771–1839, GROUNDBREAKER

Mary Breillat was the very first person to be buried at Arnos Vale Cemetery and the 12–foot high Bath stone obelisk that marks her grave is now considered to be a Grade–II listed monument by Historic England.[36]

35   There were different classifications of fitness for men who were considered for service during World War One. These ranged from A1, which meant the man was fit enough for general service in any capacity, to C3, which meant he could be considered for sedentary work only.
36   Around eight people were buried at Arnos Vale during its first year and it is thought that Mary was the very first of those eight.

Born Mary Holbrook in Bedminster, little is known of Mary's life until she married John Breillat at St Nicholas Church in July 1795. During 44 years of marriage, Mary and John had six children and, given that John is credited as being the person who brought gas street–lighting to Bristol, it is safe to assume the family lived in relative comfort.

Prior to John's involvement, Bristol's street lighting had been largely oil-based meaning that the streets were usually dark after sunset. John had previously worked as a silk dyer but he had tinkered with gas experiments as a hobby since 1811. After being invited to set up the Bristol Gas Light Company in 1815, John established the city's first gas light factory in Temple Back and set to work with his experiments. He earned £150 a year and was given the use of a house for his family in Merchant Street.

John experimented with making gas from coal but this failed to catch on. However, once his son Ebeneezer joined him they had a breakthrough with a coke/coal blend which meant that Bristol was illuminated by gas to honour the coronation of King George IV in 1821. As a result of this, John's gas lighting techniques spread from Bristol to much further afield in the UK. When John died in 1856, he was buried beside Mary at Arnos Vale and Ebeneezer carried on his father's work.

FRANCES FREELING BRODERIP
1830–1878, WRITER

Born in Enfield to poet Thomas Hood and his wife Jane Reynolds, Frances Freeling Broderip was named in honour of her father's friend Sir Frances Freeling, who was the Secretary to the General Post Office. In 1849, Frances married Rev John Broderip who was a Rector in Somerset and the couple had four daughters together.

While her family was growing up, Frances began her writing career and went on to publish 11 books for children, starting with *Chrysal* in 1861 and concluding with *Excursions into Puzzledom* which was published posthumously in 1879. In 1860, Frances and her brother Tom Hood edited and published several volumes of their father's memoirs and poems. Frances died in Clevedon in November 1878 aged just 48, having already survived her husband by 12 years.

PRISCILLA BROTHERHOOD
1815-1888, MATRIARCH

Following her 1835 marriage to Rowland Brotherhood, who worked as a contractor for the Great Western Railway under a certain Isambard Kingdom Brunel, Priscilla Penton exceeded the child-bearing abilities of the then-reigning Queen Victoria by giving birth to 14 children (the monarch had a mere nine, what a lightweight) between 1836 and 1864. All of the children survived to adulthood, which was astonishing for the time. However, the Victorians were very much in favour of large families, believing that to have as many children as possible was a way of showing God what a good and virtuous woman the mother was.

At the time, it was Rowland who received all the credit for bringing such a large family into the world, with many joking that he had fathered a cricket team, yet no mention was made of who had mothered said team. Indeed, Rowland and his sons did go on to form a cricket team in which they filled all the positions themselves; perhaps Priscilla and her daughters were allowed to make the teas? However, Rowland did acknowledge the help and support that his wife afforded him, writing in his memoirs: "I must here say that if I had not been blessed with one of the very best of wives I never could have gone through all I have nor carried out the works I have done without her help. She acted as my cashier, throughout nearly all the works, sometimes drawing the money from the banks, and collecting silver from other sources, and often had to sit up until midnight, counting and tying up many hundreds of pounds in small bags for me to throw out of the trains to the gangs on the maintenance and other works along the line. This she continued to do until the family got too large and the work increased, when her brother came down and took it out of her hands. And I am bound to say that if there was any credit due in carrying out work or bringing up our family, the greater share belonged to my devoted WIFE."

Priscilla had grown up in London where her father William was an excise officer and, after marriage, she and Rowland settled in Chippenham where they raised their large brood. For many years, Priscilla and Rowland would have been at the top of the social ladder in Chippenham, but in the 1860s Rowland's business failed and he lost a great sum of money. The family relocated to Cardiff where Priscilla had to start running her home without the domestic help she had grown used to. Once things picked up, the family moved again, this time settling in Clifton where Priscilla and Rowland enjoyed his retirement with one of their daughters living with them. After living as a widow for five years, Priscilla died in Bristol in 1888 and is buried at Arnos Vale Cemetery.[37]

37   Huge thanks to Lucy Whitfield of The Women Who Made Me project: thewomenwhomademe. wordpress.com/2018/05/22/priscilla-ps-story

RUBY AND ELSIE BROWNE
Ruby 1884-1917; Elsie born 1893,
DISCARDED DAUGHTERS

On 18 September 1896, during a heavy rain storm, sisters Ruby Emily (aged 12) and Elsie Winnie Browne (aged three) endured an horrific ordeal at the hands of their father, Birmingham-based grocer Charlie Browne. Facing bankruptcy and feeling utterly desperate, Charlie took his two daughters to the Clifton Suspension Bridge in the middle of the night and threw them over the edge, thinking that by reducing the size of his family (he had left a third daughter and two sons at home in Birmingham with his wife) he would reduce the size of his living costs.

By an astonishing twist of good fortune, a boat was passing underneath the bridge in the wee hours, the crew picked up the unconscious girls and brought them to the shore. Once on land, the sailors rushed the girls into a nearby hotel before the police were summoned. Two policemen picked up the girls and, carrying one girl each, ran with them to the Bristol Royal Infirmary. Ruby suffered spinal injuries and Elsie had badly hurt her leg but, after spending six months convalescing at the Clifton home of Greville Edwards, both made full recoveries.[38]

The day after the incident at the bridge, the elder daughter Ruby gave a report to a newspaper via a hospital nurse. Ruby explained that their father had brought them to Bristol for a day out and they believed he was taking them home in the evening. However, by the time that evening came their father said he was undecided about returning home and instead, at midnight, took the girls to the bridge and paid the penny toll for each of them to walk across. Ruby recalled how, early in the morning, her father

---

38   Greville Edwards would later become the High Sheriff of Bristol, so he has some interesting tales of his own to be told.

had told her she was tired and offered to carry her, which she had refused. She explained that he then picked her up and she said: "Papa threw me over the bridge." She added: "I clung on to him, he loosened my hands, and I fell down to the road. I thought I felt blood coming out of my mouth, and then I remembered no more until I was taken to the hospital." She went on to explain how their mother Emily had begged the girls not to get on the train to Bristol with their father, and that Ruby's main reason for going with her father was to look after her younger sister Elsie who had been crying as their father dragged her away from home.[39]

At the ensuing court hearing where Charlie was charged with attempted double murder, he was declared insane and temporarily placed in an asylum. Back with his family several years later, two further sons were born in 1902 and 1904, the first of whom was named Greville in gratitude to the man who had paid for his daughters' medical treatment. In 1904, with his business back on track, Charlie returned to Bristol to formally thank the man who had helped to save his daughters' lives.

Ruby died in 1917, aged 33. It is not known what she died from, and the last report we have of her is from the 1911 census in which she is living with her family and working as a Shop Assistant in the 'India rubber trade'. Her younger sister Elsie appears on the same census and is working as a Clerk for a furniture company. We don't know what became of Elsie, but Charlie died in 1909 leaving his widow Emily with two young children to bring up as well as the older children to look after.

---

39   'Terrible occurrence in Bristol', *Bristol Times & Mirror*, 19 September 1896.

GLADYS BROWNLEE
1880–1950, PHOTOGRAPHER

Known to pretty much everyone as 'Brownie', Gladys Methven Brownlee was an esteemed photographer and businesswoman based in Bristol who was fully immersed in the city's arts and culture scene and was an ardent supporter of women's equality.

The eldest of three children, Brownie had two younger brothers – Leigh and Wilfred – who were both cricketers; Brownie herself seems to have been a dab hand with a cricket bat and played for Clifton Ladies. When Wilfred died at just 24 after contracting meningitis, he had made enough of an impact to warrant an obituary in the cricketing magazine *Wisden*. Leigh went on to play professionally for Gloucestershire, Somerset and the University of Oxford before becoming a journalist and the editor of the *Daily Mirror* in the 1930s.

Their parents were Anna and William Brownlee; William's mother had the surname 'Methven' before she married which explains Gladys' unusual middle name. In the 1891 census, the family lived at 12 Trelawney Road in Westbury and William is listed as a wine merchant and author, which is a fun combination of jobs. By the 1901 census, they had moved to Lansdowne House, at 49 Savill Place, Clifton, and William had trimmed his role down simply to wine merchant. He died in 1903 but Anna survived until 1919, and the 1911 census sees her living with Brownie at 24 Sion Hill, Clifton.

Between 1915 and 1940, Brownie had set herself up at 18 Charlotte Street, off Park Street, which had latticed windows with a view across Brandon Hill. And she would remain here for quite some time, working as a Portrait Photographer. *The Independent* has subsequently billed Brownie as "the life and soul of literate Bristol between the wars"[40], which is quite some claim. She worked first with Photographer Audrey Pearson, and later with Nellie Baker. The ground floor of the property housed a bookshop belonging to the BBC Radio Producer Douglas Cleverdon, while the first floor was home to the Bristol Arts Club between 1924 and 1940, of which Brownie was a keen participant.

Brownie loaned out her studio space, which fitted up to 50 people, to organisations she felt sympathetic to, including the Venture Club (which would later become the Soroptimists), of which she was President from 1922 to 1923. Before then, in January 1921, the *Western Daily Press* reported on one fascinating sounding Venture Club evening held at Charlotte Street, at which the topic was the history of floorcloth. The topic of linoleum was also, ahem, covered.

However, in 1940, the property at Charlotte Street was badly damaged during the Blitz and Brownie took up a residential post as a Warden at Oldbury House on St Michael's Hill, which was a hostel for young women working at the nearby BBC. But the women who stayed there felt there was something spooky about the place and there were so many complaints about things going bump in the night that they were moved to new accommodation. But what was so wrong with it?

Well, it was believed that Oldbury House had previously been used by Prince Rupert[41] and that it was connected to the nearby Royal Fort via a system of underground tunnels. Brownie told the *Western Morning News* that she and her wards were convinced the property was haunted: "Several times I saw the apparition of a man dressed in white monastic robes with a bunch of keys

40   independent.co.uk/news/obituaries/nest-cleverdon-37751.html
41   Who's Prince Rupert? He was an English/German naval officer who used the Royal Fort to hide out during the siege of Bristol in 1643, during which time he briefly became the city's governor after his uncle, King Charles I, appointed him to the role. In 1644, he was trapped by parliamentary forces and faced a court martial in September 1645. Rupert didn't die at the Royal Fort, though, so it's unlikely he would have returned to haunt it.

hanging at his side. There were also the figures of five women apparently talking among themselves and always seen together. I would hear strange dragging footsteps and doors would open and shut."

She continued: "I said nothing at first to the 28 or 30 girls who were living at the hostel because I did not want to scare them. But one day eight of the girls came to me and said they had seen the ghosts at various times. The curious thing was that none of the other girls ever saw them at all. I am afraid that at last the apparitions and the weird noises and happenings got on our nerves, and we were very glad when we were moved to Weston-super-Mare. We were more afraid of the ghosts than the air raids."[42]

Incidentally, Brownie also claimed that poltergeists had troubled her at her previous address on Charlotte Street, and she wondered if spirits simply followed her around wherever she lived and that it was she who was haunted rather than her properties.

By 1945, Brownie had moved to London. She was killed in 1950 following a car accident. Brownie had remained unmarried and child-free throughout her life.[43]

EUNICE BRYANT
1903–1998, DOCTOR

For almost half a century, Dr Ivy Eunice Bryant, generally known as Eunice, of the Christian Medical Mission worked in the St Jude's and Old Market districts as the Medical Superintendent. When she retired in 1981, the Christian Medical Mission opted

---

42 'Haunted Hostel', *Western Morning News*, 27 October 1941.
43 With thanks to Marion Reid for the nomination of Gladys Brownlee to this book.

not to replace her and a valuable service for the community was lost. Upon her death in 1998, at the age of 94, the *British Medical Journal* published an obituary for Eunice which stated: "She was a much loved, conscientious doctor, who also attended the down and out and homeless men in the city's Salvation Army hostel, on occasions even washing their feet."[44]

Before the purpose–built medical centres that we are familiar with today, doctors usually worked from private houses. Which is why the Christian Medical Mission, established in 1872, operated out of what had been a residential house at 7 Redcross Street. As well as the doctor's consulting room there was a nurse's room and a sunray clinic for the treatment of rickets. There was also a mid-morning prayer service several times a week. For decades, Eunice provided a service not only as a family GP but also supporting those in the city who were less fortunate but still required medical care. Prior to the establishment of the NHS, the Mission was the only place in east Bristol where poor people could receive free medical aid. Long after the NHS was founded in 1948, the Mission continued to provide free medical care to those who needed it.

Writing on Facebook, a former patient called George Jefferies said: "Dr Bryant was a formidable woman, slightly eccentric but well respected by most of her patients. On entering her consulting room she would look at you over the top of her glasses and wish you 'good morning' in a voice that was so well spoken and plummy that it distanced her from her patient and would have been more at home in Buckingham Palace. Her manner, although friendly, was condescending; she spoke at you rather than to you and heard nothing you had to say in return.

"Thinking back, I can still see her sitting at her desk surrounded by medical instruments with prescription pad at the ready and wearing a big unbuttoned outdoor coat and all the windows in the room wide open regardless of the weather. On several occasions, she invited Mum, my sister and myself back to her surgery in the evening where she and the other missionaries would eagerly show us photographs and other artefacts from their time doing the Lord's work in Africa."[45]

Although I have struggled to definitively track down Eunice's family heritage or her birth surname, it looks likely that she married a man named Henry Bryant, whom she outlived, and they had four children.[46]

SARAH BUCHANAN
dates unknown, EMIGRANT

Author's note: Why is Sarah Buchanan's story shared in a book about Bristol women given she spent so much of her life in New Zealand? Because Sarah was not unusual in being a woman who emigrated from the UK in search of a better life. And just because she left Bristol, it does not discount the fact that she was born here and was originally a Bristolian woman.

What led a working-class woman from Clifton to become one of the earliest settlers in a small New Zealand town? An 1880s portrait photograph survives of a respectable looking older woman wearing typical Victorian clothing and sitting in a chair. However, as researcher Heidi Whiteside[47] has found, Sarah's seemingly respectable studio portrait does a good job of concealing the life of hardship that she endured.

45   facebook.com/groups/bristolthenandnow/posts/1566605110211519
46   With thanks to Jean Erskine for the nomination of Eunice Bryant to this book.
47   With thanks to the work of Heidi Whiteside in her MA thesis, 2017, 'We Shall Be Respectable: Women and Representations of Respectability in Lyttelton 1951–1893', University of Canterbury.

Born in Clifton to a working–class family, Sarah and her husband James emigrated to Australia before relocating to Lyttelton in New Zealand in 1866, bringing their five young children with them. The Buchanan family lived in a hut in Shin Bone Alley, which was one of the structures built by the first settlers in Lyttelton. However, a fire in 1870 destroyed not only the Buchanans' home but also almost all of their possessions. An economic depression followed in the town, meaning that work and income was scarce, leading James to seek work back in Australia where he died. Left with a young family to support, Sarah took in laundry and did char work. Researcher Heidi Whiteside also finds evidence that Sarah had two of her children baptised at this time, which was a requirement before an orphanage would accept them. Imagine the pain of having to give up your children to an orphanage because you cannot afford to support them.

Further struggle came for Sarah when, in 1876, she was called up in the Magistrate's Court for unpaid rent and her home was repossessed, leaving her and the children who remained with her homeless. Quite how she coped is not recorded, but it seemed she had remarried by the early 1880s when the surviving photographic portrait of her was taken. A few years later, Sarah and her new husband moved away from Lyttelton, leaving behind some of her children and grandchildren. She ended her days in a pauper's grave in Wellington, New Zealand. That was an awfully long way from Clifton for this woman to travel.

ALICE BUNCE
died 1937, SINGER

Born Alice Mary Wensley, this woman lived a musical life. A gifted singer, she joined the Lewin's Mead Chapel Choir at the age of 14 and sang soprano there for 40 years, eventually becoming the Choir Mistress. Alice was also a participant in the first ever Bristol Music Festival in 1908 and spent an impressive 28 years as the singing teacher at Colston's Girls' School. Alice married the composer and hymn writer Henry Bunce in 1878 but she opted to keep the name 'Wensley' for professional engagements. Recording her death, the *Western Daily Press* noted: "Mrs Bunce possessed much personal charm and was popular with the Bristol public who she so often delighted with her beautiful singing. Her passing will be much regretted by a number who had the privilege of knowing her."[48]

MISS EM BURNELL
dates unknown, HEADTEACHER

Miss EM Burnell had been a teacher for her entire life and had become the headteacher at Southville Primary School[49]. Reflecting on her career, she wrote the following in an article for the *Jubilee Southville Star Magazine* in 1958:

"I am in the unique position of having spent the whole of my teaching career in this one school, having done my teaching practice as a college student and returning later as a qualified teacher. As I look back on those early days I am reminded of the many, many times I crossed the water of the Cut in the ferry boat, long before the Gaol Ferry Bridge was built. Older readers will remember the cheery personality of Mr Dick Thomas who took us over for 1/2d toll.

"The passing of the years brought many changes of all kinds – the introduction of the Milk in Schools scheme, school dinners

48   'Former Bristol singer of great charm', *Western Daily Press*, 15 January 1937.
49   Southville Primary School remains in the same location on Merrywood Road.

etc, and a gradual change in school methods and organisation. I sometimes sigh for the days when children knew how to sit still and the classroom really was a quiet place.

"I have recollections of countless children who spent their early years with us here, many of whom stand out in memory very clearly. It is with pride and pleasure that I hear of their achievements – some following in the steps of their teachers, two now serving in the Church of Christ, another a successful artist, while another is making a name for herself in the world of theatre."[50]

ELIZABETH BURNS
1871-1925, RECORD BREAKING MOTHER

Elizabeth Ann Bowen (as she was born), also known as Lily, did not have a comfortable upbringing. Her father was a labourer and the family lived in St Augustine's, and although that city centre address would come with a hefty price tag today, back in the late Victorian era it was far less salubrious. Her father Richard had died before Elizabeth was 10, meaning that her mother Eliza became the head of the household.

In 1888, when she was just 17, Elizabeth married Avon Street Gasworks labourer Thomas Burns, who was 11 years her senior, and the couple quickly started a family. In the coming years, Elizabeth and Thomas would have 11 children: all of them girls and all of them surviving to adulthood. The large family lived at 22 Frogmore Street (now demolished), not far from where Elizabeth had grown up, and Thomas worked for the Gasworks for 40 years.

---

50   CLASS, 2004, *Southville People and Places*, Fiducia Press, p40.

Elizabeth's daughter Elsie Stokes, who worked as a cigar maker, recounted her mother's story in the 1977 booklet *Up Knowle West*, saying how a reporter from the *News of the World* came to visit them in 1910 because word of Elizabeth's impressive brood of girls had spread, and a doctor in the US who had 11 sons had claimed that nobody could beat him for the most number of children of the same sex. Elizabeth, heavily pregnant with her eleventh child at the time, was so busy doing the laundry that she barely had time to stop and talk to the newspaperman. However, she made time and was rewarded with £60 from the doctor as well as a willow plate from the *News of the World* that was decorated to say: "Britain beats the world family".

Elizabeth brought her children, who slept three to a bed, up to be Christians and insisted that they attend Sunday School at St Augustine the Less Church.[51] She also took them for walks around the churchyard where she would highlight a gravestone that had belonged to a woman who met a grisly death at the hands of her servant... who would have got away with it if it hadn't been for those pesky kids, sorry... if it hadn't been for a talkative parrot. The murder had taken place while the woman's husband was away at sea but, when he returned, he asked the servant where his wife was. The servant pleaded ignorance until the parrot squawked: "Under the hearth stone, under the hearth stone." And that indeed was where the woman's body lay. Apparently the servant was hanged and the old lady was buried at St Augustine's churchyard, where Elizabeth would take her children.[52]

51   Following extensive damage in the Blitz, the church, which had first been built in 1240, was demolished in 1962. It had once stood close to Bristol Cathedral.
52   This story is not to be confused with that of servant Sarah Thomas who also murdered her mistress and is profiled in Volume Two of *The Women Who Built Bristol*. Regrettably, I have been unable to locate any newspaper stories related to the story that Elizabeth shared with her children, suggesting it may just be folklore. However, if you Google the term "parrot murder witness" you may be surprised to find that there are quite a number of instances of parrots giving the game away for murderers throughout the years. Aviculturists who are contemplating murder should consider themselves warned.

Elizabeth died in 1925 at the relatively young age of 54. However, after the number of children she had raised and the harshness of the life she had lived, her early death is not entirely a surprise.

MARGERY BUSH
1885–1960, WARTIME NURSE

In 1907, Margery Scott became the second wife of wealthy sheep farmer and politician Robert Bush, a widow who was 31 years her senior. Margery had been born in Perth, Western Australia, and this is where she met her future husband, who had sailed to Australia and stayed there for around 30 years. However, their courtship did not begin until 1905 when Margery sailed to England with her parents. Margery and Robert married on 27 May 1907 at St Mary Magdalene Church in Stoke Bishop when Margery was 21. Children quickly followed and, over the next 13 years, the couple had five children.

With Margery being Australian and Robert having a great affection for that country, when World War One was declared they wanted to do their part to support Australia. As such, they converted their house at Stoke Bishop into a 100–bed hospital for Australian servicemen and Margery oversaw everything. This transformation took place with impressive speed and, less than three weeks after war had been declared, Bishops Knoll Hospital was ready to receive patients. During the course of the war, around 2,000 men received treatment at this hospital and the cost for everything was wholly met by the Bush family.

As the Quartermaster, Margery oversaw the work carried out in the kitchens for the soldiers and nurses, and often helped with meal preparations. She was assisted by her step–daughter Charlotte (Robert's daughter from his first marriage), who also worked at the hospital as a Nursing Auxiliary. During the course of the war and while supervising the hospital's management, Margery gave birth to two further babies, which was no small undertaking while running a hospital in wartime. After the war, Margery received an OBE in recognition of her efforts.[53]

AUDREY BUTLER
1941–2021, SPORTS ENTHUSIAST

Before she died at the age of 80, loyal Bristol Rovers fan Audrey Butler had become the club's mascot Captain Gas. But she was more than that, she was also a keen marathon runner who had raised thousands of pounds for charity over the years.

Audrey, who had four children with husband Christopher, lived in Filton and Lockleaze and worked for Rolls-Royce. She had even sat in the cockpit of Concorde when it landed after its last flight and wore a silver Concorde necklace for many years. After retirement in the 1990s, Audrey became a cleaner for Bristol Rovers at their Memorial Stadium in Horfield. She also became the club's mascot Captain Gas, wearing an oversized pirate costume, and would hand out trophies on the pitch after games.

Her daughter Christine Butler told Bristol Live in 2021: "She was amazing, colourful and she always helped others – she also encouraged people to be whatever they wanted to be. She was also a true Bristolian and dedicated Rovers fan – she knew everybody at the Rovers ground, from the players to the people working behind the bar." After learning that Audrey had become too ill with Parkinson's and dementia to be able to attend matches anymore, her friends at Bristol Rovers sent a video message for

---

53   With thanks to Clive Burlton for his help with this entry.

her to watch at home.

Adam Tutton from Bristol Rovers added: "I was lucky enough to know Audrey for about 13 years, since I was head of education at Rovers and we would go around Bristol primary schools doing assemblies together. She was an inspirational and incredible woman who has done so many marathons for charity, she did runs all over the country to raise money for various charities – running was a massive passion and she was still running them into her 70s."[54]

Audrey was a member of the Great Western Runners club. At the age of 40, she completed her first marathon, which was in Greece. Audrey also took part in cross country runs, an Ironman triathlon and she cycled from Land's End to John O'Groats. She once ran the London Marathon dressed as a nun.

CARROTY KATE
dates unknown, GANGSTER

With a name like Carroty Kate, you already know the story is going to be a goodie. Although technically more of a Bath woman than a Bristol one, her story is too good to miss out. And her story may make you think twice about dismissing Bath as a city of gentle and peaceful folk.

Kate's true name or dates have never been identified, so all we know is her pseudonym of 'Carroty Kate' and that she was wreaking trouble on the good people of Bath around the 1830s and 1840s. As well as 'Carroty Kate', she was also known as the 'Mistress of Bull Paunch Alley' and the 'Queen of the Slum'. Clearly not a woman to be messed with, Kate was the leader of a gang

54   bristolpost.co.uk/news/bristol-news/tributes-paid-inspirational-bristol-woman-6451380

deemed to be "the most brutish and criminal mob in England".

By way of introduction, here's a description of the red–haired woman courtesy of travelling circus proprietor George Sanger, who ran Wombwell's Menagerie[55], which fell foul of Kate's reign of terror one evening in August 1840: "The roughs were led by a red–headed virago, a dreadful giantess of a woman, known as Carroty Kate. She was an awful creature, strong as a navvy, a big brutal animal, caring nothing for magistrates or gaol, and had long been the terror of every respectable person in Bath and its neighbourhood. With the majority of her followers, she hailed from Bull Paunch Alley (which no longer exists), the lowest slum in the cathedral city, where no policeman ever dared to penetrate, and innumerable horrors were committed nightly."[56] You wouldn't want to cross her path on a dark night.

The story goes that Wombwell's Menagerie was part of the Bath Fair held at Lansdown in 1840 and, as everyone was packing up for the night at around 10pm, Kate and her crew descended upon them with Kate shouting orders to "Wreck the fair!" The gang set about looting the stalls for booze and throwing punches at anyone who tried to stop them. Anything that couldn't be drunk or carried was smashed, including the stalls. Almost everyone fled in terror.

After the gang turned back for Bath, Sanger and his men set off in pursuit armed with a blunderbuss.[57] They caught 12 of the troublemakers including Kate. As punishment, the men tied everyone up with rope and led them into a deep pond, in which they were dragged back and forth until almost drowned, at which time they were hauled up to the wagons. Here, the captors tied

55 The Menagerie was a travelling zoo, with tigers, elephants and other exotic animals, as well as stalls, sideshows and rides.
56 George Sanger, 1910, *Seventy Years a Showman*, p43.
57 A blunderbuss is a short-range firearm that was commonly in use from the 17th to 19th centuries and it is considered to be a predecessor of the contemporary shotgun.

two people to each of the wagon's wheels and set upon them with whips. After this, they let almost everyone go to stagger back to the city, where they were met by the police. However, the men kept hold of Kate, who was stripped to the waist and laid over a table while several women beat her with whips. "She screamed and swore horribly," Sanger wrote. "But the young women flogged on till they were tired and the red-haired wretch was allowed to limp away, cursing us as she went in the most dreadful fashion."[58]

But the events at Lansdown Fair were not the first of Kate's misdeeds to be reported. An incident a few years earlier in 1832 is also likely to be her handiwork, when "a gang of the most desperate and inhuman monsters committed outrages that would have disgraced a nation", according to a report in the local paper.[59]

They were also – possibly – not the last of Kate's actions. Between the 1860s and 1890s, there are reports of a woman (or women) named Carroty Kate in the London, Kent and Essex areas committing petty crimes, but I am unconvinced that this is the same woman as our Kate would be rather elderly by this time, and simply a lack of imagination on the part of police officers and journalists at the time when trying to come up with a nickname for a red–haired woman.

ANNA CAMPBELL
1991–2018, ACTIVIST

This young woman lived a short but a full life. Originally from Lewes in East Sussex, Anna Campbell moved to Bristol after dropping out of university. Here, she trained as and then worked as a plumber while also working at Cafe Kino in Stokes Croft.

58   somersetlive.co.uk/news/somerset–news/carroty–kate–bath–gang–leader–1570099
59   With thanks to Eugene Byrne for the nomination of Carroty Kate to this book.

She was very politically motivated and Bristol was clearly a good base from which to find like-minded activists. Soon, Anna was involved with campaigns such as the 2010 student protests (opposing spending cuts to university fees alongside a rise in tuition fees), the Hunt Saboteurs Association (opposing the act of fox hunting) and she was a member of the Anarchist Black Cross (supporting class struggle prisoners) among others.

Anna went on to join the Women's Protection Units (known as the YPJ) in the Rojava conflict during the Syrian civil war where she underwent a month of intense training before going to fight. The YPJ is an all–female militia that is largely made up of Kurds as well as a few women volunteers from other countries, including Anna. One of her passions was campaigning for equal rights for women in Kurdistan.

On 15 March 2018, Anna became the first British woman to die in Syria. She had been in Syria since May 2017 and had been fighting in Afrin against Turkish forces that were trying to push the Kurdish troops out of parts of northern Syria. She was killed by a Turkish Armed Forces air strike. Anna was 26 at the time of her death. When her friends and comrades in Bristol heard what had happened, they sprayed slogans in her memory onto the side of buildings in the city and staged a demonstration at British Aerospace Systems in Filton, which was believed to be one of the companies supplying weapons and fighter jets to Turkey.[60]

---

60   With thanks to Howard Davies for the nomination of Anna Campbell to this book.

ELIZABETH CASBERD
1741–1802, MATRIARCH

Although I would rather not define a woman by what her husband did, in Elizabeth Frances Casberd's case it is unavoidable. Born in Glamorgan as Elizabeth Matthews, she married Jacob Elton in June 1761 at St Augustine's Church in Bristol, although this was a brief marriage because Jacob died the following year. Picking up the pieces, in December 1765 she married again at the same church, this time to the Rev Dr John Casberd, who was also the vicar of this church. She must have been dedicated to and respected within her parish because she is memorialised with a plaque inside Bristol Cathedral.

BEATRICE CAVE
born 1864, WAR SHERO

Marrying into Mangotsfield's wealthy Cave dynasty in 1892, Beatrice Julia Williams (as she was born) lived at the family's Rodway Hill House from 1900 to 1922. Lady Beatrice, originally from Cornwall, and her banker husband Sir Charles Cave were devastated when one of their three sons, Walter, was killed in 1915 while serving in the Army during World War One. He was only 20. Charles' father had already offered Rodway Hill House to the authorities for use as a war hospital so, in honour of Walter, Beatrice made the running of the establishment – known as Cleeve Hill Hospital – very much her business. She also became the Commandant of the Lawford's Gate Division of the Gloucestershire Branch of the British Red Cross Society, which managed the hospitals in a wide area. The hospital was staffed by a combination of detachments from the British Red Cross

Voluntary Aid Detachment, alongside nurses from Downend, Frenchay and Frampton Cottrell, as well as civilian kitchen staff. For her part in the war effort, Beatrice was made an OBE in 1918. The hospital, and the house in which it was based, was demolished in 1930.

PAT CHARLES
born 1936, SWIMMER

Patricia Charles made a massive splash as an international swimming champion. She grew up at 2 Brougham Street, Barton Hill, with her parents and three siblings, although this street was later demolished, along with much of central Barton Hill, as part of a slum clearance programme. Pat attended Avonvale School and Redfield Girls' School, and was always a talented swimmer. Even when she was 12 in 1949, the *Bristol Times and Mirror* was championing Pat for her achievements at a school swimming gala where she swam in times that were faster than the boys in the same category. Pat triumphed at the gala again the following year and, by 1950 she was representing Bristol at a Swindon gala, before becoming the Gloucestershire freestyle champion later in the year.

The wins kept on coming and they kept getting bigger and bigger. In June 1955, Pat set a new Gloucestershire record for the 100m freestyle in an intercity race. However, her biggest triumph would come in May 1956 when, at a major swimming tournament, Pat came a close third – being beaten only by two former Olympians, which is fair enough as presumably it's pretty hard to beat an Olympian at their own sport. There was no end to Pat's talents, and the newspaper reports reveal further wins for the girl from Barton Hill. By the early 1960s, Pat had moved into the world of water polo, becoming not only a player but also a referee. During a gala at the Filwood Baths in Knowle in October

1967, there was a bizarre incident where Pat was among those who were victims of a group of vandals who tore the petrol caps off the cars outside in the car park, trashed the cars and threw lit fireworks at the parked cars and the swimming pool windows.

Pat's memory is honoured by the Pat Charles Memorial Cup which is presented annually by the Gloucester County Amateur Swimming Association, an organisation of which Pat had been President in 1980.[61]

FELICITY CHARLTON
1913–2009, ARTIST

After growing up amid the comforts of Clifton, Felicity Charlton became an acclaimed artist, admired for combining elements of fantasy and realism in her watercolour and oil paintings. Felicity attended the West of England College of Art between 1932 and 1937, which is where she met her husband Evan Charlton, who was one of her teachers. During World War Two, the couple relocated to Wales, and Felicity did her bit for the war by working as an agricultural labourer before returning to art after the conflict ended. Felicity participated in many exhibitions throughout her career, both as a solo artist and as part of artist groups. In 1986, alongside Evan, she was profiled in an exhibition at the Royal West of England Academy in Bristol called 'Evan and Felicity Charlton: Paintings 1937–1986', which was exactly what it said it was. The *Bristol Evening Post* described the exhibition as "surrealism and imagination from a pair of remarkable painters"[62].

61   With thanks to Garry Atterton for his research into Pat as part of the Voices of the Past project. voicesofthepast.org.uk/women-that-made-barton-hill/y7jcesrxzwhbybrjkhvgg208zxgmkt
62   'Pick of the Week', *Bristol Evening Post*, 13 September 1986.

SARAH CHATTERTON
1731–1791, TEACHER

If you have even a passing interest in poetry and Bristol, then the name 'Chatterton' will surely be familiar to you. Thomas Chatterton (1752–1770) was a precocious young man whose poetry has endured in history, despite – or because of – his death by suicide at the age of just 17. Sarah Chatterton was his mother and an extraordinary character in her own right.

Sarah Young had married the musician, poet and schoolmaster Thomas Chatterton Snr in April 1748 at Sodbury Church in South Gloucestershire. They lived behind Thomas' charity school on Pyle Street and they had a daughter Mary, and then a son who died shortly after he was born in 1750. Their third child, Thomas, was just 15 weeks old when Thomas Snr died, leaving Sarah in a very vulnerable position both emotionally and financially. She was looked after by the sisters of the writer Hannah More[63], who, as an act of charity, cared for women who were in exactly the sort of predicament that Sarah found herself in.

To help make ends meet, Sarah took in sewing and ornamental needlework as well as establishing a Dame School on Redcliffe Hill. Sarah was assisted in her work by her mother-in-law and by a third woman who helped with the sewing. The three women lived together at the school along with Sarah's two children. After a while, they relocated to a smaller house at 50 Redcliffe Hill. The house was opposite the church of St Mary Redcliffe, where the Chatterton family had been hereditary sextons[64] for more than 200 years, and young Thomas had loved to play among the tombs of the church as a child.[65]

---

63   Hannah More is profiled in Volume One of *The Women Who Built Bristol*.
64   A sexton is an officer of a church who helps maintain the building and churchyard. Larger churches, such as St Mary Redcliffe, would have had a team of sextons.
65   With thanks to Dawn Dyer for the nomination of Sarah Chatterton to this book.

MISS CLARK
dates unknown, TOBACCO FACTORY WORKER

In its heyday, the Imperial Tobacco Company had numerous factories around Bristol and, in 2025, it still maintains one factory on Winterstoke Road. Miss Clark remembers working at the Mardon factory[66] by Temple Meads for 46 years, where she worked on the machines, work she enjoyed. In 1979, Miss Clark said: "I worked half past seven in the morning 'til five or half past at night. Then during the war I done shift work. I started at Mardons at the end of the First World War. I can remember when the war finished. We all stood on the steps and watched all the people outside hooraying. I started with five shillings a week and I had 6d pocket money. I used to buy stockings and all odds and ends out of that 6d."

She continued: "I done the cartons which the cigarettes go in. When I first started I had to glue up the parcels. They came out of the machine and the girl on the table put them in the parcels and I had to glue them up. Then as I got better I was put on the table where the work came out. And from there I was put on what was called running out. Then I was put on the feeding. That was the tough job – feeding. During the war I done a man's job. Wages went up to 35s during the war. Then when I done a man's job, they gave me an extra 10s a week, but that was took away as soon as I was took off. There wasn't a union then. They did try and start one."[67]

---

66   Mardon, Son & Hall was bought out by Imperial Tobacco to manufacture packaging and create collectible cigarette cards.
67   Miss Clark, 1979, in *Looking Back on Bristol*, Bristol Broadsides, p8.

SARAH CLARK
dates unknown, FISHMONGER

After being widowed and needing to look after her young children, enterprising Sarah Clark established a wholesale fish business in Bristol in the 1800s. This was eventually to be a business that the whole family became involved in. Sarah's son and grandsons took over the business after she retired but, once World War Two broke out and the men had been called up, the women returned to the fish market in force, with Sarah's granddaughter Evelyn Clark and daughter-in-law Rose Clark stepping up to the (fish) plate.

Every morning at the break of day, Evelyn and Rose would go from their home in – appropriately enough – Fishponds to the market on St Nicholas Street and wait for the deliveries.

Evelyn's daughter said: "Fish was boxed in ice and, with little in the way of heating in the exposed expanse of the market, things were not easy for anyone, especially the girls. It was especially difficult for them with the additional worry of where their husbands were and would they ever see them again. This, together with rationing, not to mention bomb attacks on the city, made life extremely stressful."[68]

ROSEMARY CLINCH
c1936-2020, FLANEUR

'Flâneur' is a French term that was coined by the poet Charles Baudelaire to identify an observer of modern urban life. And Rosemary Edith Clinch, who lived in Littleton on Severn, was nothing if not an observer of modern Bristolian life. In her 1985

---

68   bbc.co.uk/history/ww2peopleswar/stories/38/a3799038.shtml

book *Unknown Bristol* she simply stated: "My brief is to wander the streets."

In her pursuit of discovering the most extraordinary parts of Bristol, Rosemary wrote a great number of local history and local interest books, despite her day job being a book seller rather than a book writer. Rosemary's career had begun in magazine publishing before she became the Avon and Somerset sales rep for Bossiney Books in Cornwall, who would later become her publisher. In 1985, Rosemary said: "Photography is my great hobby. I do my own developing and printing at my home ... My next book really will be all my own work: I wrote it, illustrated it and I shall publicise it and sell it."[69]

While some of Rosemary's books extend to areas beyond Bristol's boundaries, there are also plenty that concentrate on this city. Highlights include: *Unknown Bristol* (1985), *Curious Bristol* (1987) and *In Search of Bristol* (1988). These were volumes that detailed the small curios that Rosemary spotted on her walks through the city, which she then researched and photographed to share with her readers. Those stories she retold included the tale of the Bristol High Cross, which has had a long and troubled history since it was first established in the 1370s and has been sold and moved too many times to mention. She also unearthed a neglected and unsuccessful Victorian shopping arcade in Clifton, which has more recently been restored as the architecturally significant Boyce's Arcade but, at the time Rosemary wrote about it in 1985, was an abandoned furniture warehouse.

She was also a keen researcher of the supernatural and devoted several books to studying the spookier phenomena linked to areas such as Glastonbury.

---

69   'Rosemary goes into the unknown', *Western Daily Press*, 25 November 1985.

NORA COCKBAIN
1877–1955, DISTRICT NURSE

Nora Cockbain spent her whole life in Bedminster. Her father Robinson Cockbain was a city missionary and, with his wife Emma, had 11 children. Nora was somewhere in the middle of this large brood. She became a much-respected member of the parish of St Michael's in Bedminster, and her death in 1955 was recorded with great sadness in the parish magazine. For the final 20 years of her life, Nora had worked hard as a district nurse in the area. She was employed by the Bristol District Nursing Association but her salary was so small that it was necessary to call on some of those she looked after to help support her financially.

PHYLLIS COCKLE
1914-2005, WELDER

Things almost got off to an international start for Phyllis May Stallard, who was only born in Bristol at the last minute due to a family tragedy. The plan had been that she would begin life in Canada, where her parents Amy and Herbert Stallard were temporarily living due to Herbert's work as a master carpenter. However, fate intervened. The couple already had two older children but sadly their son died as a toddler while Amy was pregnant in Canada, and bereaved Amy was desperate to return home to her family in Bristol without delay. Which was why she made the long trip back to the UK without Herbert, but heavily pregnant with Phyllis and accompanied by her surviving infant daughter. Without easy access to aeroplanes for civilians, this is a journey that she would have undertaken by ship, making it even more arduous and uncomfortable. As a result, baby Phyllis was born in Bristol: the city she remained in for the rest of her extraordinary life.

After a fairly comfortable upbringing in Bristol with Amy, Herbert and her older sister, Phyllis had to grow up quickly and care for her beloved mother, who died from cancer in 1933. After Amy's death, Phyllis needed to find paid work and briefly went into service, although she absolutely hated it and didn't last long. "[Mum] came round to the table with some soup and it went into somebody's lap", recalls Phyllis' daughter Denise Hillier. "She said the people were horrible to her, the way they treated their staff. So she didn't want to stay there anyway." Phyllis then worked in Woolworths until the start of World War Two in 1939… when the war led Phyllis to become a welder. And it is this role that really helps set Phyllis apart from her peers.

At a time when everyone was doing their part for the war effort, and with so many men away and fighting on the front line, women were called upon to do jobs that were traditionally seen as male roles. And this was how Phyllis ended up training to be, and working as, a welder for the Bristol Aircraft Corporation, which was based at the Ministry of Defence's site in Filton. It was a position that Phyllis loved, as she later told her daughter Denise: "It was a lovely job, I absolutely loved it."

Denise says that welding on the bomber planes was clearly her mother's vocation. Like so many people during the war, but for a chance of fate Phyllis only narrowly escaped death. Denise recalls: "She had a call of nature. But the toilets were not in the building that she was in, she had to go to another block. And the building she'd just left got bombed, so she was lucky to be alive. It wasn't her time to go."

From Filton, Phylis moved to work for the Ministry of Defence in Corsham at the underground tunnels there, commuting by a specially laid-on bus every day. The workers saw very little daylight during those years: "It was dark when we went, and dark when we came back up and went home," Phyllis later told Denise.

The Corsham Tunnels were created out of an old Victorian quarry in Wiltshire. After quarrying ceased around 1910, the tunnels were repurposed by the Central Ammunition Depot who wanted to find a way to protect ammunition stocks from attacks by hostile aircrafts. Once completed, the Corsham Tunnels were a vast network of ten 'districts', each occupying five acres of floor space. Fresh air was drawn in from the outside via fans, which also expelled stale air back outside again. By 1941, a barrack block was developed in the Corsham Tunnels to accommodate up to 300 people, and this included a bar and mess area. For those who 'lived' in the Tunnels, there were few reasons to go above ground and they remained underground for lengthy periods to help protect the secrecy of the place's existence.

By 1942, a military communications depot was added to the facilities in the Tunnels, and another depot was created as a factory for the Bristol Aircraft Corporation to help protect their work from the Luftwaffe, and it was in this area that Phyllis worked. This new area was decorated with bright murals by the British artist Olga Lehmann (1912-2001), who had trained at the prestigious Slade School of Art in London, to help raise the spirits of the workers who were confined to otherwise gloomy conditions. Olga became a prominent war artist and undertook a number of commissions for the Ministry of Defence. Because art materials were difficult to obtain during the war, the colours that Olga used in her murals were those that the Bristol Aircraft Corporation already had available for use on the planes. The whole project took eight months to complete and many of Olga's murals have survived and been recorded in photographs that can be viewed online. The Tunnels were not abandoned by the military until the 1960s.

Like so many people who lived through the war, Phyllis was left with a slight nervous tendency and was always very jumpy, even decades later, which was a hangover from the years of doodlebugs[70] coming over the roofs.

Not long after the war ended, Phyllis married Stanley 'Sam' Cockle in 1946 when she was 31. Phyllis and Sam had known each other since they were children because they grew up in neighbouring houses and the families became friends, and that friendship blossomed into romance. Sam made metal window frames, and the couple initially lived in Horfield. This was an era when married women were not expected to work which meant that when a man whom Phyllis had worked with at Corsham during the war invited her to come back and return to work as a welder, she had to sadly turn him down because she was now a pregnant and married woman. "She always said she would have liked to have done it, she loved welding," says Denise.

Phyllis and Sam had two daughters, one also called Phyllis and, seven years later, a second daughter called Denise. But because Phyllis hadn't married until she was 31, and she was 40 when she had Denise, she was deemed an older mother: something Denise says she never noticed until she started attending school and realised her mother was a little older than the mothers of her friends. Denise remembers a childhood trip to Jones' department store in Broadmead where the sales assistant mistook Phyllis, who would have been about 50, for her grandmother rather than her mother: "Her face dropped and she went so white," recalls Denise, adding that Phyllis was quick to reassure the sales assistant not to worry about her faux pas.

As well as having a passion for welding, Phyllis loved to dance and took tap dancing classes. She enjoyed going to tea dances,

70   Doodlebugs were flying bombs that had no pilots.

which became a real pleasure for her and something that she kept up after Sam died in 1992. The couple had moved into a council house in West Town Lane in Brislington by this time, which was where they had lived for most of their marriage and brought up their daughters. Phyllis went almost blind towards the end of her life due to glaucoma, meaning she could only really see the difference between day and night, but she wouldn't let that dampen her independence and she still went out to the shops and to see people.[71]

KATHLEEN COLE
1886–1958, DOCTOR

The first woman to obtain a degree from the Medical School in Bristol was Kathleen Cole, who had been a student at Redland High School and had then obtained a dual-honours degree in Botany and Physiology in London. But when Kathleen applied to the University of Bristol's Medical School in 1907 she was told that women were not admitted. Evidently, this policy was overturned and, in 1909, Kathleen was allowed to attend the school.[72]

In 1913, Kathleen married the London-born Gottlob Heber, a fellow 'physician and surgeon' (according to the 1939 Register), and became Kathleen Heber. Early in their marriage, Kathleen and Gottlob spent time working on the borders of Tibet as missionary doctors. Their first daughter was born in India. They had a further three children, two of whom also became doctors. During World War Two, Kathleen and Gottlob volunteered as Air Raid Precautions medical officers.

71   With thanks to Phyllis' daughter Denise Hillier for providing so much information about her mother. Thanks also to David Parker for the nomination of Phylis Cockle to this book.
72   See the entry for Hilda Adams in this volume for more about the Medical School in Bristol and its lack of enthusiasm for female students.

QUEENIE COLES
dates unknown, MUNITIONS WORKER

Along with women from Birmingham, Devon and Cornwall, Queenie Coles began munitions work at the Rolls-Royce No 4 Shop in Patchway during World War Two, "entering a man's noisy working world of large machinery". The women were given brown overalls, arm sleeves and wooden clogs to wear, and Queenie's first job was to make spark plugs. Later on, she would become one of the first women to be transferred to a "man's job": grinding huge crank shank sleeves that would become part of an engine. "With a man's job came man's wages, which some of the men objected to," remembered Queenie. "They brought in their union who eventually agreed that women could also work on large machines if taught properly. Their loss was my gain and I remained there until the end of the war."[73]

MARY COMPTON
1951–2018, TEACHER, TRADES UNIONIST

With more than three decades of work clocked up for the National Union of Teachers (NUT), which she had joined in 1985, it was perhaps inevitable that one day Mary Compton would become the union's President: a role she held from 2004–2005.

Mary, a modern languages teacher, was born in Bristol and attended Redland High School for Girls. She graduated from Southampton University in 1971 and achieved her PGCE from Bath College of Higher Education in 1976. Mary soon found work at the John Beddoes School in Presteigne, Wales, where she

73   bbc.co.uk/history/ww2peopleswar/stories/01/a5206501.shtml

stayed for the rest of her career.

Mary was Secretary of the Radnor branch of the NUT, progressing to become an Executive NUT Member for Wales, a National Officer by 2002 and President in 2004. So committed was Mary to the cause that, in 2010, she began studying for an MA degree in International Labour and Trade Union Studies at Ruskin College at the University of Oxford. She firmly believed that the privatisation of schools was having a detrimental effect on education and needed to be addressed. Mary also maintained strong socialist roots and was a life-long attender and organiser of marches, lobbies and strikes around her adopted home country of Wales. Mary kept marching until two years before her death from cancer in 2018.

FRANCES CONY
died 2017, ILLUSTRATOR

Before her untimely death from cancer, Bristolian artist and illustrator Frances Cony became a fierce fundraiser for the charity Above & Beyond, which continues to raise money to support all of the hospitals across Bristol. Frances wanted to give something back to the staff at the Bristol Haematology & Oncology Centre who had supported her during her own cancer treatment.

Frances wrote and illustrated a number of books for children, and also illustrated one of Bristol Zoo's Wow! Gorillas for the city-wide 2011 gorilla trail, which raised funds to help protect gorillas from extinction. She called her gorilla Bert and illustrated him wearing pyjamas decorated with endangered animals. Frances explained: "Despite the jolly pyjamas [Bert] is to wear, this gorilla design is meant to illustrate how some of our planet's most recognisable species — as well as lots of lesser known ones — are in danger of dying out. Red is for danger and is also for the Red List of endangered species produced by the International Union for the Conservation of Nature, which is why I chose to make the background red. It also looks good. Why I chose pyjamas is to do with the euphemism 'going to sleep' meaning dying."[74]

JEAN COURT
dates unknown, OPEN AIR SCHOOL PUPIL

On 20 October 1913, Bristol's first open air school was opened on Broadfield Road, Knowle.[75] Also known as the Knowle School, the Knowle Open Air School remained in use until 1940. Open air schools were very popular throughout the UK in the first half of the 20th century as an alternative method of educating children who were deemed too unwell to attend a traditional school for fear that they might infect the other children. But as a consequence of this, children in less robust health were condemned to a life of potential illiteracy, and that was on the assumption that they even survived to adulthood. Open air schools were founded on the concept that fresh air, good ventilation and exposure to the outside contributed to an individual's improved health.

The Bristol Civic League began considering the idea of an open air school as early as 1910 as a means of educating and including the otherwise excluded children. It was felt that by holding classes outside, there would be less risk of cross-infection from pupils. Open air schools also had a more flexible timetable than traditional schools, and provided medical support and nourishing meals for attendees.

74   franwowgorilla.blogspot.com. With thanks to Dawn Dyer for the nomination of Frances Cony to this book.
75   The former site now houses the Knowle Clinic.

At a meeting on 21 April 1913, Fanny Townsend[76], a respected member of the Bristol Civic League, proposed the need for an open air school for the education and treatment of sick children. She said: "It is proposed to start an open air day school for Bristol schoolchildren who are in the early stages of phthisis[77], and for those who are predisposed to the disease by weakness or ill-health; children for instance who are suffering from anaemia, malnutrition, tubercular glands and other ailments. For such children the conditions of ordinary school life are unsuitable, even injurious. They need fresh air, plenty of nourishing food, some hours of rest each day and special medical treatment. If these needs can be supplied, the children already attacked by tuberculosis will have a good chance of recovery, while those who are only threatened with the disease can be built up in health and rendered sufficiently strong to fight the scourge successfully."[78]

Fanny told the meeting that, in April 1913, there were 120 children with tuberculosis in Bristol, as well as 347 with anaemia and 104 with serious malnutrition. All of these children were receiving no education and little medical attention. As an aside, by 1938, some 1,035 children in Bristol were reported to be infected with tuberculosis, partly as a result of the malnutrition prevalent among the poor during the economic depression of the 1930s. And the 1939 Register of the nation showed that half of the children in the newly-built housing estate at Knowle West lived below the poverty line, with one in four heads of household being unemployed or dependent on casual labour to scrape by.

One of Knowle Open Air School's earliest pupils was Jean Court from Kingsdown, who later wrote about her experiences there. Jean had previously attended Kingsdown Council School

76 Fanny Townsend has her own entry in this volume. And I love her.
77 'Phthisis' is another name for tuberculosis and other wasting diseases.
78 Knowle Open Air School, *The Bristolian*, May 1913, p120.

but she found the lessons a struggle, would sometimes get into trouble and end up being caned as a punishment. Her treatment at school meant Jean ended up living in a state of anxiety but, when her mother offered to go and talk to the headmistress and complain, Jean worried this would make things worse. When Jean started fainting and becoming ill at school, it was suggested that she transfer to the Knowle Open Air School.

Every morning, Jean would take the tram to Knowle and would pay for her fare with one of the red tokens she was given by the mixed-sex school. She ate a nutritious breakfast and dinner there, which were served in a large hall with a kitchen at one end and the meals were delivered on plates through a serving hatch. "The food was very good on the whole and I began to regain my lost appetite," remembered Jean. "We used to get lovely plum duff and cottage pie there, the best I have ever tasted. We were also given large mugs of milk. I love milk and always drank mine, but it was served hot and some of the children hated it, so we used to slide along a full cup for an empty one and that way I ended up having three or four cups instead of one."

The school day included an hour's rest on a camp bed outside the classrooms, although the children were usually too busy chattering to get any sleep. A cold shower followed the rest, which was intended to toughen the children up. Educationally, Jean says the school allowed the children to progress at their own rate and didn't impose stressful exams on them. She recalls the teachers as being "gentle and encouraging". The pupils were motivated to tend the garden and were each given a small plot outside to cultivate flowers, mustard and cress in. The gardens also included a large pond with goldfish. The school broadened its pupils' horizons in many other ways, too. Jean recounts: "While at this school I heard my first radio programme. We didn't have a radio at home and listening to it was a real thrill for me. It was a schools programme about the slave trade and I was enthralled."

Jean was sorry to have to leave the Knowle Open Air School when her health improved, although her family then moved to Hill Avenue by Victoria Park and Jean soon found herself attending a makeshift open air school in the park's disused bandstand.[79]

EDNA COUSINS
1879–1949, SWIMMING POOL CARETAKER

With her husband George, Edna Cousins (who had been born Edna Nash) looked after the open-air swimming pool in Warmley, which had been there since 1910. The couple, who married in 1905, had four daughters and they lived nearby at 5 Stanley Terrace, Station Road.

Benefactors had raised £1,000 to build the pool, including members of the Fry and Goldney families who were local business owners. Fed by spring water that flowed from Cock Road and was diverted to the pool, the Cousins were the pool's first caretakers. They kept the pool area clean and tidy, maintained the billiard room where the green baize needed to be ironed once a week, and looked after the reading room upstairs.

In the 1910s and 1920s, the water in the pool, which had changing cubicles down one side, was emptied once a fortnight so that the white tiles could be cleaned of algae and other debris that had blown in. It was noted that, after cleaning, the water was crystal clear but, by the end of the fortnight, it could be rather murky so George would clamber down a manhole to open a valve and release the water. By the 1930s, this system had been improved so that every Saturday evening the pool water was

---

79   Jean Court, 1988, 'Living in the Lane' in *More Bristol Lives*, Bristol Broadsides, p105–125.

emptied out and refilled by 11am on Sunday, at which point the waiting queue of eager swimmers would plunge into the freezing water with glee.

Records suggest the pool was mainly used by men and boys for swimming. However, on Thursday afternoons a woman named Mrs Shackleton ran a swimming class for women and girls, although young men would line up outside the fence and peer through the cracks to see the women in their swimwear.

Whist drives were held during World War One and 100 guineas were raised to refurbish the baths. By 1920, Hanham Road, Kingswood and Staple Hill schools each had weekly swimming lessons at Warmley, despite it being icy cold to swim in. In summer months, up to 400 people a day would visit the Warmley pool. However, once the indoor — and heated — Soundwell Swimming Baths opened nearby in the 1960s, the Warmley pool fell out of favour. As a result, the Warmley pool was filled in and grassed over, and the Warmley Social Club and Community Centre was built on the site.[80]

EDITH COX
1899–1997, MATRIARCH

Edith Cox from Speedwell heard about her husband William's death in the most awful manner. She was at the seaside in Weston-super-Mare with her young children and heard a newspaper boy calling out the headline: "Disaster at Bristol Coal Mine!" A closer look at the front cover of the paper brought Edith the dreadful news that her husband William was the victim of the disaster. He had worked at Deep Pit Colliery in Speedwell and, on that fateful

80   Olive Bryant, 1989, in Cadbury Heath History Group, *Life As It Was: Vol 2*, p8–12.

day, William had been given permission to leave his job early so that he could meet Edith for an outing to Weston. He was coming up from the pit in a cage, but the gates were not closed properly and a jolt caused William to fall out of the cage.[81] He died from massive head injuries. William was just 27 at the time of his death in June 1923, and Edith was left a widow and a single mother at the age of 24.[82]

CARRIE CROAD
born 1840, SPIRITUALIST

In 1880, a devout woman named Carrie Croad travelled from Swindon to Bristol. Carrie lived with a number of serious medical conditions which had started during her teenage years when she began having epileptic seizures. The medical profession was left baffled as to the cause of Carrie's condition.

Carrie was born into a nautical family. As a child, she claimed that when her father was away at sea, she received visions from him when he was in danger or at risk of shipwreck. When she later relayed these visions to him, he confirmed them to accurately reflect what had happened.

Aged 19, Carrie married a captain in the merchant navy with whom she had a daughter. Carrie later said that she and her husband had agreed that whichever of them should die first would keep in touch with the other. Following her husband's death at sea, Carrie said that at the time that he was drowning she had a vision of him saying, "Goodbye, Carrie, I'm going".

In 1864, Carrie had a fall down some stairs which left her partially paralysed and in great pain. The condition worsened

81   A 'cage' is the lift that workers used to get in and out of the mines.
82   Dave Stephenson et al, 2003, *Images of England: Crews Hole, St George & Speedwell*, p117.

until 1866, when the entire lower half of her body was completely paralysed and Carrie was left bed bound. By 1870 she had also become blind. The doctors were scratching their heads about how to help Carrie and they reported that strange things had happened since Carrie became fully paralysed. For instance, despite being blind and her eyes permanently closed, Carrie possessed unusual powers of perception known as 'blindsight'.

News of Carrie's ability reached Dr Davey, who sent for Carrie to be relocated to his home at 38 Park Street in 1880. Using Carrie as a case study, Davey wrote a detailed report about blindsight for the *Journal of Psychological Medicine*. He had conducted experiments where he blindfolded Carrie and then held a series of 50 picture cards in front of her face. Every time, she was able to correctly say what was on the card. On another occasion, Carrie was able to correctly tell Davey the history of his life despite knowing nothing about him.

More than 40 doctors, clergymen and experts visited Carrie at Davey's address, and every single one was stumped by what they found. The *Western Daily Press* described her as "a lady whose nervous system seems to have acquired extraordinary sensitiveness in proportion to the decay of her physical powers"[83]. Despite Carrie becoming deaf and mute in addition to being blind, she was also able to communicate with others via writing and touch.

But this wasn't the first time that Carrie's second sight had been investigated. A nonconformist minister named Mr Westlake wrote a pamphlet called 'A Service of Suffering' in 1882. Carrie had lived with him and his wife for several months in Swindon, during which time she barely ate a thing. However, her stay gave Mr Westlake ample opportunity to find out more about what Carrie

---

83   'A Service of Suffering' in *Western Daily Press*, 13 July 1880.

saw. He wrote: "I often think that, physically, she is maintained in a miraculous manner, especially when I see how little food she takes. In the month of December last, for three weeks, she did not take nourishment equal to half a pint of milk."[84] Mr Westlake further reported that Carrie claimed to be able to receive psychic messages from friends who had died, as well as from friends who lived far away.[85]

BESSIE CROSS
1890–1917, MURDERED

Three years into World War One, pregnant Bessie Cross from 5 Henry Row, Baptist Mills, was shot dead by her husband, Private Albert Cross, on the platform at Temple Meads Station.

On 17 October 1917, former decorator Albert had been in Bristol on leave for ten days where it had seemed that he and Bessie were getting on well, despite Albert not being the father of her unborn child.

However, as they stood together on the platform with Bessie waiting to wave him back to service in France, Albert took out a rifle and shot her in the stomach. Bessie died shortly afterwards at Bristol General Hospital. In his defence in court, Albert claimed that he had only been messing around and had not realised there was a bullet in the chamber: he was found not guilty, even though he had made no effort to help Bessie after 'accidentally' shooting her. Albert quite literally got away with murder, despite telling the Military Police: "I have shot my wife. She is in a certain condition by another man."[86]

---

84   allabouttheaven.org/observations/croad–mrs–carrie–the–testimony–of–the–nonconformist–minister–mr–j–g–westlake–eating–no–food–024282/221

85   With thanks to Eugene Byrne for the nomination of Carrie Croad to this book.

86   'Murder most foul on platform five', *Western Daily Press*, 14 June 1997.

Given that Albert was fighting for king and country, the media coverage of the murder portrayed Bessie as an immoral harlot who got what she deserved after being unfaithful to her husband, and the media portrayed Albert as nothing but a brave war hero... despite the fact he had, unprovoked, shot his pregnant wife in the stomach. One witness told the court that she had heard Bessie shout: "Don't do it! Oh my god, don't do it!" And then, after the initial gunfire, Bessie cried: "I'm hurt, I'm hurt". The bystander then saw Albert take aim a second time and, this time, he fired the weapon at the collapsed woman's abdomen.[87]

The case attracted enormous public interest, perhaps as a distraction from the endless horror stories of war. The courtroom was filled with members of the public wanting to watch the spectacle unfold. Albert's solicitor refused to put his client in the witness box, instead telling the court that it was not his job to prove Albert innocent but the job of the prosecution to find this saintly war hero guilty. Lord Justice Coleridge told the courtroom: "There is much in the case to move the most callous to sympathy. I would be sorry to see the day when all sympathy was banished from the jury box."[88] He then called on the jury to find Albert innocent. When the not-guilty verdict was announced, the courtroom went wild with excitement and it took several minutes to quieten everyone down.

While I do not want to pass judgement on Bessie's infidelity, it is worth remembering the times that she and Albert were living in. The war had been unfolding for three years, everyone was living with phenomenal stress and uncertainty, and couples were separated for long periods. These were difficult and unsettled times and, while not necessarily right, infidelity was far from unusual.

87   'Bristol station tragedy', *Western Daily Press*, 24 October 1917.
88   'Incredible verdict', *Western Daily Press*, 21 June 1997.

MAUD CUNNINGTON
1869–1951, ARCHAEOLOGIST

Welsh-born Maud Cunnington was one of seven children born to a notable doctor. She was educated at Cheltenham Ladies' College. From 1897, Maud became interested in archaeology and, over the next five decades, her work included digs at some of the most important sites in Britain: including a neolithic enclosure at Knap Hill, an Iron Age village at All Cannings Cross and, most interestingly for us, Woodhenge in Wiltshire. Woodhenge is a neolithic circle of 168 timber posts that is two miles north-east from the better known Stonehenge. It was discovered in 1926 by Maud and her husband Ben Cunnington thanks to an aerial photograph taken by Gilbert Insall. Woodhenge is well worth a visit because the formations and history are quite spectacular — it is also a lot less crowded than its more famous stone sibling. For two years, excavations were carried out that uncovered concentric rings of holes that had once held timber uprights and formed a structure similar to Stonehenge. Maud was nominated for a CBE in 1948 and the *Western Morning News* noted that for more than 50 years she had been "one of the leading explorers into prehistoric Britain"[89].

STELLA MARTIN CURREY
1907-1994, WRITER

The offices of the *Bristol Times & Mirror* would turn out to be inspirational for one bold reporter. Helen Estella Martin Currey, whose father had been the nonsense writer JP Martin, worked on

---

89   'Tributes to long lives of service' in *Western Morning News*, 10 June 1948.

the paper between 1926 and 1932 and used her experiences there to fuel her debut novel, 1934's *Paperchase End*.

Stella was an apprentice at the *Bristol Times & Mirror* in the 1920s and was soon working as a reporter as well as writing her own column. That column was called 'Apples of Eve' and Stella used it to subvert the old-fashioned idea of a 'woman's page', as researcher Sarah Lonsdale notes: "[Stella] took the opportunity to write a series of humorous and gently subversive articles which, at their heart, contained a sustained critique of women's magazines and women's pages in newspapers." Sarah later comments: "Other columns by [Stella] suggested that expensive cosmetics and potions were not worth the money women spend on them; that long walks in the country provide a more natural shade of rouge than powder; that home-made face masks from oatmeal and orris root work better than shop bought ones; and that the vogue for adding food supplements to every meal was a waste of time and money."[90]

One of her first assignments for the *Bristol Times & Mirror* was to report on Bristol's soup kitchen that had been set up after the General Strike in May 1926. Stella later remembered: "The sight of the women and children queuing for soup and the pervasive air of quiet misery made me feel angry and guilty. My editor wrote, 'Re–write more objectively.'"[91] In later years, Stella became the paper's Bristol Zoo correspondent and her articles included pieces on Betty the bag–snatching chimpanzee, and inventing a slimming diary for Judy the overweight elephant.

When Stella was at the *Bristol Times & Mirror*, the paper was fighting to survive in the face of rivalry from the *Bristol Evening World* (which would eventually win out), so Stella dedicated her debut novel *Paperchase End* (1934) to "those who have known the

90   Sarah Lonsdale, 2020, *Rebel Women*, Manchester University Press, p344 and p353.
91   Quoted in Sarah Lonsdale, 2016, *The Journalist in British Fiction and Film*, Bloomsbury.

comradeship and suffering of a newspaper war".

Paperchase End is about Susan Calvin and the fictional *Ravenport Courier* newspaper, which is threatened by the arrival of the *Dispatch* newspaper. It is an interesting examination of the real struggles that local newspapers were facing from rivals – in an era when local newspapers were an essential source of both local and national news and did not have to worry about competition from digital sources. Susan is faced with the dilemma between factually reporting on a dry meeting and losing readers, or sexing the same meeting up by twisting the truth and gaining readers. As Sarah Lonsdale notes: "The novel is an intelligent mediation on the responsible journalist's tightrope walk between giving the public what it wants and fulfilling his or her nebulous and ill–defined role in informing citizens on council affairs, court proceedings and health and scientific advantages. It was a tightrope the author herself walked."[92]

Stella's other novels included *Prelude for Six Flutes* in 1937, about a girl who brings up her younger siblings when their parents are killed, and *One Woman's Year* in 1953, a sort of memoir divided into the 12 months of the calendar, about life as a middle-class wife and mother in the post-war years and includes recipes, short stories and diary entries alongside beautiful woodcut illustrations by Malcolm Ford. Amusingly, when the *Bristol Evening Post* reviewed *One Woman's Year* in 1954, they did so under a big headline warning: "This book is for women."[93]

South African-born Stella moved to England with her family when she was six and attended a boarding school for daughters of the clergy (as well as being a writer, her father was also a Methodist minister). In 1932, Stella married the South African teacher and poet Ralph Nixon Currey with whom she had two

---

92   Quoted in Sarah Lonsdale, 2016, *The Journalist in British Fiction and Film*, Bloomsbury.
93   'This book is for women', *Bristol Evening Post*, 25 February 1954.

sons. They lived in Colchester. Over the course of her career, she wrote five novels as well as *One Woman's Year*, a biography of her father (illustrated by Quention Blake), short stories for magazines, and plays for stage and television, including *Love and Miss Figgis* in 1959.

HESTER DAVIS
1784–1883, ACTIVIST

In 1880, the UK was affected by a great famine that caused the cost of food to rise out of proportion to people's wages. One ingredient that particularly shot up in cost was flour and, when opportunity presented itself, the good people of Warmley were among those forced to take drastic action. One day, a merchant with a wagon full of flour was passing through the village when he was stopped by a group of women led by a grandmother named Hester Davis. The women caused such alarm in the driver that he promptly unhitched his wagon and galloped off on the horse to tell his employer what was happening. When he returned to Warmley, he discovered that Hester and her group had taken all of the flour and sold it to their neighbours for 2 shillings and 2 pence: a price that the women deemed to be fair and reasonable, unlike the extortionate costs the markets were charging at the time. The women had left the coins on the cart for the driver to collect when he returned. And, for the first time in a long time, the people of Warmley ate and slept well that night. Hester lived to be 99 before being buried at St Anne's Churchyard.[94]

94   With thanks to Allen Bridgwood for the nomination of Hester Davis to this book. Thanks also to the Bristol & Avon Family History Society website for information used in this entry.

MARIA DAVIS
died 1802, DESTITUTE MOTHER

On 20 January 1802, two schoolboys were heading over to Brandon Hill to play when they spotted a small basket lying a few yards away from the footpath. Peering inside, they found the dead body of a 15-month-old baby boy. The baby's body was taken to St Peter's Hospital on Castle Green ahead of an inquest.

A few days later, Maria Davis and her friend Charlotte Bobbet, both aged 20, were arrested for the murder. Maria was baby Richard's mother. Maria's husband had been killed in Ireland a few days after Richard's birth and the young woman was destitute. She had been given a charitable donation to pay a nurse in Clifton to look after Richard, but by 15 January the nurse returned the baby to his mother claiming that she was owed money for the care she had provided. Desperate, Maria asked her friend Charlotte for help, as Maria had no money and no home. They turned to a market trader called Susanna Avard for help, explaining that Maria and the baby had nowhere to live.

Susanna allowed Maria and Richard to stay with her at her home in St Phillips and the mother and child moved in on 16 January. But Maria found it very hard to care for her baby and had no money to buy food for him or for herself. So Charlotte suggested they leave the baby in St Mary Redcliffe churchyard for someone to find and take in and, after dark, they set off. Upon reaching the church, Maria began to have second thoughts, worrying that wild animals would find Richard in his basket and attack him. So they instead left him in his basket further up the road. But after they left, Richard cried so loudly and insistently that they returned to him and took him back to Susanna's home with them.

The next evening, 19 January, Maria and Charlotte bundled

Richard into one of Susanna's baskets and again took him out with the intention of leaving him. This time, they decided to head to Brandon Hill and hoped that his cries would attract the attention of someone from one of the big houses nearby, who would come and take care of him. But after Maria and Charlotte left him, Richard's cries didn't attract anyone's attention. Instead, he died of exposure on Brandon Hill.

After the newspapers broke the story, Maria initially denied that this was her missing baby but people who knew both Maria and Richard quickly identified her and she was sentenced to be hanged for murder. Charlotte met the same fate for her part in helping Maria. After their executions in April 1802, the bodies of the two women were given to medical students to use for dissection practice.[95]

JOAN DAY
1928-2019, CYCLIST, ARCHAEOLOGIST

For 49 years, Joan Day was a valued committee member of the Keynsham and Saltford Local History Society, which she had helped to found in 1965. Originally from Bath, as a young woman Joan was an impressive cyclist who held the record for cycling from Lands End to Bristol. She achieved this feat in 1954, completing the 195-mile cycle ride in 10 hours and 59 minutes — thereby knocking more than an hour off the previous record. Clearly an adventurous soul, Joan also held a glider pilot's licence and was an accomplished horse rider.

Alongside her husband Roy, Joan began to attend lectures about industrial archaeology which were organised by the University of

95. 'A freezing death for baby boy', *Bristol Evening Post*, 17 November 1989.

Bristol in the mid-1960s. The lectures were intended to inspire students to make their own local history investigations and Joan duly sought out older residents from Keynsham and Saltford to quiz them about their memories of working in the brass mills. In time, Joan became a renowned expert on the history of brass making in the UK and wrote two books on the subject. From the 1980s, Joan was a prominent voice in the campaign to preserve the former Saltford Brass Mill, which had closed in 1925, and to prevent the shell of the building being destroyed by developers: this was the last remaining mill in this part of the country. The Saltford Brass Museum now occupies the building as a testament to Joan's hard work.

By 1970, Joan and Roy had taken over responsibility for the university's industrial archaeology course and Joan became a tutor at the University of Bristol for 38 years until she retired in 2008. Joan and Roy joined the Bristol Industrial Archaeological Society and, within a few years, Joan joined the committee and assumed a number of key roles over the following decades, ranging from Secretary to Chair.

AUGUSTA DEANE
1871-1936, CIVIL SERVANT

Augusta Deane had the intriguing nickname of 'Pussie' but I think I'll stick to calling her Augusta on these pages. Born in London to a middle-class family, she was living in Clifton by the late 1880s and was employed as a teacher and parish worker. By 1903, Augusta had become an advocate of the Bristol branch of the Lend a Hand club, which had a strong link to the Young Women's Christian Association.

By the time of the 1911 census, Augusta was living independently in a flat that she owned at 2 Saville Place in Clifton and her profession was listed as 'Supervisor of Board of Trade Labour Exchanges, South West division'. This was in response to the Labour Exchanges Act 1909, which saw the creation of labour exchanges around the UK to help unemployed people find work. In 1918, Augusta was awarded an OBE for her war work at the Ministry of Labour and for her service to the agricultural committee. She was also a regular speaker to meetings of young women, inspiring them to pursue good works in their own careers.

In 1921, Augusta was elected as the second President of the Bristol Soroptimists, where she led a committee that was devoted to supporting and fundraising for people in need. In 1934, Augusta was made the first ever Honorary Member of the Bristol Soroptimists and, when she died in 1936, the club's members paid for a plaque to be erected to Augusta's memory in Bristol Cathedral above where her ashes were buried. But this isn't the only tribute to Augusta in the Cathedral. At the time of her death, the Bishop dedicated a prayer rail to her memory and, two years after her death, £91 was raised to install two carved oak prayer desks and a small gravestone above where her ashes were interred.

DINA DOBSON-HINTON
1885-1965, HIGH ACHIEVER

One of the joys of researching *The Women Who Built Bristol* books is discovering the extraordinary array of industries that many of these women were involved with, and Dina Portway Dobson-Hinton certainly falls into this category. I initially put 'archaeologist' next to her dates above but she was so much more than that and I had to change it. As well as being an archaeologist, Dina was also a speleologist (someone who studies caves), a city councillor in Bristol and a staunch advocate for women to be involved in the justice system. And then some.

Born Dina Portway in Essex, she was the eldest of six children. Dina was an early female student at Newnham College, University of Cambridge, which she joined in 1903 and studied the Historical Tripos. But while women at Cambridge and Oxford could sit for their degree exams, they were not entitled to wear a cap and gown or receive the degrees they had earned. And without their degrees, women were denied the same qualifications and job opportunities as the men who had completed the same education. However, Trinity College at the University of Dublin gave all students, regardless of sex, the opportunity to achieve their degree and therefore the chance to further their life chances. Women restricted by Oxbridge's archaic policy leapt at this lifeline and, in this way, Dina became a 'steamboat lady'.

This was the nickname given to female students in the years between 1904 and 1907 who took the steamboat to Dublin. Trinity thought only Irish women who had studied at Oxford or Cambridge would take them up on this opportunity. However, by 1907 there had been 720 steamboat ladies who had travelled to Dublin from Oxford and Cambridge to receive their degrees: something that their male peers achieved in Oxford and

Cambridge without having to pack a bag and travel overseas, nor pay the travel and accommodation costs, nor pay extra graduation fees to a second university.[96] Historian Susan Parkes explained: "They took one day off, they came on the overnight steamboat, stayed one night in Dublin, got their degrees the next day and went back the following night."[97]

With her degree in hand, Dina became a teacher, working in Edgbaston and Manchester between 1906 and 1910. Then, in 1911, she married John Dobson, who was Professor of Greek at the University of Bristol (he would later become Pro-Vice Chancellor there), so the couple relocated and set up home on Cambridge Park, Redland. Dina and John were extremely interested in the exploration of study and caves, and John was the President of the university's Speleological Society, a title he retained until his death in 1947. Dina shared his passion for caves and archeology and she became the Vice-President of the Speleological Society in 1946. As a cave explorer, Dina had a number of distinctions, including being the first woman to go down Eastwater Cavern in Somerset, which she did in 1920; and in 1922 she was the first woman to descend the 40ft pot in Swildon's Hole in Somerset.

In 1931, Dina wrote an impressive tome called *The Archaeology of Somerset*, which was republished in 1982. However, while Dina had written her version of the book single-handedly, it took 13 researchers to compile the updated version, which is an indication of how much work she was capable of undertaking. The introduction to the new edition states that Dina's book was "widely regarded as one of the best in the county archaeological series". She also wrote a number of other books, including the illustrated *A Book of Prehistory (1933)* for children, *A Book of Ancient*

96   When Dina's daughter attended Newnham College at the University of Cambridge in 1937, she was also denied a degree on account of being a woman. Newnham did not grant full degrees to women until 1948.

97   trinitynews.ie/2021/12/the-steamboat-ladies/

History (1934), another children's book called *Early Man* (1950), and *Clothing And Costume* (1955).

Alongside all of this, Dina was a member of the Historical Association before and after World War Two, was President of the Bristol Soroptimists in the late 1930s, and a member of a great many professional and academic societies, including being one of the few women accepted as a Fellow of the Royal Society of Antiquaries. In addition, Dina regularly spoke on the radio on the topic of prehistoric archaeology. When Dina became a Justice of the Peace in 1937, she was one of the first 12 women in Bristol to be appointed to a position that was usually reserved for men. In 1938, following an unsuccessful previous campaign, Dina was elected as the councillor for Hillfields as a member of the Citizens Party; this was a political group that existed in Bristol from 1925 to 1974 and was largely a coalition of politicians with Conservative and Liberal views who teamed up in opposition to the Labour Party. She remained a councillor until 1947.

With John, Dina had five children. After John's death in 1947, Dina married Martin Hinton in 1949, who had been a Palaeontologist and the Keeper of Zoology at the Natural History Museum in London. Dina was known to be a fearsome character who took no nonsense from anyone; she wore trousers, even when women were not usually seen to do so; and would cycle all over Bristol regardless of the fact it was considered unseemly for a woman from her educated station to travel in this way.[98]

98   With enormous thanks to Dina's grandchildren Celia Scott and Stephen Scott.

FLORENCE DOLLING
1896–1989, GROCER

When Florence Hathway married George Dolling in 1920, she joined him in running the general store and bakery that his grandparents had established many decades previously. The Dollings Shop in Warmley was run by the third generation of the family when it passed to the hands of Florence and George, who also worked with George's sister Emily Jefferies.

Before marriage, Florence had lived in nearby Cadbury Heath, where she was one of three children to Sarah and William Hathway, who worked as a boot maker. By the age of 14, Florence was working as a corset maker. After marriage, she moved to Tower Road South in Warmley, to work with her husband. George, who had served in World War One, also worked as a dairyman having set up a dairy business before the war.

Shop life was everything to Florence. While her husband was out delivering milk, Florence worked hard in the store, assisted by her children Margaret and John. Margaret recalled: "We sold everything a good village shop should sell and even on Sundays, when the store was closed, customers would often come to the back door for the odd item which had been forgotten during normal trading hours."

After World War Two, everything changed. Food was rationed and it was hard for Florence to manage customers and their needs, but she kept her wits about her to ensure everyone had enough to keep going, even if it sometimes meant forgoing the rations allotted to her own family. Margaret remembers Florence sitting up late counting out points or food coupons to help make everything go that little bit further. She said: "I did learn during the war years people became friends and not just customers, and we all helped each other and shared our sorrows.

The comradeship was unbelievable."[99]

George sold the dairy business in the mid-1940s when his health declined and he died in 1953. This put extra pressure on Florence and Margaret to keep the shop afloat, which they did until 1966 when the council decided that the area was to be redeveloped and the property was to be demolished. Florence unsuccessfully tried to appeal the decision.

MABEL DOWNING
1870-1950, MUSICIAN

A gifted musician, Mabel Downing, who was born in Weston-super-Mare but lived in Clifton, graduated from the Belgrave House School, Clevedon, in harp and piano at the age of just 15. By 1896 when she was 25, Mabel had become established as a Professor of the guitar, mandolin, harp, zither and philomel.[100]

Guitar and mandolin bands originated in Italy in the early 1880s and soon became fashionable elsewhere. Mabel picked up the trend in the UK, no doubt latching on to the fact that while respectable Victorian women were not encouraged to play conventional orchestral music in public, it was acceptable for them to play in all-female guitar and mandolin bands so long as it was for charitable purposes. So that's exactly what she did, becoming one of the most notable guitar and mandolin band leaders of her era. Mabel performed regularly with her group of 18 women at concerts and was a much in demand instrumentalist. For instance, after a pre-Christmas concert in 1898, the press coverage referred "to the great esteem in which Miss Downing is

99 Margaret Ann Rees, 1993, in Cadbury Heath History Group, *Life As It Was: Vol 3*, p50–51.
100 A zither is a stringed instrument with a flat soundboard, and a philomel is an instrument similar to the violin.

92

held throughout the West of England, where she has conducted and established ladies' mandolin bands at Clifton, Bath, Weston-super-Mare and Taunton"[101].

Mabel performed regularly with her band until 1910, when she emigrated to Winnipeg, US, where she continued her work as a music teacher who specialised in, and I love this term, plucked instruments. However, despite a life filled with making people happy with her music, Mabel met a sad fate when she died from food poisoning at a hospital in London.[102]

SARAH DUNN
1920-2010, HEADTEACHER

Between 1954 and 1980, Amy Margaret Sarah Dunn was the formidable headteacher of Colston's Girls' School.[103] Her passion for this school led her to document the first 100 years of the establishment in a book published in 1991. One year after her retirement, Sarah received an honorary Master of Arts degree from the University of Bristol in recognition of all she had done for the education of girls in the city. Sarah had grown up in Coventry, the only child to Amy and William Dunn. She attended Coventry University where she trained to be a teacher.

101   'Clifton Ladies Guitar and Mandolin Band' in *Bath Chronicle and Weekly Gazette*, 22 December 1898.
102   With thanks to Dawn Dyer for the nomination of Mabel Downing to this book.
103   The school was renamed Montpelier High School in 2019.

MARY EASBY
1914-1960, DOCTOR

Living and working from 209 Wells Road, Knowle, Dr Mary Easby was a GP who was much admired and respected by her patients and community. Mary Lena Hunt was born in Bristol. While completing her medical studies, she lived at 32 Lower Redland Road with the Williams family, who rented out rooms in their substantial house to a number of students. In 1942, newly qualified as a doctor, Mary married Richard Easby and the couple set up home on the Wells Road. Tragically, their 21-month-old son Ian died after he fell into a pond near their home. The couple had two elder daughters, Pam and Jackie. Following her own untimely death in 1960, Mary was buried at Arnos Vale Cemetery.

GWENDOLINE EVANS
1902-1958, SINGER

The contralto singer Gwendoline Florence Evans appeared countless times in the local newspapers due to her impressive singing talents. Hers was a life clearly lived on the stage because Gwendoline also sang live on BBC radio shows and performed in local theatrical productions. Despite this, the 1939 Register, which was collated at the height of Gwendoline's success, lists her profession as simply being "unpaid domestic duties": how many times those three words have been used in documentation to belittle a woman's achievements.

Gwendoline's first BBC appearance was in 1925 and she continued to sing for the broadcaster until 1956, from its studios in Cardiff and London as well as more locally in Bristol. She also taught singing to children and was the founder of the Beechwood

Ladies' Choir. Alongside her musical achievements, Gwendoline was a member of the local Tuberculosis After-Care Committee and had been the President of the Kingswood Inner Wheel. She lived with her husband David Evans, a commercial traveller, at 38 Beechwood Avenue, Hanham, and was a valued and respected member of the community.

BRENDA FOWLER
1933-2008, ADMINISTRATOR

The role of the secretary is much more demanding than outsiders may presume. And that is certainly the case when working in a university, as Brenda Fowler did.

Brenda joined the University of Bristol in 1975 as a Secretary in the Department of Biochemistry, where her husband Malcolm was already known to the team as the Medical School's Glassblower. While people may assume that a secretary does little more than type letters and file papers, Brenda's role was certainly more encompassing than that. In addition to her day-to-day duties, she also arranged dinner parties and social events for faculty members, as well as any other task that needed someone to just get on and do it. By 1989, Brenda's job title was upgraded to Office Manager, which was a better reflection of the role she played. By 1991, her job was again changed and she took over the task of dealing with the administration of admissions to the university and looking after new students who attended interviews. The following year, Brenda took a leading role in helping to plan the department's Lilian Hawker wing, before her retirement in 1996.[104]

104 Lilian Hawker is profiled in this volume of *The Women Who Built Bristol*.

At home in Winscombe with Malcolm and their two daughters, Brenda enjoyed tennis, amateur dramatics and playing a part in community events.

SARAH FOX
1742-1811, PHILANTHROPIST

When Sarah Fox (born Sarah Champion) died, she left behind 40 detailed diaries documenting her life. Although those diaries have since been lost, what has been found is a 502-page handwritten manuscript that a family friend and fellow Quaker called John Frank compiled in 1873. In 2003, academic Madge Dresser edited that manuscript into *The Diary of Sarah Fox*, and this book gives us an extraordinary insight into the life of a Bristolian woman living in an era that has been so little documented from a woman's perspective. Sarah met fascinating people of the day such as the evangelist John Wesley, politician Edmund Burke, newspaper editor Sarah Farley and acclaimed writer Hannah More.[105] Sarah also met many anti-slavery campaigners in Bristol, including a number of American activists who were staying in the UK. She counted as friends the families of some of the leading local businesses, including members of the Fry family (chocolate), the Galton family (guns) and the Lloyd family (banking).

Sarah's sharp mind and intellectual curiosity, as well as the illustrious shoulders that she rubbed up against, are what particularly set her diary apart from many other memoirs from a similar period, oh, and the fact that she's a woman. The Champion family were active in the Society of Friends, which by the time of Sarah's childhood no longer experienced the political persecution

---

105 Hannah More and Sarah Farley are profiled in Volume One of *The Women Who Built Bristol*.

that persisted until the end of the 1690s. Even so, during Sarah's lifetime Quakers were still denied access to university or from holding any political office.

For most of her life, Sarah lived in Bristol and enjoyed the social circle she shared with her brother, porcelain manufacturer Richard Champion. Their mother had died in 1745 when Sarah was just four, and their father Joseph moved to London a year later, leaving Sarah in the care of her maternal grandmother, Sarah Rogers. This was better than the fate her siblings received: Richard was sent to a nurse in Westbury until he was eight, and then he was sent to a school in London, at which point six-year-old sister Esther joined Sarah with their grandmother. The girls usually saw their father only once or twice a year.

When grandmother Sarah died in 1754, the girls were split up and sent to live with different aunts while their father Joseph focused all of his attention on Richard, and his new wife and their younger son. Taking pity on their largely abandoned nieces, Joseph's half-brothers helped provide for Sarah and Esther financially. When she was 17, Sarah was finally invited to stay with Joseph in London and discovered her father and his family lived a far more sophisticated and luxurious life than she had been doing in Bristol.

But the London visit was a short one and Sarah returned to Bristol to live with an aunt in Castle Green in the city centre, and later at a country house in Stoke Bishop. When Richard was sent to Bristol by their father to learn a trade, Sarah was very excited to be reunited with him. As for the problem of what to do with his two daughters, Joseph was keen to try and marry them off, because a daughter remained the legal responsibility of her father up until the point that she married (at which point, of course, she became her husband's legal responsibility). Joseph tried to find Sarah and Esther any number of husbands but they managed to avoid the problem... for a few years at least. Esther was 29 before she finally married, while Sarah dodged the marriage bullet by moving in with Richard and his wife Judith at their home in Castle Green.

Sarah concerned herself with philanthropic work in Bristol and gave freely of her time to various charities. She supported the Quaker workhouse, the Bristol Blind School and a penitentiary for 'fallen women'. She was a visitor to prison inmates, ostensibly offering them comfort but really attempting to educate them about how their lives would be improved if they joined the Society of Friends. She also took up the cause of animal welfare, worrying about the mistreatment of horses as well as the cruelty of fishing.

When she was 48 in 1790, Sarah married the banker Charles Fox, a widower 12 years her senior. The marriage seemed to be companionable but it was brief; Charles died in 1801 leaving Sarah to live the final decade of her life alone, having also outlived her brother and sister.

AA FRANCIS
born early 1940s, MATRIARCH

Born in Jamaica, AA Francis decided to travel to England in her late 20s in a search for better opportunities. She arrived in England on 13 August 1960 and, just four days later on 17 August, began work as a Nursing Auxiliary at Glenside Hospital.

AA shared her story in the Bristol Broadsides book *More Bristol Lives* and chose to write only under her initials; unfortunately I have not been able to find out what her initials stand for. However, her entry in the book, 'In a Strange Land', provides an extraordinary insight into the life of this ambitious woman who travelled almost 5,000 miles on her own, hoping to improve her chances in life.

Because her family had been unable to pay for her to stay on in school, AA enlisted in adult education classes in Bristol alongside her work at Glenside and she completed certificates in shorthand and typing, as well as studying for an English O'level. After a period of time at Glenside, she worked in catering and clerical roles, changing jobs when she needed to find something that better fitted in around caring for her children. AA was proud to say that, having grown up in Jamaica where there was no government financial assistance, she never claimed from the UK's benefits system either, even when life became extremely tough.

After marrying, AA had nine children (five boys and four girls) and was determined that they should all have a good schooling because she knew how hard it had been to claw back her education as an adult. But life threw AA a hard blow when she was widowed at the age of 37. She chose never to remarry. She wrote: "Life for me is very, very tough indeed, but with the determination not to allow another man to dominate or take me into the darkest gloom of life, I do not remarry. I have no regrets for bringing up my children on my own ... I did not like the thought of having a man in the house who was not the father of my children."

AA also writes perceptively about racism and the challenges of living in a "strange land" where there are so many "different tribes and nations". She describes racism as being like cancer and as something that is difficult to cure, so she chose to not recognise it in her life so that it could not weigh her down. Racism, she said, was more of an issue in the UK than in Jamaica and wrote: "There are so many different nations in Jamaica, and still I never heard of this awful word 'racism' until I came to this country."

Although we don't know much about AA as an individual, her biographical chapter is an insight into the hardships experienced by a woman emigrating to Bristol in search of a new life. She found it here but had to work hard to have the life she wanted. I wish we knew more about her.[106]

BARBARA FRANKS
1907-1987, VOLUNTEER

Born near Clifton Downs to a Quaker family, Barbara Mary Tanner (as she was originally called) grew up in a household that was non–conformist, pacifist and politically Liberal, and where there was no tobacco, alcohol or meat. After attending a Quaker school, Barbara studied philosophy, politics and economics at the University of Oxford, where she fell in love with her tutor Oliver Franks. The couple married in 1931 and had two children.

Barbara became involved with the committee of the Oxford Eye Hospital and was also a research assistant to the historian Sir George Clark. Oliver was inspired by his wife's voluntary work and learned about public service from her actions, and they would later work alongside each other to support different communities. During World War Two, Barbara volunteered for the Women's Voluntary Service and worked for the foreign ministry. After the war, the couple relocated to Washington DC, where Oliver had been made the British Ambassador. They returned to Oxford in 1952 and Barbara resumed her voluntary work for organisations including Age Concern, the Citizens' Advice Bureau and Oxfam.

106   AA Francis, 1988, 'In a Strange Land' in *More Bristol Lives*, Bristol Broadsides, p91-96.

EDITH FROST
1886-1980, ART DEALER

Edith Frost's father Walter Frost was a fine art dealer, living in Bristol with his wife Amy. They had a number of children including Edith and, following in her father's footsteps, she grew up to work as a fine art dealer and director at the family's globally renowned business of Frost and Reed Ltd, which had been established around 1800 and maintained offices in Bristol and London. As a respected businesswoman, Edith joined the Bristol Soroptimists and was the chairperson from 1948-1949.

But how did this woman end up being honoured in January 1947 with King Christian X's Freedom Medal? This medal is typically only awarded to foreign nationals who made a special contribution to Denmark's struggle for freedom during the war, and only 3,000 of these medals were ever issued. Edith received hers in recognition of her services to Denmark during World War Two, which included staging an exhibition in Bristol called 'Fighting Denmark' during 1945. This was a touring exhibition that told the story of the Danish resistance during the Nazi occupation from 1940-1945, and the exhibition is now on permanent display in Copenhagen. Edith's medal is kept at the Bristol Archives, along with the Frost family's papers.

Edith remained in Bristol for the rest of her life, living with her sister Eleanor at Hill Side on Bridge Road, Leigh Woods until she died in 1980.

MARY FUIDGE
1820-1842, GLASS WOMAN

In St Stephens Church, close to St Nicholas Market, there is a stained glass window honouring Mary Fuidge and her baby daughter Frances. But who were Mary and Frances and why are they immortalised in a window?

Mary Canning from Wiltshire married sugar merchant and land owner Thomas Fuidge in Bristol in January 1841, and the young couple set up home at Cradley House in West Clifton. Daughter Frances was born later that year, followed by a second daughter Mary a year later. In the Victorian era, it was common for wealthy families to memorialise their dead loved ones and this was the action grieving Thomas took when Mary died at just 22 years of age, less than two years after their marriage.

It is not known what caused Mary and Frances to die so close together, but Thomas paid for the stained glass window in their memory, with the inscription: "To the Glory of God and in Memory of Mary wife of Thomas Fuidge Born 5th November 1820. Died 29th November 1842. Also of Frances Ann their infant daughter who died February 1842." Thomas remarried in 1847 and had a further two daughters with his new wife, while also bringing up his eldest daughter Mary.

JEAN GEORGE
1953–2016, LIBRARIAN

Originally from the Lake District, Jean Dixon was only 15 when her mother died, and young Jean quickly took on the domestic burdens of shopping, cleaning and running the family home alongside her school work. Clearly adept at multitasking, Jean excelled at school and went on to study German at Exeter University, as well as completing her PGCE the following year.

At university, she met her husband Robin George and their first years of married life were spent in Preston, where Jean worked as a teacher. However, by 1977 they were living in Yate and Jean found a job at the *Bristol Evening Post* as a Library Assistant. It was in this way that she discovered her passion for library work and completed a postgraduate course in librarianship.

This qualification led Jean to a role at the University of Bristol's library where she quickly rose through the ranks to become Chief Cataloguer in 1986, a post she held until her retirement in 2011. Even after retirement, Jean chose to stay busy and took a voluntary role at the Bristol Regional Environmental Records Centre, entering thousands of wildlife records into a new database.

Remembering Jean's devotion to the library, former colleague Dr Peter King wrote: "Jean was perfectly suited to her work. She was professional and meticulous. Her attention to detail was legendary, but her very high standards were maintained with humour and grace. She was faithful and loyal, a manager who took a genuine interest in her staff without being intrusive. She was approachable and fair but not soft, never having to raise her voice to exert her authority."[107]

SARAH GIBBONS
1634-1659, PREACHER

One of the first British Quakers to travel to the US to preach was Bristol's Sarah Gibbons. But, of course, her path was not smooth.

107 bristol.ac.uk/news/2016/august/jean–george.html

Sarah was one of the British Quakers who boarded the 'Speedwell' in 1656, which was bound from Gravesend, Kent, for Massachusetts Bay Colony, an English settlement in the US. However, on arrival 21-year-old Sarah and her fellow Quakers were arrested, interrogated and detained in prison for 11 weeks, before being deported back to England for religious reasons: the leaders of Massachusetts Bay Colony were worried about the influence of the Quakers on the other members of the British colony. It is thought that Sarah may have been illiterate because her statement was taken on her behalf and signed only with the letter 'Q' for 'Quaker'.

In 1657, Sarah took part in a second voyage to the US, this time on board the 'Woodhouse' and this time bound for New Amsterdam (now called New York). However, on arrival, three of the party were judicially executed for their religious beliefs. Sarah, along with five others who were permitted to settle in New Amsterdam, helped to establish a Quaker group on Rhode Island. She used this as her base for the following two years to travel as a preacher to locations including Barbados, Boston, Manhattan and Salem.

However, Sarah's life was cut short in 1659 following a canoeing accident in Providence, when the canoe she was travelling in sprung a leak and, unable to swim, Sarah drowned at the age of 25.

SARAH GIBBS and ELIZABETH BURRIDGE
Sarah born c1822; Eliza born c1850, DRAPERS

Living at 1 Frederick Street in Totterdown, at the time of the 1881 census Sarah Gibbs was listed as a draper and the head of the household. Hers was a household of three women, who were three generations of the same family. Sarah, 59 in 1881, was living with her daughter Elizabeth Burridge, 31 and listed as a 'draperess', and Elizabeth's one-year-old daughter Minnie. Where were their menfolk? Well, we know that Sarah was widowed by this point but I have not been able to find out what had become of Elizabeth's husband. However, from the census report of 1891 it seems that Elizabeth was now a resident of St Peter's Hospital (a workhouse) in the city centre. Her daughter Minnie is nowhere to be found in the records, which suggests that Elizabeth's life took a very sad turn.[108]

LOUIE GOFFE
1902-1997, WAR SHERO

Many thousands of lives were lost during World War One and a great number of memorials and tributes were erected to those people around the UK. One such memorial stands in Shirehampton and was unveiled on 4 September 1921. Of the 58 men named on the memorial, almost all were seamen, which is not surprising considering Shirehampton is a port. For more than 70 years, well into the 1990s, that war memorial was attended by a local woman.

Louie Kathleen Sansum (as she was originally called) was born in Shirehampton in 1902. Her father George was a dock labourer and, with his wife Louisa, he had 12 children, of whom Louie was the youngest. Five of her brothers fought in World War One and two of them were killed in action.

During the war, Louie worked at the munitions factory in

---

108   It was not uncommon for young children to be separated from their parents who had entered the workhouse, and for the child to be sent to a workhouse school and prepared for a life in service. But it is mere speculation as to whether or not this was Minnie's fate.

Kingsweston Lane, Avonmouth. The factory began producing mustard gas in January 1918, and at the tender age of 15 Louie had become a 'gas girl' involved in the production of this highly toxic substance.

After the war, Louie would regularly walk from her home at 8 Old Quarry Road to tend the memorial, often bringing a lawn mower and gardening tools with her to keep the area tidy, and she bought flowers to make the site colourful. Her brothers Roy and Nelson Sansum were named on the memorial, but Louie said she also tended the area because she knew every single one of the young men named on it. Louie later told the *Bristol Post*: "I've looked after that memorial because I loved all those boys. [Shirehampton] was only a small village and everyone knew everyone else. I still feel very sad for them. It was terrible what happened to them. In my street alone 13 boys were killed."[109]

In September 1923, Louie married George (known as Jim) Goffe at Shirehampton Parish Church, with whom she had four children. After their home at Old Quarry Road was destroyed in the Bristol Blitz Good Friday air raid during World War Two, the family moved to 59 Coombe Dale, Shirehampton. When Louie became too infirm to manage the walk to the memorial herself, her daughter would give her a lift in her car so that Louie could continue to maintain the site.

Louie was awarded an MBE in the 1995 New Years Honours list in recognition of her dedication to the community of Shirehampton and her extraordinary care of the war memorial. She received her medal at the Mansion House, Bristol, in a ceremony carried out by the Lord Lieutenant of Avon, Sir John Wills. During her retirement, and following George's death, Louie moved to live in Westbury-on-Trym.

---

109 'Sadness behind a lifetime's devotion', *Bristol Evening Post*, 19 November 1988.

ELINOR GOLDSCHMEID
1910-2009, SOCIAL WORKER

Following her early schooling at Clifton High School, including serving as Head Girl, Elinor Violet Sinnott (as she was born) attended the London School of Economics from where she qualified as a psychiatric social worker. This work led her to Milan, Italy, where she worked in a home for illegitimate and abandoned children. Here she conceived the idea of the 'treasure basket', which contained multi-sensory items for children to play with on their own, without needing an adult to supervise them. Elinor met her future husband, Guido Goldschmeid, while working in Italy, and the couple later relocated to London. Elinor devoted her whole career to working with young children and developing ideas for evolving the way that children play.

ELIZABETH de GORGES
1578-1658, HEIRESS

In 1629, aged 51, Dame Elizabeth Smyth became the fourth wife of Sir Ferdinando de Gorges, a soldier (also her cousin), and the couple lived at Wraxall Court. Here's a fun fact: during the 1620s alone, Ferdinando had already married three times. And here's another fun fact, Elizabeth was the goddaughter of Queen Elizabeth I.

Elizabeth Smyth, who was descended from Swedish nobility and was an Elizabethean courtier, had been widowed in 1627 following the death of her first husband, Sir Hugh Smyth of Ashton Court. This marriage does not seem to have been a particularly happy one, and she is recorded as having written to her son about life at Ashton Court saying: "God increase my patience to endure it still."[110] Reportedly, Hugh was more preoccupied with his health and his horses than he was with anything else, including his wife and children.

Her second marriage, which was to Ferdinando, may or may not have been happy for Elizabeth but it was certainly profitable for him: Elizabeth's inherited wealth helped to bolster Ferdinando's ailing finances considerably. Despite a subsequent position as Governor of New England in the US, Ferdinando's financial situation struggled to improve sufficiently and he remained financially dependent on Elizabeth throughout their marriage. His biographer CM MacInnes wrote: "In addition to all of this, he was now virtually penniless and lived mainly on the bounty of his wife, but ... nothing could daunt this gallant old soldier. It was appropriate that the device on his coat-of-arms should be a whirlpool."[111]

MEG GRIMES
1951-2011, CHARITY PIONEER

In 1986, Meg Grimes set up the Julian Trust Night Shelter in St Pauls to help address the issue of homelessness in the city, taking inspiration from Dame Julian of Norwich: "To love a human being is to accept him as he is. If you wait until he is different you are only loving an idea."[112] As well as being the Chair of the Julian Trust, Meg was also the founder of Bristol's Night Shelter and she is recognised as the driving force of the charity's first 25 years.

Born and raised in Avonmouth, Meg spent many years

---

110   ashtoncourt.wixsite.com/mansionfriends/women-stories
111   CM MacInnes, 1965, *Ferdinando Gorges and New England*, Bristol Branch of the Historical Association, p22.
112   Dame Julian of Norwich (1343-1416) was an anchoress (someone who lived in seclusion due to their religious devotion) during the Middle Ages. Her surviving texts are thought to be the earliest surviving English language examples of writing that has been attributed to a woman.

working as a nurse at the Bristol Royal Infirmary before becoming the manager of a residential care home, which was the paid role she held alongside running the Julian Trust Night Shelter as a volunteer. At home in St George, she was mother to two sons and was known for her love of Christmas, for which she usually spent six months preparing. It is also claimed that Meg never once missed an episode of *EastEnders*. As a keen baker, Meg would make a cake for anyone staying at the night shelter who had a birthday and would bring it in, bedecked in candles, and everyone would sing 'Happy Birthday' to the recipient.

The Julian Trust Night Shelter began as a soup kitchen on Pennywell Road. Meg gathered a small but strong team to help her and, before long, they had expanded to set up Caring at Christmas, offering extra support to homeless people in the harsh winter months. From this, the shelter grew into the impressive organisation that it is today, now based on Little Bishop Street, St Pauls.

Meg's principles for the shelter were to keep things simple, meaning no forms, no questions, no names and no charges. The shelter offered emergency beds in dormitories as well as hot drinks and food, and everything was run by volunteers. She wanted the shelter to offer the basic essentials to those who needed them most and to ensure that anyone who came to the service received a warm welcome. To that end, the more formal complexities of running a charity were less appealing to Meg: while she enjoyed talking to the people staying at the shelter and preparing meals in the kitchen, she did not enjoy chairing meetings or speaking at the charity's AGM.

In 2001, Meg received the Lord Mayor's gold medal in recognition of her work with the homeless people of Bristol.[113]

---

113   With thanks to Debbie Frith for the nomination of Meg Grimes to this book.

LUCILLA GROSSMITH
1939-2022, HEIRESS

Author's note: This is an unusual entry but please indulge me. I met Miss Grossmith, as she preferred to be called, in December 2019. I had heard from a friend that she wanted to buy the first two The Women Who Built Bristol *books but she didn't use the internet, so he gave me her phone number and address to make contact. I tried the number a few times but there was no answer. Having been told that Miss Grossmith was quite elderly, I thought she might not have heard the phone. Because her address was fairly near my home, I walked around one afternoon and knocked on her door...*

Lucilla Grossmith lived in a mid–terrace house on Redcatch Road, Knowle, almost facing the park. It had a slightly shabby exterior, and the front door and windows were covered with stickers for cat charities. It was a large property, quite big for one woman to live in on her own.

Miss Grossmith invited me into her living room and I ended up staying and chatting with her for a few hours, she was quite a talker. It turned out that Miss Grossmith had some strong opinions that she was not afraid to express; this was a woman who had no time for fools. But her interests, as well as cats, extended to local history and catholicism. She told me she had bought her house decades previously owing to the fact it was around the corner from the Society of St Pius X, one of only four such convents and retreats in the UK and a canonically irregular traditionalist catholic church.

I found Miss Grossmith to be a captivating and fascinating woman. And the most interesting thing of all was when she explained that the reason she had never had to work in her life, and the reason she had been able to afford to buy this house in Bristol and devote her life to worshipping at the convent, was because she had inherited a great deal of money from her ancestors: George and Weedon Grossmith, who had co-written the comedy book *The Diary of a Nobody* in 1892, which has never been out of print. Fun fact, the first publishers of the book were JW Arrowsmith of Bristol, who remained in business until 2006. To my disappointment, I haven't been able to work out how Miss Grossmith fitted into the family tree.

I include her here because you never know who is living in that unassuming house down the road from you, and which you walk past numerous times a week without a second thought. There are some extraordinary people living among us and sometimes we have absolutely no idea about them.

EMILY GOUGH
Born 1849, DRESSMAKER

Author's note: There are many women I wish we knew more about. There are women who have remained in my 'in progress' document for many months, returned to every so often in the hope that I can somehow uncover more information about her. And Emily Gough is one of those women.

Born in Cosham, Wiltshire, Emily Gough's surname before she married is not known. Nor is the date of her marriage. But the 1871 census has her married to shoemaker Edward Gough and living with their two-month-old daughter, also called Emily, at 44 Herbert Street, which is behind Dame Emily Park in Bedminster. We know that Edward died, leaving Emily as a young widow with a clutch of small children to bring up, and she supported her family by working as a dressmaker. That information on its own is remarkable enough but that information is not on its own. Emily was involved in the community, particularly with regards to organisations committed to the betterment of conditions for working people.

The Bedminster Industrial Co-operative Society was formed in 1881 and located at 88 West Street and then, from 1886, on Dean Street. There were many co-operatives throughout the area, all formed with the intention of working people supporting each other by pooling their skills and resources to set up shops from which the profits would be shared. Food was expensive in the 1880s and some less scrupulous traders would adulterate their products in order to increase their profits. Co-operatives run by working people addressed this, supplying good food at fair prices. As a dressmaker, it would make sense for Emily to have been a part of this system by trading her sewing skills to help feed her family. In 1899, Emily was listed as one of the 'committee men' at the co-operative. However, the refusal of the Bedminster Industrial Co–Operative Society to support the Women's Trade Union Society may have been a factor in Emily deciding to move on.

Hence why we quickly find Emily as the Vice President of the Bedminster Women's Guild, as well as the Treasurer and Secretary of that organisation. The Bedminster Guild began in 1895 and was a spin-off from the Bedminster Industrial Co-operative Society led by wives of the co-operative members. Mrs Martin was the initial President, and the Guild met every other Monday evening. It seems that the Guild was similar to a Women's Institute, in that women would meet regularly, enjoy guest speakers and raise money for local causes. However, with their roots in the reality of life for working women, it was found by the head office that members of the various Women's Guilds across the country, including Bristol, were strong supporters of the campaign for votes for women that was raging across the UK at this time. A legacy of the Guild that contemporary readers are likely to be familiar with is the white peace poppy, which was introduced by the Guild as a pacifist alternative to the British Legion's red poppy. After 133 years, the final UK Guild closed in 2016.

Emily also held strong views about education and she gave lectures on the topics of employment and social affairs. However, on the census her employment is simply listed as 'seamstress and mantle maker'.[114] By the time of the 1911 census, Emily had moved to Weston-super-Mare to live with her married daughter Lillian.

GRANNY MARIA
dates unknown, SHOPKEEPER

How does an unmarried woman with no children of her own come to be known as 'Granny Maria' by everyone in her community? How does an illiterate woman successfully run a fish shop? How indeed, but that's Granny Maria for you.

We don't know Maria's full name, but we do know that she ran a small shop in Stillhouse Lane, Bedminster. Despite being unable to read or write, or to do maths, Maria created her own basic accounting system on slates that were fixed to the shop walls. And she would show the price of each piece of the fish that she sold by cutting a different number of notches into the fish's skin.

The main item she sold was 'tea fish', which is salted cod, and this was a popular item as it was easily available in Bristol and cheap to buy. On Good Friday, tea fish was widely accepted to be the standard family meal, served with white sauce, chopped

114 CLASS, 2004, *Southville People and Places*, Fiducia Press, p3.1

hard boiled eggs and mashed potato. Another popular item she sold was a treat for children: boiled rice sweetened with dried fruit. Children would bring in a small container and Maria would measure out a teacup full.

Another unusual feature of Maria's shops was the 'death cards' that adorned the walls. These were cards that undertakers supplied as part of the cost of a funeral, and were beautifully ornate, illustrated with flowers or crosses, and verses of scripture or poetry that described the deceased person as well as giving information about the time and location of the funeral. While traditionally sent only to close family and friends of the deceased, once word spread of Maria's collection, people would save extra copies of the cards to give to her. At Christmas time, Maria added colourful paper chains to her collection of death cards to make them more jolly.[115]

MARJORIE GROVE
1915-1998, COTTON FACTORY WORKER

Marjorie Grove worked at the Great Western Cotton Factory in Barton Hill, starting there in November 1929. Her mother was a single parent to three children and was seemingly an angry woman at the best of times.

She dragged Marjorie along to work at the mill, even though the girl was terrified of the prospect. Marjorie later explained what it was like: "The rough domineering Judd Haye was teaching me to weave ... He swore and bullied me mercilessly each day. He chewed tobacco endlessly and spat it into a pool of slimy brown spittle between the heaving looms ... The din of the endless

---

115 windmillsoftime.wordpress.com/2014/03/03/bedminsters–backstreets–part-3/

looms, row upon row in the fluff laden atmosphere, the reek of raw cotton and hot machine oil made me feel sick.

"Several times a day I was expected to carry great laps of cloth to the warehouse below, cringing between madly waving picking sticks and flying shuttles, and huge whirring leather fan belts, which it was said had ripped hair from many an unwitting girl's head. I was terrified of the youth whose task it was to sweep beneath the looms. He would have a grimy hand up your drawers before you knew it. He rejoiced in the nickname of 'Pinch Bum.'"

After being threatened with the sack for lateness by her supervisor, a tearful Marjorie fled the mill to the stream and wept miserably, knowing she would soon have to face her furious mother. But as Marjorie says, she "determined never to enter a mill again" and she never did.[116]

NATALIE GURNEY
c1890-c1960, REVOLUTIONARY

As the Secretary of the Bristol branch of the Society for Cultural Relations with the USSR, Natalie Gurney had a distinctive role to play in the revolution. She was born in Russia and raised in the UK, but Natalie felt a strong kinship to the country of her birth and devoted her adult life to advocating for it.

With her husband Ronald Gurney, Natalie was linked to the German physicist and atomic spy Klaus Fuchs who notoriously supplied information about atomic bombs to the Soviet Union around the time of World War Two and was imprisoned for nine years in 1950. Klaus had come to Bristol as a refugee fleeing the Nazis in 1933 and found work as a Research Assistant to a

116   Marjorie Grove, 1987, in *Bristol Lives*, Bristol Broadsides, p51-56.

Physics Professor at the University of Bristol. It was here that he met Ronald, a Theoretical Physicist who also came to work at the University of Bristol in the 1930s.

Ronald and Natalie were members of the Communist Party so their beliefs aligned with those of Klaus, who was a member of the German Communist Party. They became close friends and socialised regularly until 1937 when Klaus left for Edinburgh having completed his PhD in physics. The Gurneys later reunited with Klaus in 1947 when they visited the US where Klaus was working prior to his imprisonment.

Natalie was the Secretary of the Bristol branch of the Society for Cultural Relations with the USSR[117] and took an active role with the organisation.[118] The Society was founded in 1924 (the Bristol branch was set up in 1934) and members sought to collect and disseminate information in both the UK and USSR on developments in science, education, philosophy, art, literature, and social and economic life. The Society was non-political and shared work via exhibitions, meetings, film screenings and lectures. Despite its good intentions, some people were suspicious of its motives, prompting Natalie to write a letter to the *Western Daily Press* which set out the objectives of the Society and said: "This Society is not the instrument 'skillfully disguised by Russian duplicity' which [a previous correspondent] appears to fear." She added: "Many new things are happening in Russia in the present day, some of which may be deplorable. Others, however, are interesting, and among them may perhaps be found valuable additions to man's accumulated store of culture and knowledge."[119]

117   Artist Doris Hatt, who has her own entry in this book, was a member. Acclaimed actor Sybil Thorndyke was also linked to the Society and is profiled in Volume One of *The Women Who Built Bristol*.
118   The Society is now known as the Society for Cooperation in Russian and Soviet Studies, following the breakup of the Soviet Union.
119   'Objects of Bristol Society', *Western Daily Press*, 22 December 1934.

The Society sometimes held meetings on the Downs in Bristol and journalist Hubert Nicholson, who was working for the *Bristol Evening World* in the 1930s, remembered attending some of the meetings which, he said, were attended by "some of the most interesting people in the city". He wrote: "I think I was doing a composite description of the scene for my paper, with a snatch of every speech. 'Come to one of our meetings, at my flat,' Mrs Gurney invited, and I went, not to one but to many. It was a huge and beautiful flat in one of Clifton's fine old houses, packed with people always, mostly middle-class or upper-middle, with a small sprinkling of working-class members. They ranged from energetic communists to timid right-wing liberals. They were university professors, authors, painters, even a big business executive or two. They had play-readings and short talks and lots of discussion; and I have never found any group of people anywhere among whom the level of discourse was so high, the quality of debate so good. It was extremely stimulating."[120]

Klaus was a member of the Bristol branch in 1936 and 1937. However, when he was questioned for leaking top secret information, he threw the Gurneys under the bus and claimed that their membership of the Society, which Klaus claimed was a Communist front organisation, made the couple — especially Natalie — a security risk. In an official memo, it is noted of Klaus: "He did not know of any espionage activity on [Natalie's] part nor that she would actually engage in such activity but believed that other people might get in contact with Soviet espionage through her. He was of the opinion also that she was not sufficiently discreet."[121] Of course, there's the possibility that Klaus said this of his former friend simply to deflect some of the heat that he

---

120   Hubert Nicholson, 'Half My Days and Nights', quoted in Adrian Webb et al, 2019, *Doris Hatt: Revolutionary Artist*, p40-41.
121   archive.org/stream/KlausFuchs/fuchs62_djvu.txt

was attracting while under interrogation. It does not seem that Natalie faced any repercussions as a result of Klaus' comments.

Natalie remained a fierce advocate for Russian culture and regularly gave talks to various groups around Bristol in the 1930s promoting the works of Russian creatives and thinkers, and attempting to counter some of the negativity towards Russia that some people felt in the UK.

In the 1940s and 1950s, the Gurneys were living in Baltimore, US, where Ronald was teaching and Natalie was a student at the Walter Hines Page School of International Relations. When questioned during the investigation prior to Klaus' arrest, Natalie was suitably vague about her connection to him and betrayed little useful information. The school Natalie was studying at was closed in 1953 as part of the 'Second Red Scare': the moral panic of McCarthyism that caused a number of left-leaning institutions to close due to fears of communist espionage.

EMMA GUYTON
1825-1887, WRITER

The novelist Emma Guyton met her end while living in Clevedon, following a battle with alcohol addiction: a sad end for this once acclaimed writer. Born Emma Jane Worboys in Birmingham, her father was a gunsmith. Emma was brought up with strict Congregationalist values which were demonstrated throughout the 50+ books she wrote. Although Emma described herself as a widow of the Baptist minister Etherington Guyton, no record of this man's existence has been found although Emma claimed he died in 1861.

Emma published as Emma Worboise (an alternative spelling of her birth surname) and her first book was a novel called *Alice*

Cunningham (1946). Some 50 more novels followed, all with a definite Christian undertone, and the books were popular in their time. Some of them are still available as print-on-demand titles, such as: *Thornycroft Hall* (1864), *Crystabel* (1873) and *A Woman's Patience* (1879). Alongside novels, Emma also published several biographies, including one for Dr Thomas Arnold in 1859, who was an educational reformer and a headmaster in Rugby. In addition, Emma was the editor of *Christian World* and *Family Visitor* magazines, in which several of her novels were serialised.

MRS L HALLIDAY
dates unknown, SUFFRAGIST

Living at 12 Ashton Gate Road, Mrs Halliday (oh, how I wish we knew her real name - this entry would be so much longer if we knew her first name and her original surname) would become one of the women to pass a resolution in favour of votes for women in 1896. She was also the Secretary of the Bedminster Women's Guild for many years. As well as campaigning for the vote, Mrs Halliday and her sister suffragists were working to strengthen the position of women in the workforce. This was pertinent locally given the growing dominance of the Wills tobacco factories and the increasing employment of women in the retail sector as North Street developed into a shopping district.[122]

122   CLASS, 2004, *Southville People and Places*, Fiducia Press, p31–32.

ELIZABETH HAM
1783-1859, WRITER

Born in North Perrott, Somerset, Elizabeth Ham was the middle child of a farming family. She had a sporadic schooling but the education she received ignited a passion for culture. In 1804, when she was 21, Elizabeth's father moved the family to Ireland where he set up a brewery. During this time, Elizabeth fell in love with an officer called Mr Jackson, but he broke her heart and she vowed never to love again. And it was while living in Ireland that Elizabeth became aware of the tough conditions that poorer people were living in and she began to write down some of her thoughts and observations. These notes would inform much of her later writing.

Back in England, Elizabeth lived with relatives in Somerset and Dorset as well as spending time in Clifton working as a governess to the children of the poet Charles Elton. With Charles' help, Elizabeth published her first book anonymously: *An Infant's Grammar.* When the book sold well, Elizabeth regretted not having given her name to it because the income would have been enormously beneficial.

Elizabeth's 1845 novel *The Ford Family in Ireland* was inspired by her time there, and by 1849 Elizabeth had started work on her memoirs. She was living in Brislington and working as a housekeeper, and the book described important historical events as well as details of Elizabeth's personal life. However, *Elizabeth Ham by Herself* was not published until 1945, when an abridged version was issued by Faber & Faber. She is buried at Arnos Vale Cemetery.

BETTY HARES
1921-1999, MISSIONARY

Ever since she was a toddler, the Bible played an important role in the life of Gwendoline Betty Hares: something that would stay with her until the day she died at the age of 78.

Talking about how she discovered God, Betty said: "I could not have been very old, because our kitchen table was not very large, it only needed to accommodate four: my parents, my young sister and me. I was sitting comfortably underneath, the Bible storybooks open at a picture of the crucifixion, the tears rolling down my cheeks. I can still feel the pain; what it meant or where that picture would take me I could have no idea, but my bumpy journey had begun."[123]

Betty grew up on Seneca Street, opposite St George Park, and attended Summerhill Infants' and Junior School before moving on to St George Secondary. However, the church was an important part of her education, and it was while she was attending the Salem Methodist Chapel on Church Road that the words of a missionary visiting from Africa piqued her interest and she knew that it was her calling to become a missionary herself.

When World War Two started, Betty did her part by training as a nurse, and then moved to China to work as a Methodist missionary nurse. When the communist revolution made life in China impossible for her, she relocated to Africa and stayed there until 1981, working as a missionary for several decades.

After returning to Bristol, she taught at the Wesley Theological College while indulging her passions for art and poetry.

In 1993, Betty contributed several essays on her choice to live a life without any romantic attachment in an anthology published

---

123   Dave Stephenson et al, 2003, *Images of England: Crews Hole, St George & Speedwell*, The History Press, p51.

by Bloomsbury called *Single Women: Affirming Our Spiritual Journey*. The book was a way of demonstrating how women from a range of faiths "found great fulfilment in aloneness and reached significant literary and professional achievements" in the process.

In 1992, Betty contributed to an oral history project about her life as a Methodist missionary and this can be accessed via the British Library.

ISABEL HATHERLY
1867-1939, THE WOMAN WHO BUILT (BITS OF) BRISTOL

Author's note: "I know this is being literal, but do [your books] include any builders? When we got the deeds to our house, I was pleasantly surprised to find the builder was Mrs I Hatherly." Alex Craven sent me this message on social media in 2019. How could I refuse? Alex had already done quite a bit of digging into Mrs Hatherly and I was pleased to pick up the shovel and include a woman who – quite literally – built Bristol in this volume.

The house which started this exciting line of enquiry is one of nine properties on Belmont Road in Brislington for which the builder is named as I Hatherly. Brislington was also where Isabel Hatherly lived and based her business at the end of the Victorian era. However, a newspaper advert shows that 'I Hatherley: Building Contractor and General Decorator' had been established in 1830 and had previously been based at 41 City Road, Stokes Croft. But it was only known as 'I Hatherly' in its final years, having previously been 'JA Hatherly'.

Carpenter John A Hatherly established the firm in 1802. It was later run by his son Edward John, before his eldest son Edward

Tom took over. All of them were members of the Bristol Master Builders' Association so they were clearly a respectable firm.

Edward Tom married a young woman called Isabel Ashford in 1892 and she is the 'I' of 'I Hatherly'. As you'll agree, it is very unusual for a business in the Victorian era to have a woman's name, albeit her initials, especially a building company. And it seems the reason for the business to be renamed using Isabel's initials was that the men ran into financial troubles in 1895, forcing them to declare bankruptcy and rename the business before they could resume work with a clean slate.

Isabel and Edward had two children: Edward and Christobel. And by 1911, the census shows the family having moved from Penarth Lodge in Brislington to Penarth, Wales, where Isabel's profession is listed as 'builder and boarding house keeper': to reinforce the second point, there are three lodgers living with the family. But this does pose the question of why the family left Bristol and took a different direction?

While it turns out that Isabel wasn't really a builder in anything more than name, it seemed too close a connection not to include her small contribution to the world of women building Bristol, given there are at least nine buildings in Bristol that bear her name as the builder. Even if she didn't personally build them.[124]

DORIS HATT
1890-1969, ARTIST

One of the pioneers of Modernism was a Clevedon-based social realist artist called Doris Brabham Hatt. A painter and printmaker, Doris grew up in Bath as part of a family that, appropriately

124   With thanks to Alex Craven for nominating Isabel to this book and for doing much of the initial research.

enough, ran a wig-making and hairdressing business. She was educated at Bath High School before going to finishing school in Kassel, Germany, from 1906 to 1907. It was in Germany that Doris first became interested in art, and took inspiration from paintings she had seen at the Neue Galerie. Back in the UK, Doris attended Bath School of Art from 1911 to 1914, and then she went to Goldsmiths College and the Royal College of Art in London, graduating in 1919.

While in London, Doris designed the winning poster for a World War One recruitment campaign, although she would become staunchly opposed to war. Describing the poster 'St George and the Dragon', Mr Tucker of the Parliamentary Recruiting Committee said: "When Miss Hatt submitted her design to me it had 'winner' written all over it. It appealed without being bullying, it was strong but not crude, it was dignified without being dull. Those are the essentials of the successful recruiting poster."[125]

During the 1920s, Doris visited her brother Richard in Austria and attended printmaking classes at the Vienna Art School for Women and Girls. She was also a regular visitor to Paris where she moved in the same circles as the male artists Pablo Picasso and Henri Léger.

After World War One, Doris and her widowed mother moved from Bath to Clevedon where they commissioned a bungalow called Littlemead to be built on a small plot of land. Following an inheritance Doris received in 1938, Littlemead was extended and built into a stunning Bauhaus/Art Deco house. It survives today and is a glorious example of unique architecture. Doris loved her home and used Littlemead as a base for meetings with like-minded radical thinkers to discuss art and politics, and as a space

125   'Girl poster artist', *Shepton Mallet Journal*, 23 July 1915.

to hold free art classes and lectures.

Doris exhibited her work regularly from 1918, and her paintings showed a clear influence from twentieth century Modernism, including cubism, purism and abstraction. Portraits, landscapes and still lives were recurring subjects in her work, and the scenery of South West locations such as Clevedon, Watchet and Wedmore feature frequently in her pieces. Across more than five decades, Doris' work appeared in almost 40 exhibitions both locally and further away, including in London and Paris. Ahead of a retrospective exhibition about Doris in 2019, Sam Astill at the South West Heritage Trust said: "Doris Hatt was a woman ahead of her time – a feminist and socialist whose remarkable life and artistic achievements have remained surprisingly little known."[126] While in 2000, *Country Life* magazine described a series of Doris' paintings showing women workers: "She swept into a series of large canvases featuring powerful women workers, their limbs rounded out in a style that was part Wyndham Lewis, part Léger. She applied her paint thinly to the canvas but created an artificial impasto by a thick sprinkling of silver sand. In fact, the rhythmic solidity of the forms needed no depth of paint to give her women presence: they command because they were the Revolution."[127]

World War One had a clear influence on pacifist Doris' outlook and particularly her politics, which had already been shaped by the suffrage movement. Initially a member of the Independent Labour Party, by the 1920s Doris was asserting her position as a socialist feminist and, in 1935, she joined the Communist Party and could be found selling copies of the *Daily Worker* in local pubs. She visited the Soviet Union with her partner Margery Mack Smith in 1937.

In 1946 and 1947, Doris ignored the fact that Clevedon

126   facesofclevedon.com
127   Timothy Mowl, 'Power and the people's painter', *Country Life*, November 2000.

Urban District Council had no women members and stood (albeit unsuccessfully) as a candidate for the Communist Party in elections in both years. Doris was also a member of the Bristol branch of the Society for Cultural Relations with the USSR.[128]

Doris and Margery, a textile artist and teacher, enjoyed hosting Sunday afternoon salons at Littlemead, inviting great thinkers to come and discuss all manner of topics. The couple also enjoyed travelling together, whether in the South West of England or further afield in Europe.

After Doris' death in 1969, her wish that her body be donated to medical science was honoured, and she has no memorial other than her artworks. Fearing that the government might get hold of Doris' correspondence with comrades in Russia, Doris' sister-in-law burned many of her letters and writings after her death. Fortunately, Margery preserved as many sketchbooks and drawings as possible and kept them safe.

LILIAN HAWKER
1908-1991, MYCOLOGIST

The subject of spores may not sound all that exciting, but Dr Lilian Hawker made it her life's work to study fungal physiology, particularly spore production, becoming a leading expert in her field.

Lilian grew up in Reading and found her passion early in life. She studied Botany at the University of Reading, which she furthered with a Masters and a PhD. These were no small achievements in the 1920s and early 1930s when it was still difficult for women to gain access to further education, never

128 For more on this Society, see Natalie Gurney's entry in this volume.

mind on the subject of science.

After 13 years working at the Imperial College of Science and Technology in London, Lilian came to the University of Bristol in 1945 where she stayed until her retirement in 1973. During her time in Bristol, Lilian held the Chair in Mycology from 1965 to 1973 and was the Dean of the Science Faculty from 1970 to 1973; Lilian was the first ever woman to hold that position in Bristol. She also helped to develop the university's degree course in mycology. In addition, she was the President of the British Mycological Society, and an honorary member of both that organisation and the Mycological Society of America. As you might expect, Lilian published widely on the subject.

Having never married or had children, Lilian instead left a large legacy in her will to the University of Bristol, which has since named a laboratory in her memory.

MAUD HEATH
born c1400, PHILANTHROPIST

For centuries, the mystery of a 15th century widow in the Chippenham area remained unsolved, even after a stone statue was erected in 1838 beside a field at Wick Hill. The statue depicts a seated woman in a large bonnet beside a basket and represents Maud Heath as a peasant trader. But Maud remained the subject of numerous myths and tall tales for centuries. Until now.

In 2024, researchers from the University of the West of England and Chippenham Museum finally unravelled Maud's history… and why this ancient philanthropist is such a significant character in local history.

For many years, a story circulated that Maud was a poor market trader who tramped the dirt path to Chippenham to sell eggs. Frustrated at constantly stumbling on the rutted path and breaking her eggs, she saved up enough money to buy the causeway. But this is not true. After all, someone would need to sell a heck of a lot of eggs to buy that much land.

What is true is that as the childfree widow of the wealthy merchant John Heath, Maud was entitled to own the freehold of property that had previously belonged to John, and as such she had a lot of status in society.

During the 1470s, Maud, sometimes referred to as Mathilda Hethe, gave gifts of property and land in the town, including the land for the four-and-a-half-mile causeway in order to create an alternative to the river crossing, so that goods could be transported in all weathers. In addition to the causeway, Maud endowed money and land to various good causes and Maud Heath's Trust remains a registered charity.

In 1698, trustees of the Maud Heath Charity erected a memorial pillar by Kellaways Bridge with an inscription that read: "To the memory Of the worthy Maud Heath of Langley Burrell Widow Who in the year of Grace 1474 for the good of Travellers did in Charity bestow land and houses about Eight Pounds a year forever to be laid out on the Highways and Causey leading from Wick Hill to Chippenham Clift. This Piller was Set up by the feoffees in 1698 Injure me not."[129]

Maud endowed a great deal of property in Chippenham to the care of trustees, most significantly Bristolian MP John Bagot, who was also a prominent merchant in the city. It is believed that John was Maud's step-nephew, and that John's uncle Nicholas Bagot (a former Sheriff of Bristol who died in 1422) had been Maud's first husband. After his death, she married John Heath: a Bristolian merchant who inherited a fortune in 1423 meaning

---

129 bremhillparishhistory.com/article/maud-heaths-causeway

that he was considered a good husband for a recently-widowed and well-connected young woman.[130]

Maud was the subject of an exhibition at the Chippenham Museum in August 2024 and the museum's Melissa Barnett said: "We can see in her what we want and project onto her our own beliefs and opinions, particularly surrounding the role of women." She added: "Part of Maud Heath's appeal is this mystery. The name Maud Heath is well remembered, and most local people will have used and seen her causeway and the monuments to her memory. There are even poems, stories and songs written in her honour."[131]

HAZEL HENDERSON
1933-2022, ENVIRONMENTALIST

Born in Bristol, Jean Hazel Mustard attended Clifton High School until 1950, after which time she took various jobs such as Hotel Receptionist and Telephone Operator. But it was after moving to New York City in 1957 that her life really took off.

While living in New York with her husband and young daughter Ali, Hazel was prompted to take an interest in environmental affairs. She and Ali would be frequently left covered in soot from the incinerators on the streets, but her complaints about the pollution to City Hall were ignored. With another concerned mother, Hazel set up a group called Citizens for Clean Air in 1964 and, in doing so, became an early advocate of clean air activism. The group's biggest achievement was seeing the air pollution index included in weather reporting. Citizens for Clean Air eventually grew to include 20,000 members, of

130 bbc.co.uk/news/articles/cxe2dny06lyo and wiltshirehistory.org/news/the-real-maud-heath
131 bbc.co.uk/news/articles/cg669k6549do. With thanks to Clare Meraz for the nomination of Maud Heath to this book.

whom 75% were women.

Despite leaving school at 17, Hazel began teaching herself the subjects that interested her and was so successful at doing this that, despite having no formal higher education, she became a Lecturer at the University of California, while also working as a guest lecturer and travelling speaker. In 2004, she formed Ethical Markets Media LLC to share information on environmental issues, before publishing a book called *Ethical Markets* in 2007.

IVY HEPPELL
1887–1918, SUFFRAGETTE

Born in Chippenham and raised in Bristol, Ivy Gertrude Heppell caused quite a stir in the rank of the Women's Social and Political Union (WSPU). Ivy came from a middle-class family, where her father Lancelot was a supervisor for an insurance company, and Ivy was the youngest of his four children.

Although Ivy trained and worked as a school teacher, she quickly developed an interest in the votes for women campaign and joined the WSPU early on.[132] In December 1906, aged just 19, Ivy was one of the women to take part in the suffragette raid on the House of Commons, for which she was one of five women who were arrested; the arresting officers had to literally drag her out of the building because she was clinging to the furniture in an effort to stay put. One newspaper reported, in bizarre language: "In spite of the tender efforts of two burly policemen, she clung tenaciously to the wall surrounding the Cromwell statue shouting: 'I want the vote, I want justice for women.'"[133]

Before she was arrested, Ivy made her way into the Strangers'

132   The WSPU was formed on 10 October 1903, so Ivy joined just three years later.
133   'Suffragist raids', *London Evening Standard*, 21 December 1906.

Lobby at the House, jumped onto a bench and began making a speech calling for votes for women. When she later appeared in court, Ivy was asked if she had any questions for the magistrate, to which she replied: "I should like to ask him if he was a working woman what would you do to get justice for women and children?" She continued: "What would you do to try and make things better for people who are worse off than yourself, for poor old people who are not able to get any work, and for poor children who go to school hungry?" The unsympathetic magistrate replied: "'I see you are only 19 years old. I don't think you would have the vote anyway. They don't get the vote until they are 21." To which Ivy replied: "I want the vote for other people."[134] She was sent to Holloway Prison for two weeks and, at that time, she was the youngest woman, and the first Bristolian woman, to be imprisoned for the cause.

A copy of Ivy's 1917 diary is in the Bristol Museums collection and a section from her time in prison reads: "Tuesday Jan 1st: Miss [S] Allen & Miss H came to see me yesterday afternoon, the last day of the old year, they were at the court when I was tried & got the wool and needles for me. The knitting needles have been most useful to eat boiled rice with, much better than a wooden spoon … Wednesday Jan 2nd: Mrs Martin showed me proofs of a photograph she has had taken in clothes she has had made similar to these grey prison clothes (I shall not be wearing them tomorrow thank goodness) and also one taken in her cap & gown. She is from Cheltenham & said is glad I am from the West Country as most of the imprisoned suffragettes are from the north. The four who will be released tomorrow, Miss Fraser, Mrs Drummond, Mrs Jones (who has been in the infirmary during the whole fortnight of our imprisonment) and I are to be

134 collections.bristolmuseums.org.uk/stories/womens-suffrage

entertained at Anderton's Hotel Fleet St at breakfast tomorrow. I am glad it is to be breakfast and not lunch, as the last prisoners had to welcome them, as I want to be able to be there, and if it had been lunch I could not have waited as I want to be home as soon as possible as I have so little time to be with them, how I wish I had another week's holiday instead of having to be at school on Monday morning. Mrs Martin also said that Dr Aked's letter to me had been published in the *Daily News* I think it was. I only have a vague idea what was in the letter, it was read to me so hurriedly ... Am looking forward to being released tomorrow."[135]

In the next few years, Ivy continued to work for the WSPU, travelling around the UK to speak at and organise events, often working closely with Annie Kenney who was the Bristol-based WSPU organiser for a number of years.[136] Ivy falls off the radar after around 1909 and, as you might expect, along with many other suffragettes she is deliberately missing from the 1911 census report for her address, which lists the other members of her family. Ivy died in London in 1918 aged 31, but it has not been recorded what caused her premature death.

IVY HERWIG
1909–2006, HISTORIAN

With a sharp memory and a big family who had always lived in Bedminster, Ivy Agnes Herwig was well placed to become the family historian because she was a member of several local history groups.

The youngest of 11 children to Elizabeth and William Herwig, Ivy was born on West Street and attended Parson Street School,

135 museums.bristol.gov.uk/details.php?irn=348523
136 Annie Kenney is profiled in Volume One of *The Women Who Built Bristol*.

where she particularly loved art classes. However, she was thought to be a delicate child which meant that her mother decided to delay Ivy having her smallpox vaccination. You can see where this is going... As a toddler, Ivy caught smallpox and was sent to the fever hospital in Nover's Hill, where she later made a full recovery. However, while she was a patient, visitors were denied access to prevent infection so father William would sometimes come to the far side of the wall at the edge of the hospital ground, bringing the family's whippet Prince with him, and wave at his daughter over the wall to keep her spirits up.

Ivy recalled her mother Elizabeth coming to bring her home from the hospital, bringing new clothes for her, including a pair of black patent leather shoes with shiny silver buckles. Ivy wrote: "A push-chair was brought to wheel me home and, on the way, my sister Doris and a friend, Grace, jumped out of the bushes as a surprise." Writing nearly 80 years later, Ivy said the smell of the hospital's disinfectant was still in her nose, as was the memory of being washed in the hospital's old-fashioned hip bath.

As was typical for the time, it fell to Ivy, as the youngest daughter, to stay at home and help her mother. In this way, Ivy became known unofficially as the family's carer: first for her mother, and later for her sisters Violet, Elvena, Mabel and Floss.[137] However, Ivy did manage to have some time to herself and, with her niece Nora, who was only two years younger than Ivy, she began work at the Transport and General Workers' Union, where the two girls took a keen interest in the social club and particularly enjoyed skittles, dancing and the hiking club. It was here that Ivy discovered her passion for local history. A young woman with creative interests, Ivy also enjoyed dress-making, knitting and embroidery.

137   Florence 'Floss' Sage has her own entry in this book.

In later years, with fewer caring responsibilities, Ivy, who – as was so often the case for the younger daughter who had been called upon to care – never married, indulged her passion for travel and embarked on some adventures to places such as Egypt, which was a trip she took with a party from her church at St Mary Redcliffe. Ivy recalled with fondness visiting the pyramids and riding a camel.[138]

ANNE HICKS
1928–2020, ARTIST

Living with her artist husband Jerry Hicks in a townhouse called Goldrush behind Great George Street, which they had designed themselves, Anne Hicks spent her entire life immersed in the art world. Anne and Jerry met while studying at the Slade School of Art in London and, as you would imagine, the couple shared a passion for painting. They adopted a realist style which was not particularly fashionable for the time but, nevertheless, it was what spoke to them.

After the couple married and moved to Bristol in 1960, Jerry became the Head of Art at Cotham School and Anne devoted her time to being an artist, wife and mother to their two children. She also worked as a visiting lecturer at the University of Bristol's School of Architecture and taught adult education classes.

Both held a strong connection to the Royal West of England Academy and exhibited regularly there, and Anne's work was featured in the 'British Women Painters' exhibition at the Museum of Modern Art in Paris. Her art was described as having a "delightful impressionistic style" and often incorporated children

138 Ivy Herwig, Winifred Harris, 1992, *A Tree Grew in Bedminster: An Anthology Based on a Family Tree*, p27-30.

or wild animals in dappled shade. One of Anne's murals survives by the swimming pool at the University of Bristol.

Concerned about the unsympathetic redevelopment of Bristol that was being proposed as part of the post-war changes in the 1970s, Anne began drawing sketches of buildings that were at risk because she wanted to preserve them for future generations. Anne and Gerry were involved with various campaigns, including those to save the Avon Gorge Hotel and the city docks. They also campaigned to stop the building of the outer circuit road which would have destroyed or blighted homes in several communities. As advocates for the city's buildings, they contributed to the 1980 book *The Fight for Bristol*. Talking to a historian at the Bristol Archives, Anne said: "There was no respect for anything that existed in Bristol after the bombing really. Things could quite well have been repaired, but the idea was, 'Oh! Well that's our opportunity to build new.'"[139]

ELIZA HOLBROOK
dates unknown, SHOPKEEPER

In 1915, Eliza Holbrook was running a grocery store at 63 Merrywood Road, Southville, with the help of her sister. The shop was popular with schoolchildren who would call in to buy blue tissue paper at a farthing a sheet, and haberdashery items that they needed for their school lessons. Sweets were also popular with the kids, particularly the 'everlasting strip' which cost a half–penny. And around Bonfire Night, fireworks and sparklers were added to the shop's inventory. It was remembered in a local history book by members of the Continued Learning

139 museums.bristol.gov.uk/narratives.php?irn=13982

for Adults of South Street that "the two maiden ladies who ran the shop always dressed in black. They walked silently through the long passage from the living quarters, giving the shop an eerie atmosphere when they appeared. When farthings were in short supply, they gave their customers pins for change."[140] I'm not sure how well it would be received today if people were given sewing pins instead of coins...

BETTY HUGGETT
1920-2016, PILOT

Third Officer Eleanor Keith-Jopp (as she was named on her birth certificate) was one of the final seven women pilots enlisted to the Air Transport Auxiliary during World War Two. She was known to everyone as Betty.

Born in Clifton, Betty's family was a military one. Her father had been a Major in the Indian Civil Service so she was educated at the Royal School for Daughters of Officers of the Army, which was a boarding school in Bath. Following her father's death in 1939, Betty and her mother Florence were living at 4 Rodney Cottages, Clifton, and Betty was a Secretary for the British Overseas Aircraft Corporation. However, by May 1944 she had signed up to be a Pilot with the Air Transport Auxiliary and would remain there until August 1945. After the war, Betty married Major Peter Huggett in Bristol and they lived at 26 Brunswick Square with their daughter Caroline, before emigrating to South Africa in September 1953 where their second daughter Eleanor was born.

140 CLASS, 2004, *Southville People and Places*, Fiducia Press, p22.

MARGARET IRWIN
1889-1967, WRITER

Although born in London, after the deaths of her parents when she was a child Margaret Irwin came to Bristol to live with her uncle Sidney Irwin and she attended Clifton High School for Girls. This education clearly stood her in good stead and she went on to earn a degree in English from the University of Oxford. In 1929, Margaret married the artist John Monsell and became a respected historical novelist, although she wrote under her given surname rather than her married name. John would illustrate the covers of several of her books. Those books were plentiful and included a biography of Sir Walter Raleigh, a three-part series about Queen Elizabeth 1 and at least 14 novels. Margaret was revered for the historical accuracy in her books, indeed *Young Bess* (1944) was turned into a film with the same name in 1953 with Jean Simmons in the title role as the queen. In 1939, the *Bristol Evening Post* paid her a back-handed compliment by writing: "Her historical novels appeal to many readers who do not otherwise enjoy that class of literature, as well as to enthusiasts for the historical novel." For an extra dose of the South West, Margaret's 1938 novel *The Stranger Prince* included an account of the Siege of Bristol of 1645.

JENNY JAMES
1927-2014, SWIMMER

This one is a little tenuous in terms of a Bristol connection, but given that she was the first woman to swim the *Bristol* Channel in both directions, I feel that Jenny James from Wales is definitely worth a small mention here.

Having begun swimming in Pontypridd when she was seven,

on 19 September 1949 Jenny swam from Penarth to Weston-super-Mare... and swam the journey in reverse on 9 July 1950, becoming the first woman to ever swim the Bristol Channel in both directions. Throughout the rest of her swimming career, Jenny achieved other wonderful things, such as being the first Welsh person of either sex to swim the English Channel, making the crossing from France to England in just under 14 hours.

After her retirement from long-distance swimming, Jenny worked as a coach and lifeguard at the Pontypridd Baths, where she had her first swimming lessons back in 1934. A plaque honouring Jenny now sits on the wall there.

MARGARET JAYCOCK
Died 2021, COMMUNITY MIDWIFE

Before the popular BBC drama *Call The Midwife* appeared on your TV screen, there was a documentary programme called *The Midwife's Tale*. First screened on BBC 2 on 14 April 1987, it followed the indomitable community midwife Sister Margaret Jaycock as she went about her duties, helping to look after the pregnant women of St Pauls and Easton. These were not privileged districts, and Sister Jaycock was supporting families who were making do amid bad housing, mounting heating bills and severe pressures on their lives.

The BBC film crew was apprehensive about taking its expensive equipment into St Pauls given the riot that had taken place there in May 1986, but Sister Jaycock, who had worked in St Pauls and Easton for 25 years by this point, insisted everything would be fine. At just five foot tall, she might have been small in stature but she was mighty in presence. BBC producer Sarah Pitt said: "Sister Jaycock delivered most of the young men and women who were about in the streets and so long as we were there with her we were OK. She was our passport."[141]

Margaret Anne O'Reilly was born on a farm in County Wexford, Ireland, and her mother was a midwife: clearly a family tradition, because four of Margaret's sisters also worked as midwives or nurses. Talking about her training, which she started in Cornwall at the age of 18, Margaret recalled: "My training took three years, then I had to give a year to the hospital which was four. I had £3 10s per month when I was training, and I had £7 when I was qualified. Training was good. Very disciplined and very little off duty, half a day a week."[142] Her training didn't just qualify her to deliver babies, Margaret was also equipped to be a general nurse and theatre sister.

She moved to Bristol in 1961 where she began working at the Charlotte Keel Medical Practice in Easton: she remained at this health centre for three decades until her retirement. She married in January 1965, becoming Margaret Jaycock. Her arrival in Bristol had coincided with the arrival of West Indian immigrants, many of whom settled in St Pauls. Perhaps the fact that Sister Jaycock was also an immigrant – at a time when 'No Irish, No Blacks, No Dogs' signs were widespread – also helped her to be accepted. Margaret never lost her strong Irish accent, despite decades living in the UK.

The nurse was saddened that so many urban children were still so disadvantaged, saying in the programme: "If you don't have basics when you're young, you don't respect people when you grow up."

Clearly respect was something that Sister Jaycock lived and breathed, both in herself and for others. Writing to the letters page of the *Bristol Evening Post*, an unnamed correspondent said:

141   'St Pauls angel', *Western Daily Press*, 14 April 1987.
142   'Sister Jaycock', 1983, in *St Pauls People Talking*, Bristol Broadsides, p4.

"This week's BBC programme on Sister Jaycock was a refreshing change from the usual happenings we are shown in the St Pauls area of Bristol. She can walk, safe, at any hour of the day through the area. Why? Because she does not emanate that feeling: 'I'm white, you're Black.' We can learn a lot from a person I would nominate as woman of the year."[143]

In the early years of her career, many of the deliveries Sister Jaycock helped with in Bristol were home births, but by the time the programme was aired in 1987 these accounted for just 1% of births in Bristol. She recalled in 1983: "We have some babies still that get delivered at home but the majority of them get delivered in hospital and that's where our changes have taken place. We used to be out night and day, that wasn't good either. We couldn't take the pace. In the olden days, if a midwife reached the age of 50 in the district, she was very lucky because she was worn out. They didn't have the transport that I have, the older midwives. They were wet through [from the rain], they were crippled with arthritis and they had a very bad life really, very hard times for very little money. We don't get paid for any deliveries we do at home, the doctors get paid for that."[144]

Talking about her early years in Bristol, Sister Jaycock said: "Lots of people didn't have a telephone then and often it was a matter of a neighbour running with a threepenny bit to the telephone box, or sprinting to the local police station to ask them to call for us. We carried round heavy bags of equipment and we had to sterilise all the instruments as we didn't have all the convenient packs you get now."[145] In the programme, giving advice to the next generation of midwives, Sister Jaycock said: "All a young midwife needs are eyes to see, ears to hear and hands

143 Letters, *Bristol Evening Post*, 21 April 1987.
144 'Sister Jaycock', 1983, in *St Pauls People Talking*, Bristol Broadsides, p5–7.
145 'Sister with the voice of sanity', *Bristol Evening Post*, 24 July 1990.

to touch and feel. That coupled with common sense and their general training, and they can't go far wrong."

In December 1988, Sister Jaycock, who lived on Kimberley Avenue in Fishponds, published a low-cost booklet about pregnancy and childcare called *Hints for Mother*. She decided to do this because she felt that many of the glossy books about parenting were too complicated and off-putting for new mothers, and they were so expensive that not everyone could afford the information. She was also concerned that the use of medical terminology could appear frightening to women who might not understand it, so she strove for a plain-speaking tone.

In March 1989, Margaret was awarded an MBE at Buckingham Palace for her years of devotion to midwifery. She retired at the end of July 1990, having delivered almost 3,000 babies during her 30-year career in Bristol, and many of those children – well, the adults they had become – attended her retirement party at the Malcolm X Centre in St Pauls.[146]

HILDA JENNINGS
1893-1979, SOCIAL WORKER

For 20 years between 1937 to 1957, Hilda Jennings was the Warden of Barton Hill University Settlement, having previously worked in a similar former industrial area in South Wales. Considering the need for the Settlement, Hilda wrote in 1951: "Like all those in the Residential Settlement movement, [the team at Barton Hill] recognise that despite social changes and professional social services, society still depends on individual goodwill and its texture is still woven of the values and relationships of men and

146   With thanks to Ted Fowler for the nomination of Sister Jaycock to this book.

women in their ordinary daily lives."[147]

Right from the start of her time in Barton Hill, Hilda committed herself to improving the lot for the working-class people she worked with. For instance, in September 1939 she and her colleague Winifred Gill undertook a survey on behalf of the BBC in which they examined the social changes that broadcasting could bring about. They wrote: "It may be said that no social innovation since the coming of compulsory elementary education has affected so large a proportion of the working population as has the coming of broadcasting. It is clear that it is not now regarded only as recreational in function. People are learning to use their sets with discrimination as a means to acquiring new interests and aiding individual development."[148]

Hilda did an astonishing amount of work to improve the conditions of the people who lived and worked in Barton Hill. She also worked with Bristol Council towards those goals, producing a report in 1960 suggesting ways in which the council could sensitively and helpfully redevelop the former urban area by working with the Settlement. In 1971, she wrote a booklet celebrating the first 60 years of the Settlement.

During World War Two, Hilda volunteered as an Air Raid Precautions warden for the area. And, when speaking to a journalist in 1945 about how the post-war housing boom needed to be better planned in order to consider the needs of the people who would be living in the new housing, she said: "Attempts have been made to mitigate the loneliness of the large, uncoordinated estates by the provision of community centres as an afterthought. But a community centre calls for a community, not for a conglomeration of people with no mutual interests or links with their new surroundings. These new residents need, from the

147 'Good neighbours', *Bristol Evening Post*, 15 May 1951.
148 'How radio affects social life', *Bristol Evening Post*, 1 September 1939.

outset, friends living among them who have the time, experience and neighbourly interest to help them to settle down and play their part in the new community to which they now belong. This need can be met through residential settlements such as the University Settlement at Barton Hill."[149]

The university settlements in Bristol[150] prioritised the individuals who lived in the community by incorporating the staff and wardens into the communities they served. People were asked what they wanted and what would help them, and consequently educational programmes were set up, as were recreational clubs and libraries. The programmes were geared towards people of all ages, from small children right up to retired workers. One of the earliest initiatives set up in Barton Hill was the School for Mothers, led by a surgeon called Dr Lily Baker.

Following Hilda's death in 1979, it was discovered that she had left behind reams of poetry about nature and religion. Her friends decided to publish a free booklet of these poems in her memory, with donations going to the Settlement.

GLYNIS JOHNS
1923–2024, ACTOR

Stand up, sister suffragette! In the wonderful 1964 film *Mary Poppins*, the immortal song 'Sister Suffragette' was performed by the passionate Mrs Banks, played by Glynis Johns. But why is she in this book about Bristol women? Because Glynis attended Clifton High School from the age of 12. She had a lifelong passion for dancing that began when she was five and saw her become a dancing teacher at the age of ten, such was her talent. Glynis' time

149 'Towards real community', *Western Daily Press*, 29 September 1945.
150　As well as Barton Hill, there were settlements at Shirehampton and Speedwell.

in Bristol was brief when compared to her 100 years of life, so she will only be granted a short mention here. But, given the brilliance of *Mary Poppins* and the legacy of Mrs Banks on the votes for women movement in popular culture, it seemed churlish not to give Glynis the nod she deserves.[151]

BESSIE JOHNSON
1865-1941, ARTIST

The first pupil registered at the brand new Clifton High School was Elizabeth 'Bessie' Percival (her original name). The school opened at 65 Pembroke Road on 24 January 1878 with 67 students, and founder Rev John Percival's daughter was the first of those to be enrolled. The very first headteacher of the school was Mary Alice Woods, who remained in post until 1891. Also in 1891, Bessie married Cecil Johnson, whose father had been the Dean of Wells, so he was clearly from good stock. The couple lived in Clifton and, in time, Bessie became a watercolour artist and had exhibitions in her name. Her pictures of the local area were much admired, and one was bought for the permanent collection of the Bristol Wills Arts Gallery, which is now part of the Royal West of England Academy. Bessie made a point of donating all proceeds from sales of her work to artists in need.

151   As a child, the first time I heard of the suffrage movement was while watching the film *Mary Poppins* which, by the way, is in the top five of my list of all-time favourite films ever. And I genuinely believe that the Disney film of *Mary Poppins* has done a great deal to raise the awareness of the suffrage movement among children and adults who might not otherwise have given it much thought. Stand up, sister suffragette!

EMMELINE KING and ZOE KING
1770-1843 and 1803-1881, LITERATI

Emmeline Edgeworth (as she was born) was the younger sister of novelist Maria Edgeworth[152] and the older sister of poet Anna Beddoes[153]. Emmeline lived at 6 & 7 Dowry Square in Hotwells, the home of the Medical Pneumatic Institute where the Chemist Humphry Davy was living while working for Emmeline's brother-in-law Thomas Beddoes and where the discovery of therapeutic and hallucinogenic properties of nitrous oxide (aka laughing gas) was discovered.

Emmeline later married Dr John King who also worked at the Medical Pneumatic Institute. They lived at 26 The Mall, Clifton which backed onto Anna's home at 3 Rodney Place. John became a popular GP in Clifton and his correspondence with patrons of the art, romantic poets and influential friends gives a lot of information about their social life in Bristol in the early part of the 19th century.[154]

The list of friends and acquaintances that Emmeline would have met in Bristol reads like a veritable who's who of intelligent society: the poets Robert Southey, Samuel Taylor Coleridge and William Wordsworth, author Sara Coleridge, chemist Humphry Davy, Dr Peter Mark Roget (he of *Roget's Thesaurus* fame) and writer Anne Yearsley[155] to name but a few.

Emmeline's oldest daughter Zoë King was just four when, during a visit to 3 Rodney Place, she was immortalised in a poem by Sarah Coleridge who was visiting at the same time. Zoë was sitting very still and Sarah mistook her for a china doll rather

152   Maria Edgeworth is profiled in Volume One of *The Women Who Built Bristol*.
153   Anna Beddoes has her own entry in this volume.
154   Michael Whitfield, 2021, *John King: The Bristol Surgeon and Friend of Artists and Poets*.
155   Sara Coleridge and Anne Yearsley are both profiled in Volume One of *The Women Who Built Bristol*. Sara's name is sometimes spelled 'Sarah' but because she is profiled in Volume One as 'Sara' I am continuing with that spelling here.

145

than a living child. Years later, in 1874, when Zoë was writing a letter to the lawyer Thomas Forbes Kelsalin, she describes how Sarah's poem was written: "When I was a very little thing I was on a rocking horse at the end of the Hall – And seeing strangers at the door sat quite still (rather an unusual thing with me) – the little girl – when I spoke – said to her mother – 'why it isn't a doll'."[156] In 1805, Humphry also wrote a poem for Zoë as did her cousin Thomas Lovell Beddoes.

Emmeline and Zoë are buried at Arnos Vale Cemetery. The epitaph on the gravestone is by the writer Walter Savage Landor.[157]

JANE LANE
1626-1689, ACCOMPLICE

When King Charles II was defeated by Oliver Cromwell (who sought to overthrow the monarchy) at the Battle of Worcester in September 1651, he was forced to flee to France for his life. A key woman who helped him escape was Jane Lane, later known as Lady Fisher following her marriage in 1663.

A reward of £1,000 was offered for the capture of King Charles II and anyone caught assisting the king in his escape would likely be executed for treason. Which makes Jane's assistance all the more courageous. Special patrols were enlisted to try and prevent him crossing any borders out of England. Nonetheless, when the monarch arrived at the home of officer Colonel John Lane in Staffordshire, Lane's sister Jane stepped up to assist. The Lane family was both catholic and royalist, which was a dangerous combination in a period where the monarchy was under threat.

156 HW Donner, 1935, *Browning Box or the Life and Works of Thomas Lovell Beddoes as reflected in letters by his friends and admirers*, Oxford University Press, p94.
157 With enormous thanks to John Beddoes for all of his help with this entry.

It was, at this time, illegal for a catholic to travel more than five miles from their home without a pass from the Sheriff of the County, but Jane obtained a pass for herself and a servant to travel to Bristol saying she wanted to visit a relative. It was in this way that King Charles II was disguised as a servant called William Jackson and travelled with Jane to Bristol. Their party was completed by Jane's sister and brother-in-law plus another royalist officer.

When the group reached Bristol, they unsuccessfully attempted to find a ship that would carry them to France. Instead, Jane escorted the disguised king to Dorset, with the intention of getting him on another ship. It was here that Jane left him. However, her involvement in his escape was by no means over. The Council of State had been informed that she had helped the king, meaning that Jane now had to adopt a disguise and escape to France, arriving in Paris in December 1651. Reunited with the king, he arranged for her to work as a lady-in-waiting to his sister, and the king and Jane maintained a friendly correspondence for many years.

When Cromwell's dictatorship of England fell in 1660, Charles and Jane were free to return to England. In gratitude for all that she had done, Charles supported Jane with a £1,000 annual allowance and sent her an array of gifts.

PAT LANE
born 1936, THALIDOMIDE CAMPAIGNER

In 1962, pregnant Pat Lane of Speedwell Lane, St George took the thalidomide drug Distaval on the advice of her doctor. Her daughter Julie was born in November 1961 with only one ear and with skin growths over both eyes, for which Julie underwent surgery. Talking to the *Daily Mirror* on 3 August 1962, Pat said: "Compared to many mothers I was very lucky. I was prescribed the thalidomide drug for asthma when I was five weeks pregnant, but I only took two tablets because they made me feel numb."

Thalidomide was widely prescribed for nausea in the late 1950s and early 1960s, however it quickly became apparent that the drug caused severe birth defects in the unborn children of the mothers who had been prescribed it. The drug was withdrawn in November 1961. However, by this time, thousands of babies had been born to women who had been given the drug.

Determined to get compensation and justice for the victims, Pat became one of the four co-founders of the Society for the Aid of Thalidomide Children. Launching the campaign, she told the *Daily Mirror*: "I want to hear from as many of these mothers as possible so that we can subscribe to a fund and make a test case of the worst example of deformity caused by the drug."[158]

The intention of the Society, of which Pat was the first Secretary, was to set up a national organisation to support all the children and parents who were affected by the drug and to campaign for compensation. The first official meeting was held on 20 October 1962, attended by 44 parents. The Society continued to grow and, due to the wide spread of members throughout the UK, it was decided to set up smaller branches around the country. Pat was the area representative for the Bristol region, and her address at Speedwell Road became so well known that she asked for a name plate to be installed by the street sign to help direct people to her house, such was the volume of callers that she received in response to the publicity she generated. By the end of the 1970s, the smaller groups were discontinued because the ages of the affected children meant that they needed less support.

---

158 'Drug–baby mum leads crusade', *Daily Mirror*, 3 August 1962.

In 1973, Distillers, the company that manufactured thalidomide, finally reached a settlement with parents of children affected by thalidomide. The Society still exists but is now a user-led organisation that is largely run by the children, now adults, who were affected by the drug.

'LADY JURORS'
born 1920, DECISION MAKERS

I know, I know... I'm pushing my luck here because this entry refers to a group of women rather than a named individual. But one of the things about jurors is that, by and large, their names are kept confidential to avoid them being at risk of intimidation.[159] BUT... on 28 July 1920[160] women (gasp!) were permitted to act as jurors (eek!) in a court of law (gulp!) for the very first time (faint!). And it feels like this should be worthy of some sort of mention.

The development in judicial equality was, of course, reported in the newspapers, and the *Bristol Times & Mirror* ran the headline 'Lady Jurors in Bristol' in response to women sitting alongside men at the Bristol Quarter Sessions. Be afraid, people, or these women might literally lock up your sons.

The first case that the lady jurors adjudicated concerned a man who had allegedly stolen two parcels at Temple Meads Station. Upon addressing the panel of jurors, prosecutor Mr RE Dummett began to say, "Ladies and gentlemen of the jury..." before needing to take a moment to collect his thoughts, so shocking and unusual was the addition of women to that statement. The *Bristol Times*

159   This right to anonymity might be a more recent innovation because I've found several group photos of 'lady jurors' in newspapers around the end of 1920, marvelling at this new fangled method of justice.
160   This was just four days after the UK's first ever female magistrate had been appointed, in the form of Ada Prosser of Gloucester.

& Mirror wrote: "[Dummett] said as that was the first occasion he had used that unfamiliar phrase – as far as he knew it had not been used before in the annals of jurisdiction of this country, certainly not in that city before the Recorder – he thought they would forgive him if he said a word or two of congratulations to the ladies upon at last taking their proper place in the jurisdiction of the country and also of congratulation to the cause of justice that they had done so."[161]

However, at the end of the day, Mrs Wellings of Redland asked to be dismissed from the jury because she could not spare a second day away from caring for her children. Another woman was a widow who ran a shop that she had been obliged to close for the day in order to attend the court, and she also asked to be excused from a second day in court because she could not afford to lose her income for another day. Both requests were granted and female volunteers were found to take their places.

A few days later, an intrepid reporter at the *Bristol Times & Mirror* sought out some of those lady jurors to ask them about their experiences. He noted they were mostly "ladies in business in the city, with one of two Labour representatives and social workers among their numbers". One woman told the reporter: "As a result of my experience I am satisfied that ladies serving on juries will be very useful, especially in cases in which women are concerned, because women understand women and their temptations and downfalls better than men. I found no embarrassment in the atmosphere of the court, it was much nicer than I expected."[162]

As you might expect (and, dear reader, get ready to do some serious eye rolling here), the letters pages of the newspapers were filled to bursting in the following days with condescending missives from men with their noses out of joint, either issuing

161 'Lady jurors in Bristol', *Bristol Times & Mirror*, 29 July 1920.
162 'Our lady jurors', *Bristol Times & Mirror*, 30 July 1920.

advice to the lady jurors (along the lines of being sure to remember that a court of law is a serious place), or being cheered by the fact that the presence of women in their pretty dresses and with their smiling faces will make the sombre courtrooms a more cheerful place from now on.

AGNES LANGLEY
1881-1945, HEARING IMPAIRED

There used to be many small, specialist hospitals which, over time, became consolidated into the mega-hospitals that we have now. One such specialist hospital was the Sanitary Authority Hospital for Infectious Diseases in Novers Hill, south Bristol. A nearby isolation hospital at St Philips Marsh was already in existence but, with only 44 beds, this was deemed too small. The new isolation hospital would have up to 100 beds.

Building work began in 1892 and the hospital opened the following year. It was located on the edge of the city in order to isolate cases of contagious diseases and hopefully avoid epidemics. For instance, during a smallpox outbreak in 1893, seven patients were treated at Novers Hill in isolation. At that time, patients were given a number to identify them and the newspapers would publish reports on which numbered patients were better or worse. If no number was published, it could be assumed that the patient was doing OK.

One of those early patients was Agnes Garland (as she was born) of St George, who was admitted to Novers Hill Hospital with scarlet fever when she was 12 in 1893. With no known treatment for this disease, Agnes was kept in isolation. In all, she spent two years in the hospital because her illness morphed into 'brain fever' (a Victorian term that refers to illnesses such as meningitis). As a result, Agnes permanently lost her hearing. Her son Ernest Langley later wrote: "She must have been a very strong girl indeed to have pulled through those two terrible killer diseases and, throughout the rest of her life, the manifestations of her considerable strength, physically, mentally and of will certainly showed itself."

Agnes' earliest years had been spent with her family in St George. Her father Abraham was a coal miner and later a stone mason. After Abraham's death in 1901, Agnes' mother Mary took in laundry to help make ends meet while Agnes, who still lived at home, worked as a domestic servant. In 1908, Agnes married Ernest Langley, they set up home at 13 Byron Street in Redfield and had four children. Husband Ernest worked as a Dock Labourer before becoming a commercial traveller, which meant he was away from home for much of the year, leaving Agnes to keep things running at home for the children with the help of the regular cheque that Ernest would send her.

Although she could not hear, Agnes was very involved with life in the 1910s and 1920s. She particularly enjoyed trips to the cinema to see silent movies. Ernest said: "The film stars seemed to become personal friends and she spent a lot of her leisure time in the local cinema where the whole film made perfect sense to her." Agnes also attended the local church and enjoyed community outings on the charabanc: sometimes a day out to the coast, other times an evening in the countryside.

Ernest says that his mother became an adept lip reader: "She once stood in the showroom of a piano shop, looking through the window towards a small shop selling furniture across the road. Her companion made the casual statement that a certain bedroom suite on show there looked particularly nice, to which my mother was able to tell her, quite nonchalantly, that a young couple who had been standing in the shop with the salesman had just bought it – on easy terms."[163]

The Novers Hill Hospital closed in 1936 after 40 or so years. The newly extended Ham Green Hospital, which had opened in 1927 to manage infectious diseases, meant that there was no need for some of the smaller hospitals on the edge of the city. The former site of the Novers Hill Hospital is now the site of the Knowle DGE Academy for young people with special educational needs and disabilities.

One last point to note about the Novers Hill Hospital was that, in 1920, female laundry workers were successful in their campaign to have their wages increased above that of a domestic laundry worker (which they were previously paid), owing to the fact that the washing they managed in the infectious hospital setting was not only more cumbersome in bulk and weight but also had the potential to carry infections that might harm their health. The *Western Daily Press* noted: "It was work that could not be compared with ordinary laundry women's work, but it was dangerous. [Mr Ashley] moved that the wages be increased to 50s, to be made retrospective to July 1 … and this move was adopted."[164]

EILEEN LAPHAM
1921-1989, DRAUGHTSWOMAN

Eileen Grace Bishop (as she was born) grew up with her family at 19 Muller Avenue. She married carpenter Leonard Lapham at Bishopston Parish Church on 23 August 1958 and the couple set up home at 68 Wessex Avenue, Horfield, where they remained for the rest of their lives.

After she had left school in 1936, Eileen found work as a

163 Ernest Langley, 1982, in *Bristol Writes: No 2*, Bristol Broadsides, p29–31.
164 'A claim for the women', *Western Daily Press*, 11 November 1920.

hairdresser but, when World War One broke out, she entered the engineering industry where she started her training as a draughtswoman. Her brother John had been an apprentice draughtsman at the British Aircraft Corporation in Filton, before becoming a lecturer at Rolls-Royce technical college, and he persuaded his sister that being a draughtswoman would be a good line of work for her.

Eileen continued to work as a draughtswoman for the rest of her working life, and eventually set up her own draughting and tracing service from an office on Wessex Avenue. All of Eileen's work was done by hand using ink and technical pens, and completed on tracing paper or film. This was a skillful and painstaking process, and Eileen was clearly successful at her work because she was contracted by a variety of engineering firms across Bristol.

Eileen's ancestor Murray Cameron notes: "Eileen had a lively, inquisitive mind and her own accomplishments included mastering the piano accordion, which she loved to play."[165]

ELSIE LAWRANCE
c1895-c1985, HISTORIAN

There was once a vibrant community in Totterdown, but it was completely demolished in the 1970s to make way for a ring road that was never built... by which time the community had already been displaced. The scheme was grandly, and misguidedly, called the Three Lamps Improvement Scheme. However, memories of the people who lived in Totterdown were recorded by the Totterdown Road Project.

---

165   With thanks to Murray Cameron for the nomination of Eileen Lapham to this book and for providing the information that appears in this entry.

As a teenager and then a young bride, Elsie Lawrance lived at the bottom of Park Street (the small one in Totterdown, not the big one in central Bristol), a road which still exists today. In 1979, she shared some of her memories in a significant booklet called *Growing Up In Totterdown*. Elsie, who by the time of her book was living at Beckington Close, Knowle, told the *Bristol Evening Post*: "I was sitting sewing with a church group when someone said that Harris and Tozer, the drapers on Wells Road, was closing. It came as a terrible shock because they were the last link with my childhood memories. I thought that if someone didn't sit down and write all about old Totterdown no-one will ever know anything about it."

While Elsie's booklet covers the reality of life in a poorer suburb, and the poverty, poor sanitation, overcrowding and ill-health that goes with that, she also looks at the positive and community aspects. Talking about her childhood, Elsie said: "When it was sunny, out would come a skipping rope and that would keep us playing for hours. There was no traffic in the side streets so it was perfectly safe."[166]

In the booklet she wrote about her feelings regarding the closure of Harris and Tozer, a family-run drapery that operated on Wells Road for more than 80 years until 1978, when new fire regulations would have required the company to spend more than £8,000 on upgrades to the building (approximately £65,000 in 2025 money). This was a far cry from the early 1950s, when Mr Harris was quoted in the *Bristol Evening World* talking about the problem his shop had keeping up with the sudden boom in customer spending on fashions post-war.

Elsie wrote about the shop's closure: "It was the last link in a long line of shops that had stretched from the Three Lamps

---

166 'Totting up the memories', *Bristol Evening Post*, 19 November 1979.

to Firfield Street. The expense of the new fire precautions was doing to Harris and Tozer what the Blitz of 1939-1945 and the road planners of the 1960s had failed to do. They had struggled valiantly on, with fewer and fewer customers, as the streets one by one were demolished for the new road scheme, which had not come to pass. I remember the happy days when I purchased the soft furnishings for my first home."

PATIENCE LAWRENCE
dates unknown, 'LADY DETECTIVE'

One of the first five women to join the detective branch of the Bristol Constabulary was Patience Lawrence, who did so in 1916 as a result of World War One calling for more women to step up to what had previously been seen as male roles. Dorothy Peto[167] had run the Bristol Training School for Women Patrols and Police in Berkeley Square between 1916 and 1919, and she played a key role in helping women to be taken more seriously in the police force. The recruitment of the first five female detectives was a result of the initial success of Dorothy's training school.

Patience had cut her teeth at the Chipping Camden Police Station in Gloucestershire, where her father was a police constable. Some of her early assignments as a detective involved going to shops to keep an eye out for thieves. For instance, in April 1916 she apprehended a woman for attempting to steal a leather bag and, when the case came to court, Patience was complimented for her professionalism.[168]

Patience then progressed to cases involving rogue fortune-tellers. In April 1916, Patience investigated Julia Gibson who,

---

167 Dorothy Peto is profiled in Volume One of *The Women Who Built Bristol*.
168 Nell Darby, 2021, *Sister Sleuths: Female Detectives in Britain*, Pen & Sword.

under the name 'Zakaree Ermahoff', was charging money to read people's palms in her home on Newfoundland Street. Under the Witchcraft Act of 1735, promising to tell people's fortunes in exchange for money was illegal. There is a string of reports from the same period in which other fortune tellers in Bristol are caught for similar reasons and these go on until 1923.

Even more sensational than rogue fortune-tellers, in December 1917 Patience was one of the detectives involved with rumbling a peep show, where an exhibition on Castle Street was discovered behind a screen labelled 'gentleman only', displaying 'obscene' images.[169]

Two of the other five 'lady detectives' who joined Patience in that initial cohort were Mary Richardson and Alice Robinson. The newspaper records show Mary and Alice were also largely confirmed to cases concerning rogue fortune tellers and shop thieves. In all reports about these women, they are referred to as 'the lady detective' yet their male colleagues are not referred to as, for example, 'the gentleman detective'. Ho hum.

It is thought that the first uniformed woman constable in Bristol was employed on 10 August 1917, and seven more women followed in the next 12 months. The women constables wore a less formal and more feminine uniform than their male colleagues, and their caseload seemed to mostly concern female and juvenile law breakers.

169   'Police and peep show', *Western Daily Press*, 4 December 1917.

CONSTANCE LEATHART
1903-1993, PILOT

When Newcastle's Constance Ruth Leathart, known to everyone as Connie, signed up to be a Pilot for the Air Transport Auxiliary (ATA) during World War Two, she was the most accomplished and experienced woman to do so, with more than 700 hours of flying experience under her belt. Not only was Connie one of the first 20 women to sign up to the ATA, but she was the only one of that 20 who had not gained her certificate in London, instead qualifying in Newcastle.

Connie lived and breathed aviation. Upon her death, it was said in a news report: "[At Newcastle Aero Club] she soon made a name for herself for her fearlessness and became a keen competition flyer, eventually taking part in rallies and aero events throughout Europe. Indeed, as a member of the Aero Club, she became one of the first women to fly over the Alps, in a De Havilland Tiger Moth."[170]

Having been educated at Cheltenham Ladies' College, Connie was not necessarily considered 'ladylike' by the standards of the day. Standing at 5ft 3, sister aviator Lettice Curtis described Connie as being of "generous proportions", while another aviator, Mary du Bunsen, stated that Connie resembled the music hall performer George Robey, which was hardly complimentary given George's stage look involved thickly painted on eyebrows and a partial bald cap.

Nonetheless, Connie earned her Royal Aero Club Certificate in 1927, just 14 years after the first ever female pilot had done so (Hilda Hewlett, since you ask) and was only the 12th woman ever to earn the certificate at that time. In the late-1920s and early-

---

170 'Historic basket for auction', *Blyth News Post Leader*, 17 March 1994.

1930s, Connie ran a company called Cramlington Aircraft with Leslie Runciman, which repaired damaged aircraft. During this time, Connie also designed and flew her own glider and became an experienced racing pilot. By the time that war had been declared, Connie was based in Bristol and working in the mapping department at Bristol Airport, then based at Whitchurch.

From Bristol Airport, she applied to join the ATA and, given she was one of the most experienced female pilots in the UK, this was quite a fillip to the organisation. Connie was one of the very first pilots to sign up when she did so in August 1940. Within her role she was responsible for ferrying Spitfires from the factories to the squadrons and was soon promoted to Flight Captain. Later in the war, Connie flew four-engined bomber planes.

She remained with the ATA for almost four years until June 1944, although it is clear Connie wanted to stay on and she wrote to her superiors pleading with them not to let her go: "I feel that, if I can be of further use here, the problem of how to pay me ought not to be insuperable. I like the work here and have already got in some flying so I do hope you can resolve whatever difficulties may crop up."[171] Alas, Connie was unsuccessful in her plea. However, during the course of her four years with the ATA Connie accrued a total of 800 hours in the air. She was close friends with acclaimed aviator Amy Johnson and was with Amy the night before her death in 1941.

After the war, Connie maintained her love of aircraft and she kept flying until 1958, undertaking mercy missions for the United Nations. After retirement, she moved to Northumberland where she set herself up as a cattle and sheep farmer and became an accomplished horse rider. By the time she died, Connie had amassed an estate worth more than half a million pounds.

---

171   ata-ferry-pilots.org/index.php/category-blog-1940/220-leathart-constance-ruth

In 1994, the year after her death, a picnic basket that Connie had owned came up for auction and attracted national attention. Connie had taken the wicker basket with her on a great number of her pre-war flights and continued to use it while flying for the ATA. The auctioneer noted: "The picnic basket apparently travelled with her everywhere and there are probably few such baskets in the world which have journeyed so far and in such adventurous company as this one."[172]

GERTRUDE LITTLEJOHNS
and MINNIE LITTLEJOHNS
1897-1987 and 1899-1978, HABERDASHERS

Sisters Gertrude (Trudy) and Minnie Littlejohns fulfilled a lifelong ambition when they opened a haberdashery in Westbury-on-Trym in January 1939. But the sisters, who would eventually live and work at 6 Canford Lane, had to work hard to get there.

Trudy was a school teacher in Sheffield while Minnie was the district nurse for Sea Mills, cycling from patient to patient. When their father became ill, the sisters' mother asked one of them to come home and help, so Trudy dutifully returned to Bristol to assist her mother. She continued to work as a teacher, and was based at Christchurch School in Clifton (in the building which is now Clifton Library).

It was while she was out on her bicycle one day, visiting patients, that Minnie cycled through Westbury-on-Trym and noticed the empty shop on Canford Lane. It was a newly-built property that was yet to be let. Minnie knew that she wanted that shop as the location for her much dreamed of haberdashery, and she cycled home to tell Trudy what she had found.

---

172   'Historic basket for auction', *Blyth News Post Leader*, 17 March 1994.

The sisters moved fast. Although Minnie had very little money of her own, Trudy decided that she could support them both, so Minnie gave up her nursing job, they leased the shop and opened it in 1939 as Littlejohns. Trudy kept teaching until 1952 when she also joined the shop full-time.

At the time the shop was opened, wool was rationed due to the war but, despite this set-back, the sisters managed to keep their new business afloat. Even though they had no business experience, it seemed that if they could navigate their shop through the war years then nothing could stop them. However, certain male relatives felt the sisters were irresponsible to give up their sensible jobs to focus on a dream. As well as wool, Littlejohns stocked everything a home sewer might need: fabrics, cottons, sewing materials and even clothes for small children. In time, they expanded into a second branch of Littlejohns at 248 The Kingsway, St George (now demolished and replaced with a shopping precinct).

Trudy and Minnie ran Littlejohns until 1969 when they decided to retire and the business was sold. Although Minnie died in 1978, Trudy remembered their decades together with great fondness. She said: "Minnie was the impetuous one and I was the practical one. We spent many happy years here and I miss her dreadfully. We always got on so well together. I hate to hear of sisters not getting on. But the grief has passed now and I have many happy memories."[173]

173   Beryl Tully, 2004, *Shoes and Ships and Sealing Wax*, Malago Press, p75-77.

VAL LORRAINE
1920-2001, ACTOR, WRITER

Considering she was once dubbed "the fairy godmother for the theatrical industry in Bristol" by the writer ACH Smith, we really ought to be celebrating Val Lorraine more in this city than we do. Better known for her work on the stage rather than the screen, Val was a hard-working actor who was touring the UK from the 1930s right up until the early 2000s.

Val had grown up in Wimbledon, London, and made her stage debut in that borough when she was just 11 in a production of *The Wind In The Willows*. Throughout World War Two, Val was employed at the BBC in London, working as a Broadcaster and as an Assistant to the Journalist Richard Dimbleby, who was the BBC's first War Correspondent. After the war, Val became a Music Assistant at the BBC's Pinewood Studios. She married Bob Lorraine in Liverpool in 1942, and the couple moved to Gordon Road, Clifton, in the 1950s. Their house became a magnet for other performers and creatives in the city, and the 70 house guests they welcomed over the decades included the then-unknown actors Pete Postlethwaite and Peter O'Toole. The aspiring playwright Tom Stoppward lived with Val and Bob between 1959 and 1961 and he wrote his first play at their dining-room table.

By 1967, Val was Chair of the Bristol Old Vic Theatre Club and travelled with the club to New York for a tour of *Measure for Measure*, and she reported back to the Bristol newspapers during the months that she was away. Between its formation in 1994 and her death in 2001, Val was also a committed member of the Southwest Scriptwriters group.

Talking to Andrew Kelly of Bristol Ideas in 2022, Bristolian novelist ACH Smith, who knew Val well, said: "She'd been a professional actress since wartime. I think she probably came to

Bristol to work for the BBC in the war, and she was … a radio continuity announcer and doing the jobs they do, weather and that kind of thing. And she, like so many of us, succumbed to the fatal charms of Bristol and couldn't get away and so stayed here. She went on to act a bit. She never had a big, flashy career but she got some work.

"She and her husband … acquired that gorgeous little Georgian house just behind the Student Union. And she would occasionally take a lodger. She wasn't running a boarding house, but she had a room and she would let it out if there was somebody who wanted somewhere to stay for a bit. And that's where Tom [Stoppard] was. She was charging him £2 a week, and that included supper most evenings. And I once said to her, years later, 'Val, £2 a week, even in the late '50s and early '60s, including a meal, is ridiculous.' And she said, 'I just thought he might have it in him to become a good writer.' … Val was, in effect, the mother of actors in Bristol, her house was the mecca for them. I think there's probably one of them in most big cities with a theatre company, but Val was the one in Bristol.

"Val was the fairy godmother for the theatrical industry in Bristol. She was a lovely warm woman, and Tom has remained grateful to her all his life since."[174]

VIRLIE LOUTH
born 1923, MINING FAMILY

Virlie Isaacs (as she was born) was the seventh of nine children born to a mining family off Wraxall Road in Cadbury Heath. Her father Aaron Isaacs had always been a miner and, as a young

---

174 bristolideas.co.uk/watch/ach-smith

child, Virlie remembers seeing her dad having a bath in the front of the fire and noticing the blue marks on his back caused when the coal dust got into scratches; a common complaint for miners.

The family lived a rather hand to mouth existence, and Virlie grew up in a cottage with a big garden where they grew potatoes, cabbages and other vegetables. A neighbour who worked in one of the many local boot factories would give them offcuts of leather which they would burn on the fire, and she recalled: "It would smell terrible but it helped to keep us warm." Water came from an outside tap that was shared with the house next door.

Extended family members were in the same neighbourhood, with Virlie's aunts Phoebe and Cissie, who were her mother Ethel's sisters, living very close by. As Ethel was the only one of the sisters to have children, she arranged to swap houses with Phoebe – who had one of the new council houses on the Barrs Court Road – so that she would have more space for her family. This house didn't have any carpet or lino, though, only cold flagstone flooring. And the big open fire they had enjoyed in the old cottage was now replaced with a small register fireplace. However, the new council house did have a large oven and Ethel cooked delicious meals there. But, as Virlie recalled: "I don't think any of us were really hard done by as they say. The mums and dads might have had their worries but the children were well looked after and always came first, but never spoilt."

In December 1944, Virlie married an aircraft engineer named Albert Louth.[175]

---

175 Virlie Louth, 1989, in Cadbury Heath History Group, *Life As It Was: Vol 2*, p28–30.

JESSIE LOVELL
dates unknown, WARTIME BUS CONDUCTOR

In central Bristol during World War Two, 20-year-old Jessie Lovell left her job as a typist to become a clippie, aka a bus conductor. It was hard work: getting up before dawn, walking several miles to the bus station, ferrying workers to their jobs at the docks and factories, and walking several miles home again in the dark at the end of the day. As a young woman of small stature, Jessie was teased by the drivers and the passengers on her buses, and her daughter later said: "The drivers' favourite trick being to pull away when she was off the bus, and keep just ahead of her chasing down the street. The passengers would love to chat her up, hoping that she wouldn't notice that it was yesterday's ticket in their hand."

Come hell or high water, the buses needed to keep on running, even in the most dangerous of conditions. Jessie's daughter added: "Sometimes, in the blackout, full of fog and smog from the weather and fires, Mum had to walk in front of the bus with a torch, leading the way and looking for bomb craters in the road. Roads were closed from fallen buildings and unexploded bombs, but the buses had to get through."[176] It was brave work.

SUSANNAH LOVERIDGE
born 1859, PUB LANDLADY

The Hatchet Inn on Frogmore Street dates from 1606 and, as such, is the oldest still-operating pub in Bristol. For more than 100 years between the 1830s and 1930s, it was run by members of the

---

176 bbc.co.uk/history/ww2peopleswar/stories/18/a2857818.shtml

Loveridge family. Susannah Loveridge, who had been born at the pub in 1859, became landlady after the deaths of her parents and was assisted by her younger brother John. The family's tenancy only ended in 1934 when Susannah sold the pub to a brewery chain. By this time, she had lived and worked at The Hatchet for more than 70 years.

ESTHER McEWAN
born 1887, 'SAILOR BOY'

Orphaned Esther McEwan, aged 15, took a novel approach to fending for herself: by dressing as a man and seeking work on board a boat under the pretence of being male (because, of course, the work would be too strenuous for a woman to do - despite several women doing the work with nobody realising).

However, Esther was arrested in the winter of 1902 for the offence of walking down Princes Street in male clothing with a mere 25 shillings in her pocket. When she was charged on 3 November that year, her crime was "wandering abroad without visible means of subsistence". Poor Esther. The *Western Times* later reported: "It appears that when she was left an orphan, foreseeing that she would have to fight her own way in the world, she resolved to do so as a boy. She managed to secure a lad's suit and then, without a regret, had her long dark hair cropped close to the head. The disguise was complete and such an excellent boy did she make that she had no difficulty in obtaining employment at a colliery."[177] After four months in the mines, she began working at sea as a cabin boy.

When Esther appeared in the dock in Bristol, the reporters

177   'The romance of the sea', *Western Times*, 8 November 1902. With thanks to the work of Rosemary Caldicott and her booklet *Nautical Women*, 2019, Bristol Radical History Group.

noted her "male attire" and then wrote that, after bursting into tears, the teenager "admitted" to being a girl. Impressively, Esther stated that she had already worked on three voyages as a mess-room steward and nobody had been any the wiser as to her sex. While the court decided what to do with her, Esther was taken into care in Bristol. She was eventually sent to live with a relative in South Wales, work was found for her as a domestic servant, and she was reported to now be dressed in "female costume".

JOAN McLAREN
1918-2010, DOCTOR, POLITICIAN

"I think Bristol would be a lot better if some of the people in power were women," said Councillor Joan McLaren in 1992.[178] And how right she was.

Joan was born in Poona, India, and came to England in 1937. She initially trained in physiotherapy. After several other posts, Joan came to the Bristol Maternity Hospital in 1955 and, in 1975, was promoted to the role of Superintendent. In this role, Joan was an advocate for physiotherapists specialising in obstetrics and gynaecology, and she would lead ante-natal classes.

In July 1976, the *Western Daily Press* bestowed the rather dubious title of 'Woman of the Week' upon Joan, and took the trouble to ask this intelligent and scientifically minded woman for her opinions on the current clothes fashions for women: "Today's clothes are lovely for expectant mothers, they can wear almost anything," Joan answered patiently.

However, she also said: "This is the century when mortality rates of mothers and babies dropped dramatically, when family

178 'Crisis city needs the gentle touch', *Western Daily Press*, 4 February 1992.

planning gave women control over their fertility, when equal pay and the Employment Protection Act gave those with skills the chance to use them and to have babies and then take up their careers again. I'm a feminist, though not a rabid one."[179] Joan sounds pretty staunchly feminist to me.

After retiring, Joan became a Labour city councillor in 1980 and was elected as Lord Mayor of Bristol in 1995. And despite claiming not to be a 'rabid feminist', Joan evidently had a passion for women's health and wellbeing and took up a role as Chair of the Women's Committee at Bristol City Council in 1989, which campaigned on issues including domestic violence, child benefit freezes, family planning cuts, safe transport for women and better street lighting. She also spent time lobbying to rid Bristol of its sex shops, explaining in 1991: "Pornography was, at first, thought of as harmless, a bit of fun, a release of tension. Now there is evidence it can be harmful, leading to child sex abuse, rape and the demeaning of women."[180] The committee continues in the 21st century in the form of the Women's Commission.

Joan lived in Stoke Bishop, brought up four children single-handed and, by 1976, was a grandmother several times over.[181]

MAZZARINA MACREADY–CHUTE
1824-1878, THEATRE MANAGER

The theatrical Macready-Chute dynasty that thrived in Bristol for two centuries was cemented when comedy actor James Chute married the young actor Mazzarina Emily Macready, who had followed in the thespian footsteps of her father William Macready

179 'Woman of the week', *Western Daily Press*, 23 July 1976.
180 '£20,000 to shut city's sex shops', *Bristol Evening Post*, 22 January 1991.
181 With thanks to @Pingosaurus on Twitter/X for the nomination of Joan McLaren to this book.

by treading the boards at London's Drury Lane as a child. Her first performance in Bristol was in *The Maid of Mariandorp*, for which she won "favourable reviews" according to the *Bristol Mercury*. As a young woman, Mazzarina also wrote a handful of short plays.

After Mazzarina and James' 1844 marriage, James settled down to the more steady work of theatre management and the Macready-Chute partnership oversaw both the Princes Theatre on Park Row, which they designed and built, and later the Theatre Royal on King Street (now Bristol Old Vic) from the 1850s. Mazzarina continued to act after marriage and was best known for her appearances in a series of Greek tragedies.

The Princes Theatre was built on a steep slope beneath Tyndall's Park, on a site that had previously been home to a grand mansion. However, when choosing this spot for the theatre, one key flaw had been overlooked: all the entrances and exits emerged on Park Row, which was not large enough to accommodate a theatre full of evacuated patrons. Mazzarina and James found this out to their cost on 26 December 1869 when the crowds gathered outside waiting to come in and watch a pantomime. The polite queuing system that British folks now adhere to was not adopted until the 1890s, meaning that when the doors to the pit and gallery opened the crowd surged down the steep slope to get in. Some of those at the front fell to the floor and were unknowingly trampled by those behind them. More than 40 people were injured and 14 people died. Mazzarina and James helped to lay out the bodies of the dead in the theatre's refreshment room, while insisting that the pantomime went ahead so that none of the patrons inside knew of the disaster until after the show. Consequently, tighter safety measures were introduced but neither Mazzarina nor James ever fully recovered – mentally or financially – from the ordeal. The building was destroyed during the Blitz in 1940.

Mazzarina died aged 53 in 1878 when she suddenly fell ill after supper one day. She was diagnosed with Bright's Disease, which affects the kidneys. Her obituary in the *Bristol Mercury*, headlined 'Death of Mrs James Henry Chute', is an astonishingly detailed account of the achievements of the various men in Mazzarina's life (by which I mean her father, step-brother, husband etc, rather than romantic attachments) instead of the achievements of Mazzarina herself. Which tells you everything you need to know about the role of women in Victorian England. However, at the end of the obituary, the writer did remember to say something about Mazzarina: "Her undeviating purity of taste and character has exerted a refining influence on many stage representations … Exemplary in her discharge of all the duties of domestic life, she had a heart which was ever full of that spirit of charity which we have divine authority for saying is the greatest of human virtues."[182]

She is buried at Arnos Vale Cemetery and her funeral was attended by an enormous number of theatrical friends and associates. It was reported that out of respect for Mazzarina, almost everyone in the streets surrounding their home and theatre kept their shutters closed for days following her death. James died a few months later and is buried in the same plot.

Mazzarina and James had nine children, of whom the most well known is George Macready-Chute who also ran the Prince's Theatre. His eldest daughter was blessed with the name Mazzarina Macready Chippendale Chute (1885–1921), which is the kind of flamboyant moniker that most performers are obliged to make up. Because George died when his daughter Mazzarina was two, her mother Adelaide Chippendale ran the Princes Theatre and Mazzarina Jr and her younger brother Edward grew up surrounded by actors, props and scripts.

---

182 'Death of Mrs James Henry Chute', *Bristol Mercury*, 28 March 1878.

ELLEN MALOS
1937–2023, ACTIVIST, ACADEMIC

Author's note: I had the pleasure of meeting Ellen Malos on numerous occasions. In fact the first time I ever spoke at an event was in 2011 on a panel with Ellen talking about the history of feminist activism in Bristol. We met several times over the following 12 years, and she was supportive of The Women Who Built Bristol *project and always gave generous feedback. It was with enormous sadness that I heard of Ellen's death at the age of 85. She remains an inspiration to me, and Ellen was one of the few people in whose presence I would feel completely tongue-tied with awe. Although she would have been embarrassed to know that.*

Born in Australia to a socialist family, Ellen Scarlett (as she was originally called) was a natural at school who earned a place at Melbourne University to study English and History: a place she had to support by working as a supply teacher because, as a recently married woman, she was ineligible for a student grant. Worse, her husband John Malos was a socialist and this caused him to lose his job. Nonetheless, both continued with their studies, with Ellen earning a Masters and John a PhD.

The couple emigrated to the UK in 1962 with their two-year-old son and John took a job at the University of Bristol. This was around the same time that sister Australian feminists Germaine Greer and Lynne Segal also came to England. Ellen tried to study for her doctorate in the UK but she was forced to abandon it when her supervisor could not accept that a woman was able to both study *and* care for a toddler. But the life of a typical 'university wife' was never going to be something that Ellen pursued.

By 1969, she was starting to make her mark as an activist and a key member of the second wave of feminism. Ellen attended the famous Women's Liberation Movement conference at Ruskin College in 1970 and subsequently became a central part of the women's movement in Bristol. The basement of her house in Waverley Road, Redland, was repurposed as the Women's Centre. Meetings took place there and, significantly, this was also a refuge for women fleeing domestic violence: the first such refuge in Bristol. At weekends, the same space offered pregnancy testing in the days before home testing kits were available and in the days when GPs judged women harshly for requesting a pregnancy test: should the woman be unmarried, she was immoral, and should she be married but not wanting the child, she was monstrous. At the pregnancy testing centre on Waverley Road, there was no judgement, only support. After two years, the women who helped Ellen run the Women's Centre had acquired and were managing three houses in Bristol, and this was how Bristol Women's Aid was established.

As time progressed, Ellen broadened the campaigning to include the fight for contraceptive rights and support for working women on low pay, among other issues. A magazine called *Enough* was established which was copied on a duplicator in the Women's Centre. There were also briefings and newsletters, and a telephone tree was set up to share urgent information in a hurry.[183]

Describing a typical week at this time, Ellen said: "I would be going down to meetings, say three or four times a week. The phone would ring and somebody would come in at 11 or 12 o' clock, 3 or 4 in the morning. I would go down and give them cups of tea, settle them in, whatever. It did become very much a life, more than a job, I suppose a vocation really for a while. There

183 Before emails and social media, a telephone tree was an efficient way of getting urgent information out to a lot of people in a short space of time. Telephone trees were well-used by activists, campaigners and community groups. A telephone tree is essentially a list of phone numbers provided to a group, and each person is responsible for ringing a certain number of other people to tell them the news. And those people then are responsible for ringing a certain number of different people to further share the news, and so on.

were vast numbers of people involved. The mailing list must have been four or five double-sided pages of A4."[184]

While all this was going on, Ellen was looking after her two young children and working part-time as a teacher, and she and John were members of the Labour Party and several other campaign groups including the Campaign for Nuclear Disarmament (CND). As a writer, she had contributed to the Virago Press book *Half The Sky: An Introduction to Women's Studies* in 1979, which was collectively produced by the Bristol Women's Study Group and presented a range of writing about women's experiences of the world. Ellen also contributed to many publications, including her edited collection *The Politics of Housework* in 1980, and was one of the early members of the radical publishing group Bristol Broadsides.[185]

This led Ellen back to the University of Bristol where she completed a diploma in Social Administration. She returned to Women's Aid as a paid worker but wanted to challenge herself further and, in 1981, secured her first temporary teaching contract at the university. Over the coming years, Ellen would become a regular fixture there. In 1984, together with Gill Hague, they won a grant to study the housing authorities' responses to women experiencing domestic violence, and this was the start of a long collaboration and valuable research into an area that had previously been academically ignored. As a result, in 1990, the Domestic Violence Research Group was established. However, Ellen did not get a permanent post at the University of Bristol until she was 60 and had been working at the establishment for 18 years.

184   bristol.ac.uk/graduation/honorary–degrees/hondeg06/malos.html
185   Bristol Broadsides was a working writers' project in this city that was set up in 1976 and has been an incredible resource for finding some of the stories of women included in *The Women Who Built Bristol* books. In 2024, I wrote a retrospective of the project which is available online: bristolideas. co.uk/read/bristol-broadsides-1976-1991

Throughout the remainder of her career, Ellen continued to work with Women's Aid, helping to secure funding when the organisation was threatened with closure. She taught Social Policy and lectured on the Masters programmes in Gender and Social Policy, and Women's Studies.

EMILY MALTBY
born 1806, SUFFRAGIST

One of the 13 Bristolian women to sign the 1866 mass women's suffrage petition was Emily Maltby who was a widow and head of her household, which would have made it easier for her to speak out on such a contentious topic. The fact she lived a comfortable life at 2 Kensington Villas in Clifton also suggests that her money would have cushioned her from any negativity that her signature roused. Alongside servants, Emily lived with two nephews and a niece, who were all of school age in 1861, suggesting that she had become their guardian. It has not been possible to find further information about Emily.

ADA MANSEL
1866-1916, MUSIC HALL ARTIST

In November 1899, established music hall performer Lady Ada Mansel, who sometimes went by the name of 'Lily Ernest', decided to take a risk and bought the struggling Tivoli Theatre in what is now Broadmead. Announcing the news, *The Stage* wrote: "Under entirely new management, this popular music hall, by far the oldest in the city, enters upon a fresh phase in its career."[186]

As Ada Alice Lea, she was born in Bethnal Green, London, to Mary and James Lea. Aged 25 in 1891, she married a divorced man called Sir Richard Phillips Mansel who was 15 years her senior: Ada perhaps should have heeded the fact that Richard's first wife Maude divorced him on the grounds of his cruelty towards her. There is a suggestion that Richard, who seemed to be in financial difficulty, was tempted to marry Ada by the fact she received an annuity of £600, much of which he insisted she hand over to him. At a later court case, Ada's solicitor said: "[Ada] had the misfortune to marry a gentleman of title who, for some reason, found himself unable to live with her, and she only had the advantage of that marriage for one year."[187] The marriage was brief and Richard died the following year, leaving little to Ada who was also largely ignored by her late husband's family. In the years immediately after, Ada travelled to the US where she performed a few seasons in New York.

She was no stranger to the stage (nor was she averse to the occasional whistling solo), having made her first public performance at the tender age of just three-and-a-half. From the age of ten, Ada was a regular on the stage and, from the age of 17, she was taking leading roles in London. In addition, Ada ran her own burlesque company under the name of Randolph the Reckless and she assumed the lead role in this for several years. From 1901, Ada had a troupe called Lady Mansel and Juveniles in which she toured with up to 16 young girls whom she schooled in the art of music hall performance. Fun fact: Ada was also a champion skipping-rope dancer, which is something you don't hear much about these days.

The Tivoli Theatre opened in central Bristol 1870 as the Star

---

186 'The Provinces', *The Stage*, 16 November 1899.
187 'Actress's ill-luck', *Yorkshire Evening News*, 16 March 1914.

Music Hall. Following a fire in 1896, the hall was rebuilt. In June 1896, the Tivoli became one of the first theatres in the UK to show moving pictures, but these were very much a novelty ahead of the theatre's main offering: music hall acts. At the time that Ada took out a mortgage for £7,000 and bought the hall in 1899 (appointing William Lovell Hurst as manager), the venue had been struggling. And clearly she didn't do much to help things along because, within six months, Ada had abandoned the Tivoli and was attempting to buy a hotel in Bridlington. The Tivoli later became a dedicated cinema and thrived in the years 1912-1916, before becoming a venue for live theatre. It was demolished in 1952, along with everything around it, to make way for the Broadmead shopping area.

However, Ada didn't restrict her energies in Bristol to the Tivoli. For instance, in January 1900 she was the warm-up act at Bedminster Football Ground ahead of a Fancy Dress Football Match in aid of the Soldiers', Widows' and Orphans' Fund.

It seems the Tivoli wasn't the only bad investment that Ada made. In 1911, she was in bankruptcy court having reneged on a string of properties around the UK that she had attempted to buy and run as music hall venues: none of them successfully.[188] However, this might not have been entirely her fault. The Tivoli seems to have been the first venue that Ada attempted to run and it seems that her brief tenure there may have been prompted by the sudden death of her manager William Lovell Hurt, who died a bankrupt owing Ada almost £3,500[189] (aka, half of her mortgage for the venue): so perhaps William had mishandled the finances on Ada's behalf? This is mere speculation, of course. The bankruptcy case was not resolved until 1914 and, by the time of Ada's death in 1916, although she had been beloved by audiences

188 'Affairs of Baronet's widow', *Bayswater Chronicle*, 23 December 1911.
189 'Music hall gossip', *The Era*, 15 September 1900.

all over the country, she warranted little more than a sentence in any newspaper.

Fun fact: Ada's niece was the vaudeville performer Minnie Love (1888-1967), who was born in Bristol and learned her trade here before becoming an even bigger stage star in Australia and, in the final decade of her life, moved into television.

ANNIE MARDON
1863–1922, SAILORS' SAVIOUR

As the wife of wealthy Ernest Mardon, Annie 'Nan' Mardon of Sneyd Park House was in a privileged position to support soldiers fighting for their country during World War One. Ernest was one of the founders of Mardon, Son & Hall Ltd, a Bristolian printing company that was a branch of the Imperial Tobacco Company. Among other things, Mardon manufactured the collectible cards that would come in packets of cigarettes.[190] Bristol's printing industry was at its peak in the early 20th century, meaning that Annie and Ernest were sitting pretty when World War One hit the UK. Ernest was also the Commander of the Royal Naval Volunteer Reserve in Bristol, and so he had a direct concern for the welfare of British sailors.

Early in the war, 100 Bristolian sailors were captured and sent to prisoner of war camps in Germany and Austria. In response, Nan set up the Ladies' Emergency Committee of the Bristol Branch of the Navy League, and they would send parcels of food, clothing, books and medicines to the captured sailors as well as those who were still serving on ships. In addition, Nan would help to trace sailors who were missing, and she would write a

190 Miss Clark, who worked for Mardon, has her own entry in this volume.

personal letter once a week to every sailor who was a prisoner of war, as well as offering support to their families in Bristol.

After the war, the returning sailors threw a party in Nan's honour in 1919. One sailor commented that for some of the men, who had no relatives at home to write to them, Nan's weekly letter was "their brightest treasure". Nan was presented with an engraved silver rose bowl as a token of the sailor's gratitude. In response, she said that the work for her "naval boys" was done through love and she would always treasure the relationships she had built with them.

When Nan died in 1922, her memorial service at Bristol Cathedral was packed out with former Bristol sailors.

ELIZABETH MARLEYN
1936-2024, JOURNALIST

Some may know Elizabeth 'Liz' Marleyne better by her pen name of 'Helen Reid', under which she wrote a number of books about Bristol and its history, including the influential *Go Home and Do the Washing* (2000), co-authored with Lorna Brierly, which took a look at some pioneering women from Bristol (it was certainly an influence on the writer of this book). As Helen Reid, Liz also wrote books such as *A Chronicle of Clifton and Hotwells* (1992), *Bristol Under Siege* (2005) and *Life in Victorian Bristol* (2005). In addition to her local history books, Liz/Helen contributed to the *Western Daily Press* for decades, chiefly as a theatre and music reviewer and as a columnist, having joined the newspaper in 1960.

Liz was not originally from Bristol but had moved here in 1954 as a university student. She later recalled: "Bristol in 1954 still showed raw scars from the Blitz: Park Street was full of gaps, like missing teeth, bombsites where herb robert grew. There was still a British Restaurant on College Green; Gillows on the Triangle had not yet been built, and the Broadmead development had only begun piecemeal." She continued: "We were elderly before our time. There was no youth cult in the early Fifties: you left school and became an adult overnight ... We had no youth music of our own other than skiffle and bop, no fashions of our own. Women's Lib had not been invented, there were no drugs, and I can't remember seeing a television set in my student years."[191]

She had hoped to become a university lecturer but with no suitable openings (unless she was interested in a post in Africa, which she wasn't), Liz ended up as a junior reporter for the *Western Daily Press*, having taken some student jobs in Bristol as everything from a tomato picker to a Woolworths' sales assistant. Her job at the paper came about following a stint working for the retailer John Lewis in the publicity department, and fortunately the *Press* considered this suitable prior experience.

Despite a lack of media training, Liz soon became one of the paper's star writers, regardless of whether she was covering local or national stories, or reviewing the latest play in the theatre. She also contributed a weekly column about her home life in Hotwells, which lasted until her retirement in April 1995.

At the time of her retirement, Liz said: "No regrets but if I had my time over again I would like to be a political journalist. There have been enormous changes and womens' pages have altered dramatically from the old knitting sections. And now, thankfully, there are a lot more women in the business. I've interviewed most of the leading figures in theatre and politics, [John] Gielgud was interesting, Marlene Dietrich was a cow and Margaret Thatcher was terrifying. No matter what you asked, she told you what she wanted to."[192]

191   Helen Reid, 1988, 'Salad Days' in *Bristol in the Fifties*, p35-42.
192   'Bye, Helen Reid', *Western Daily Press*, 7 April 1995.

After Liz's death, former *Western Daily Press* editor Ian Beales said: "She was a gem: a multi–faceted journalistic diamond, by-lined – for reasons long forgotten – Helen Reid. Officially, she was the *WDP*'s chief features writer, but that is a masterpiece of understatement … At her brilliant best, Liz was one of the wittiest writers I ever worked with and wise with it."[193]

VI MARRIOTT
dates unknown, SECRETARY

Thanks to her work as a Secretary at Croydon Aerodrome, Vi Marriott was well equipped to be transferred to Bristol during World War Two to deal with military aircraft here. Because everything that the secretaries did was absolutely top secret, the carbon paper that was used in the typewriters needed to be torn into tiny pieces once it was finished with and placed in a special sack to be burned. Vi later said: "My sense of the ridiculous was enchanted, because these secret sacks came from the ex-German Embassy, and were printed in red and black with the German eagle emblem."

Bristol was heavily bombed by the Germans, and Vi and her colleagues would keep watch to see which way the planes were headed once they left Bristol. She said: "The most spectacular raid was the night the whole of the centre of Bristol went, and the air smelt of mulled ale for the next week as the brewery was burned to the ground."

However, not all raids happened at night: "The most frightening for me was the daylight raid when one of the escorting fighters was shot down and flew the whole length of Whiteladies

193 'A gem', *Western Daily Press*, 15 March 2024. With thanks to Eugene Byrne for the nomination of Liz Marleyn to this book.

180

Road, emptying his gun and barely skimming the roof of the house where I lived."[194]

JANE MARTIN
born 1910, TEACHER, WARTIME MOTHER

Born in Liverpool, Jane Martin and her family moved to Bristol in September 1923 when she was 13. Barely a teenager, Jane never attended school in Bristol because her mother said she had learned enough, so Jane had no further education until she was 39 and went to Redland Training College as a mature student to learn to be a teacher.

In her early years in Bristol, Jane struggled to fit in. She missed her friends from Liverpool and felt homesick. She missed going to school and watched as children her age would set off for school in the mornings.

Her mother kept her busy around the house until Jane turned 14 and was legally allowed to work, at which point she was employed at a photography studio in Bedminster. After two weeks, Jane knew enough to know that she didn't want to work there and left. Her second job came when she was 15 and was with another photographer who had an office at the top of a building in Temple Gate. She stayed there for 12 years, unintentionally becoming the family's breadwinner after her father lost his job during the Great Depression and her brother was on an apprentice's low wage.

In 1937, Jane married a fireman and they travelled to Germany on honeymoon, unaware of the war that was looming: "We saw, though we did not know it, the preparations that Hitler was making for World War Two. His mountains of tins grew on the skyline, he wasted nothing and his Hitler Youth marched through the streets with their spades over their shoulders singing lustily. Little did we know that those selfsame spades would be used in the murder of millions of Jews."

Back home, Jane's first daughter was born as war was announced and, as a new mother, she was horrified to have to be taught how to fit a tiny little gas mask to her newborn. Jane later wrote: "It doesn't seem quite right that 3 September 1939 [the day war was declared] was the happiest day of my life, I came out of hospital hugging my new baby. The blackouts were put up, the [barrage] balloons suddenly blossomed at the end of the road, but I couldn't see further than a little golden head nor feel anything but the clasp of little warm fingers."[195]

ANITA MASON
1942-2020, WRITER

Anita Frances Mason was the author of eight novels, including *The Illusionist* in 1983 which was nominated for the Booker Prize. Anita was educated at Red Maids' School before completing an English degree at the University of Oxford in 1963. Although she lived in Cornwall for a number of years, Anita returned to Bristol in 2003 and remained here for the rest of her life. In Anita's obituary, her friend Christine Cohen Park wrote: "Anita lived ... in a flat full of books and the art work she had collected from her travels in Latin America. She was a fine cook, an inveterate walker and someone who enjoyed the natural world almost as much as the city."[196]

After dabbling in journalism and organic farming, Anita

195 Jane Martin, 1988, in *Bristol Reflections*, Bristol Broadsides, p88-94.
196 theguardian.com/books/2020/nov/01/anita–mason–obituary

settled on writing fiction and, as well as *The Illusionist*, her novels included *The Racket* (1990) and *The Right Hand of the Sun* (2008). Her writing varied in terms of where and when it was set. For instance, *The Illusionist* told the story of a religious figure called Simon Magus and his connection to the early Christians, while her debut novel *Bethany* (1981) was set in a Cornish commune. Alternative communities and ways of life were recurring themes, as was her use of the past as a way of mirroring the present. The *Bristol Evening Post* described *Bethany* as an "impressive first novel", adding that: "Anita Mason gets deeply inside her characters in what is essentially a study of one woman under increasing stress in a shortish novel that both grips and entertains." [197]

LILIAN MEADE-KING
born 1872, SOCIAL WORKER

As an unmarried woman from a respectable family, Lilian Meade-King lived with her father Herbert Meade-King at 19 Royal York Crescent, Clifton, until well into her 40s. Herbert was a retired solicitor and they lived in great comfort with several servants to tend to them. Lilian concerned herself with helping those less fortunate than herself, and as such she was 'Chairman' of the Staff Committee of Bristol and Clifton District Nursing Society, having been a member of the committee for 25 years. She was also on the board of the Infant Welfare Council, and had been the Honorary Secretary of St Augustine's Welfare Centre since it had been established in 1913. When she had a moment to herself, which sounds like a rarity, Lilian could be found relaxing in her garden where she enjoyed tending to the flower beds.

197   'A summer of discontent', *Bristol Evening Post*, 18 March 1981.

FLO MELHUISH
born c1904, COTTON FACTORY WORKER

Barton Hill resident Flo Melhuish started work at the Great Western Cotton Factory as a 14-year-old. She had only been working at the factory for a few days when her supervisor told Flo that she was heading to the pub for a while and she asked the teenager to carry on with her work. But when the supervisor returned, she was furious to see that a streak had developed on the calico Flo's loom had been producing and told the girl it would need to be re-done or she wouldn't be paid. Flo recalled: "She got in a temper, slapped my face and left her finger marks on my face. So I thought, well the only thing I can do now is give her one back. So I picked up the bobbin and let her have one back see. So the foreman says, 'What's going on here?' So I said, 'Well, she slapped me across the face, you can still see the marks. So I got into a bit of a paddy and hit her one with this bobbin.' So he said, 'That's enough of that then. You go to the office and get your cards. You're finished.'"

Seemingly, Flo didn't lose her job, or else she returned to the cotton factory at a subsequent date, because she later writes that she worked there for several years and describes the conditions saying: "We didn't have any canteen there to eat our food. You'd sit down in the alleyways. There was nowhere to wash your hands or anything like that. I stayed there for four or five years among the cotton workers. I started about 1918 just after the war. Now all the women there worked very hard."[198]

198   Flo Melhuish, 1977, in *Bristol as We Remember It*, Bristol: Broadsides, p10–12.

BARBARA MIDDLETON
dates unknown, LIBRARIAN

The first librarian of Cadbury Heath Library was Barbara Middleton. The library was opened on 4 July 1959 and it was the first of the new libraries in the area, and originally called Oldland Parkwall Library. Prior to 1959, books were loaned via a system of wooden boxes that were circulated to schools. They were distributed in the evenings by volunteers including Barbara in Bitton, and a woman named Mrs Stone in Cadbury Heath.

When Cadbury Heath Library opened, Barbara had one part-time assistant. The pair found the work very time-consuming. The demand for the library's services was high so Barbara and her assistant were kept busy sorting out membership forms, as well as keeping records of the books that were available and to whom they had been loaned. There was no Citizens' Advice Bureau locally, so the library doubled up as an information service and the librarians found themselves trusted to keep all sorts of secrets. In addition, children would come in with creatures they had found outside and the librarians would help them identify the grass snakes, frogs, butterflies and leaves they presented.

Talking about how the library later expanded, former librarian Joyce Cormack said: "Helped by the local Women's Institute, we started a weekly service taking books to Newton House [a care home] and soon learned the type of book individual senior citizens enjoyed ... Soon we had classes of children brought to be introduced to the assortment of books and the working of a library by teachers from several local schools."

Joyce remembers how one of her early jobs at the library was to cycle around to people's houses to collect overdue books, and although she was doubtful that people would welcome her she soon found that readers were glad of the help because it meant they avoided large fines. She explained: "I found myself holding babies, admiring furniture, carpets and curtains, while the books were found, and I enjoyed my excursions."[199]

BETTY MILLARD
1910-1991, ACTIVIST

Betty Millard was known in Bristol, and elsewhere in the UK, as the voice of Britain's pensioners and she was awarded an MBE in 1979 for her efforts. Having grown up on Bright Street in Barton Hill, Betty attended Rose Green and Bristol East schools, and during World War Two she volunteered as an ambulance driver. In 1974, Betty became the first female president of the National Federation of Old Age Pensions Associations and, by the time of her retirement in 1985, she had devoted 41 years to the organisation. One of her biggest achievements was successfully lobbying for a fairer deal for women in retirement. Until 2010, women were forced to retire at 60 (rather than the male retirement age of 65), but pension benefits such as bus passes and cheaper rail tickets were not given until women reached the age of 65. Thanks to Betty, retired women began to see a better deal. Marking her death, Barbara Rees of Avon Age Concern said: "Her whole life was devoted to helping those less fortunate than herself."[200]

---

199   Joyce Cormack, 1989, in Cadbury Heath History Group, *Life As It Was: Vol 2*, p33–34.
200   'Voice of OAPs Betty dies', *Bristol Evening Post*, 26 November 1991.

BERTHA MILTON
dates unknown, CHOCOLATE FACTORY WORKER

Bertha Milton began working at Fry's when she was 14 in the early 1900s and explained the process of getting a job there: "You had to go through a thorough examination by a doctor and they wanted to know if you went to church or chapel or if you were good or no. So I had to have a tooth out and I didn't like that very much. I had to have the tooth out or else I wouldn't have gone into Fry's. I wanted to be one of their 'Angels'. If you were a 'Fry's Angel' in them days you were somebody. At Packers, the other chocolate place here, they were called 'Packer's Devils'."[201]

Bertha worked in the weight room before she learned how to cover chocolate, which was piece work. "It was to cover little creams which were called tens," she said. "We used to have to cover 120 for three farthings. A couple of weeks after they put it up to a penny. I didn't like it … but of course you couldn't leave … In those days, during the hot weather, if the work [was ruined in the heat] you didn't get any money and you were sent home. In the summer I was at home more often than I was at work … Finally I got onto chocolate creams, which are still made to this day [1977], but today it's all done by machinery. We daren't talk and we daren't laugh. If we laughed or if we talked we had to leave off. She'd tell you, 'Leave off and sit'. We had to sit on our stools and wait half an hour and then we'd start work again."

True to the Quaker origins of the Fry's factory, Bertha recalled how every day there was a service with hymns, prayers and a doxology.[202] While Bertha didn't seem to think much of the enforced worship, she did admit that the bosses – if eccentric – were at least kind. "[The boss] used to look a real sight. With a

201 WJ Packer & Co was established in Easton in 1881 by a former Fry's employee.
202 A doxology is a form of religious praise

frock tail coat and a pair of boots on that were never done up," she said. "But I must say, when he died he left us all a bit of money, so I was alright then. If you worked there five years you had £5, and for every year over that number you had an extra pound. So I had £5 and I thought it was lovely. I was very happy in Fry's but I was glad to leave."[203]

KATE MILTON
dates unknown,
TOBACCO FACTORY WORKER, DISC JOCKEY

Rather delightfully, the Wills factory workers enjoyed an in-house DJ in the form of Kate Milton at the No 4 Factory. The staff preferred to listen to music while they worked as they were not keen on all the talking on the BBC's radio stations, so DJ Kate filled the role admirably. A 1967 copy of the staff magazine *Wills World* writes: "The BBC's Onederful [sic] Radio 1 has proved less than wonderful to listeners during the music periods in the Wills factories. They find the fast talking disc jockeys with their jokes and comments cannot be heard over the noise of the machinery and long for their old favourite. The factories' own disc jockeys are playing extra sessions of gramophone records to fill the gap. At the No 4 factories at Ashton the regular disc jockey is 64-year-old Mrs Kate Milton, who takes over the turntable for four half-hour sessions and for another hour when evening overtime is being worked."[204]

203 Bertha Milton, 1977, in *Bristol as We Remember It*, Bristol Broadsides, p15–16.
204 imagesofengland.org.uk/learningzone/lz/forum_tobacco_67.aspx

JO MITCHELL
dates unknown, LAND GIRL

Women who were a part of the Women's Land Army were known as Land Girls. This was a British civilian organisation that sent women out to do the agricultural jobs that had been left empty by male farm workers and land workers who had been called up to fight. Bristolian Jo Mitchell was just 17 when she joined the Land Army during World War Two, which sent her to Cheltenham for a month to train as a thatcher. Once she had a grasp of the thatching ropes, Jo was assigned to a job in Almondsbury with a young woman from London. She said: "We did threshing in the winter and haymaking and harvesting during the summer." Jo was in the Land Army for three-and-a-half years, saying she enjoyed the experience and it was good fun.[205]

MARY MOBBS
1925–2012, MUSICIAN, ARTIST

Born into a music–loving family in Birmingham, Mary Jeanette Randall (as she was originally known) furthered her musical education at the University of Birmingham. She gained a BA from the Music Department in 1948, adding on a diploma for piano teaching in 1956 from the Royal Academy of Music. All of this was to the dismay of the Head of Art at the university, who recognised that Mary was also a gifted fine artist.

Mary spent the 1950s as a music teacher in Birmingham, before moving to the University of Bristol where she undertook a number of administrative roles, beginning in the Physics

205 bbc.co.uk/history/ww2peopleswar/stories/83/a4022083.shtml. Freda Baron, who led the Land Army, has her own entry in this volume.

Department where she worked with the Nobel Prize-winning Cecil Powell[206] making high-altitude balloons for his cosmic ray research work. It was quite a departure from the world of music. In later years, she moved to different departments at the university, ending up as the Administrative Assistant to the Registrar until her retirement in 1983.

However, Mary never lost her love for music. As well as playing in a Bristolian piano group she was a singer and performer with a local opera group, and in her mid-30s she took up the bassoon which she later played in wind trios and as part of the university's orchestra. It should come as no surprise that, when Mary did marry in 1979, her husband Kenneth Mobbs was the university's Senior Lecturer in Music.

This shared passion led the couple to amass what would become a nationally important collection of early keyboard instruments. After retirement, Mary became a harpsichord soundboard painter and, within a year, her work was exhibited in Bruges at the international Early Keyboard Exhibition. This brought a lot of attention to Mary's skills and she was soon inundated with commissions from other harpsichord owners to decorate their instruments with birds and flowers, which she did in the style of the Old Masters.

Unfortunately, a diagnosis of Multi-System Dystrophy, which is a form of Parkinson's Disease, cut short Mary's career in this precise painting. She also found it difficult to play the bassoon due to her illness, although she then threw her energies into trying to learn the oboe instead. Mary was one woman who would keep on pushing back against life's obstacles.

---

206 Isobel Powell, who was married to Cecil, is profiled in Volume Two of *The Women Who Built Bristol*.

MARY MOGFORD
born 1859, IRONMONGER

Born in Pill on the edge of Bristol, Mary Ann Paines married William Mogford in 1885 and the couple took over his father's painting and decorating shop on Blackboy Hill, Clifton. The shop, Mogfords, would remain in the family for generations to come.

Mary and William had two children, Ernest and Alberta, who they brought up in their home above the shop. And in time, Mary and William developed the shop to include ironmongery alongside the building and decorating items they already sold. Their granddaughter Renee Wiltshire remembered Mary with fondness as a straightforward woman who refused to see anything as an obstacle: "On one occasion she knocked a hole through one wall to allow for self-service of linseed oil." Which is a very practical solution to a problem. Over time, the business grew so much that it needed new premises and they relocated to Westbury Hill. At the time of publication, WH Mogford & Son remains in business in Westbury-on-Trym.[207]

MARY MORTIFEE
1860-1935, TEACHER

Bristolian through and through, Mary Bussell Mortifee's father James was a labourer and her mother Sarah a homemaker. Mary was the eldest of their six children and she never married or had children of her own: perhaps helping to bring up her younger siblings was enough to put her off?

At the time of Mary's birth, the family was living at 1 Dale

207 Beryl Tully, 2004, *Shoes and Ships and Sealing Wax*, Malago Press, p55-62.

Cottages in St Pauls, which they shared with the Masters family: an indication of their lowly income. By the time of the 1881 census, the family had moved to 59 Pennywell Road in St Pauls and Mary, 21, was working as a Certified Assistant (what we would now call a Teaching Assistant) at Redcross Street Girls School. She moved to Castle Board School in 1887 but, by 1889, had been appointed as Headteacher of East Street School in 1889 and transferred to Bedminster Bridge Mixed School in 1893, before moving to Ashton Gate Mixed School in 1899 where she remained for the rest of her career, with her younger sister Amy working there as an Assistant Teacher. By 1911, their parents had died and Mary and Amy were lodging with the Bennett family at 40 Burghley Road, St Andrews.

Unfortunately, illness forced Mary to take early retirement in October 1914 when she was in her mid-50s, prompting the Bristol School Board and Education Committee (which itself would fold in 1914) to pass a vote of thanks to Mary given she had been in their service for so many years. Alderman Elkins expressed the Board's "deep regret that she was retiring, especially as it was because of ill health". Fanny Townsend added: "Miss Mortifee has had schools in difficult neighbourhoods and has worked very hard for her children. The Committee would very much regret her retirement."[208]

MAGGIE MOSS
1952–2021, ECOLOGIST, TEACHER, WRITER

Born in Wantage, Oxfordshire, Maggie Moss was one of three daughters of Rachel and Basil Moss, a vicar. When she was three,

208 'Retirement of Miss Mortifee', *Western Daily Press*, 30 October 1914. Fanny Townsend has her own entry in this volume.

the family moved to Redland, where Basil became a parish priest and later the canon of Bristol Cathedral. After leaving school, Maggie trained as a teacher at the Loughborough College of Education, from where she qualified in 1974. Her role as a teacher brought her back to the south west, where she worked at Weston All Saints primary school in Bath for several years.

However, her itchy feet got the better of her and, in 1978, Maggie travelled overland to India on her own. This experience really boosted her confidence and her sense of independence and it generated a self-reliance that stayed with Maggie for the rest of her life. It also fostered a love of travelling that would see her visit places including Ethiopia, Mali and Iran. In this way, she was able to indulge her love of other cultures and music. Maggie's sister Jill Moss remembers how Maggie would always take some string with her so that she could make a cat's cradle hand game, as a way of helping her to connect with the local women and children she met when she was away.

In 1987, Maggie and her sister Gemma Moss collaborated to write *The Handbook for Women Travellers*, which has since been translated into three languages and updated and reprinted several times. The book offers practical advice for women whether travelling on their own or with other women, and covers topics such as how to stay safe, how to be culturally sensitive and tips for being eco-conscious. This was followed by *The Himalayan Tourist Code* in 1988, produced in conjunction with Tourism Concern. Maggie also delivered seminars to women offering advice on how to travel safely. She felt that women travellers had more cultural awareness than men, and that women were more interested in meeting local people than men were. She said: "For many older women, who never really had a chance to travel in their 20s and 30s because they were too busy being wives and mothers, this is their chance to travel. About one third of the participants on our courses are older women who want to travel in a thoughtful way."[209] She also said: "We need to step back and take a look at the way we travel. We imagine that, if we have paid for a holiday, we have purchased the right to behave in the way we wish, wherever we are. That is what we really have to re-examine."[210]

In 1984, Maggie married Mike Manson with whom she would have two children. By this time, Maggie had retrained to become a careers advisor and went to work for the Avon Careers Service with young people who were excluded or failed by the education system. She later became an outreach worker for further education colleges in Bristol. After retiring in 2015, Maggie became a schools liaison officer for St Brendan's sixth form college in Bristol.

Throughout all of this, Maggie always had a strong interest in plants and bugs and became a keen advocate of butterfly monitoring in an urban setting. Maggie felt that only monitoring butterflies in the countryside was half-hearted and so, in 2017, she created an urban butterfly transect to measure, by weekly survey, changes in the numbers and variety of butterflies in a set area. In addition, she initiated a conference programme looking at urban issues such as verge mowing management and wildlife gardening. Alongside this, she became the first wildlife officer at the Ashley Vale Allotment Association. With students from the University of the West of England, Maggie renovated a large pond, and a motion sensitive camera was installed which revealed night-time visitors such as badgers, deer and foxes.

Committed to the cause, Maggie was a passionate supporter of the Extinction Rebellion environmental movement and, in

209 independent.co.uk/travel/travel-for-women-is-a-fine-balance-between-risk-and-adventure-1318235.html
210 independent.co.uk/life-style/an-englishwoman-abroad-lisa-o-kelly-discovers-that-although-more-women-are-being-assaulted-on-holiday-or-while-travelling-few-of-them-ever-report-the-crime-1459841.html

2019, she was proud to be arrested outside the Home Office in London while taking part in a demonstration.[211]

MARY MULLER
1797-1870, ORPHANAGE FOUNDER

Born Mary Groves to a middle-class family in Hampshire, this young lady was brought up in comfort and taught how to be the perfect wife to a wealthy man. As such, her education included the necessary domestic skills of sewing, drawing and piano playing. However, following her father's financial crash when she was 16, Mary was suddenly in a situation where she needed to earn her own keep and she swiftly set up a small Dame School with a friend.

Following her mother's death, Mary moved to Exeter to live with her married brother and it was here that Mary married a deeply religious man called George Müller in 1830. They moved to Bristol in May 1932 and had four children, although only one survived past infancy.

The Müller name is traditionally associated with George alone, who is credited with the sole responsibility for five orphanages in Bristol. But, as is so often the case, George didn't work alone: Mary played a vital role in their creation and in the running of these orphanages.

Initially, Mary and George worked at Bristol's Bethesda Chapel in Redfield. This was a large missionary chapel and it had become dilapidated and the congregation numbered just six. However, under the guidance of Mary and George, the chapel's fortunes began to turn around and attendance grew. By 1835, the

211 With thanks to Maggie's husband Mike Manson and sister Jill Moss, who wrote Maggie's obituary in *The Guardian*: theguardian.com/environment/2021/jun/01/maggie-moss-obituary-environment

couple sought a new challenge and this is where the idea for their first orphanage came from.

A recent cholera epidemic had resulted in a high number of orphaned and homeless children, and Mary offered food to many of them from her doorstep, and so the Müllers called a meeting to discuss setting up what they called an Orphan Home. George asked God to help him find both £1,000 and the people to run the orphanage and, within five months, both had been found. Mary refurbished the couple's home on Wilson Street, St Pauls, to become accommodation for 30 girls, and soon another three properties on Wilson Street were found to house a total of 130 children. By 1845, the demand had outgrown the spaces on Wilson Street and the Müllers decided they needed a purpose-built home which could accommodate 300 children. The devout couple prayed that they would find the £10,000 they needed to achieve this and, somehow, their prayers were answered. The newly-built orphanage was opened in Ashley Down in 1849.

Mary's role in all of this was not insubstantial. She was involved with the day-to-day running of the homes, as well as being the chief accountant and administrator. She ordered in the necessary fabrics to make clothing and bedding for the children. Mary was also responsible for ensuring that nutritious meals were provided, as well as overseeing the sickbay where she would often sit and read stories to those who were not well.

The need for the Müllers' orphanages kept growing and, by 1870, there were five Müller orphanages in Bristol collectively providing homes for 2,000 children. Running the orphanages was not without its challenges.

Disease was rife and society was still learning about hygiene, meaning that the hurdles the Müllers needed to overcome during their decades at the helm included outbreaks of smallpox and cholera, unsatisfactory sanitary conditions, open sewers, dirty drinking water and rubbish piled high in the streets.

Following Mary's death at the age of 73, her funeral procession to Arnos Vale Cemetery was joined by 1,400 children and the sermon was read by George. It included the following words: "My precious wife died, as it were, in harness. Up to the very last she was at work for the Lord. Even when on her deathbed she gave directions for this thing and another thing to be done connected with the honour of the Lord, caring about the sick ones outside the house, and sending refreshments; caring yet for the orphans, and giving directions concerning them."[212]

JOZEFA MUNDZIEL
1919-2012, BUSINESS OWNER

As a young child, Jozefa Wozniak (as she was originally known) moved with her farming family from Poland to Belarus. It was a simple life but they were perfectly happy until the war came in 1940, at which time the whole family was arrested by the Russians and taken to a labour camp near Arkhangelsk, where they were imprisoned for two years.

Jozefa's granddaughter Gabriela Staniszewska says: "She remembered the Russian authorities being horrific but the people they lived among were very kind and helpful towards them. She told me a story that it was so cold by the window of the barracks they were kept in, and so hot by the fireplace in the middle, that the people by the fire would overheat and the people by the window would freeze to death in their sleep."

On another occasion at the camp, 21-year-old Josefa and some of the other young women came across a lone sheep. They

---

212   biblemesh.com/blog/the-christ-centered-life-of-mary-muller-george-muller-1805-1898/

were so desperately hungry that they discussed how they could kill and cook it, and ended up killing it and butchering it as skillfully as they knew how. "On the way back they met a guard from the camp, and they managed to distract him enough that he didn't notice the blood dripping from their pockets in their dark clothing. They got away with it and ate well," says Gabriela.

When the amnesty came in 1942, the Wozniaks walked to the nearest town, got a lift on a truck to the nearest train station, and then got on the first available train just to get away from that awful place as fast as possible. They travelled across Russia, Kazakhstan and Uzbekistan, reaching Iran in 1943. Josefa remembers spending Wigilia (Christmas Eve) 1942 in a train carriage in Kazakhstan. After further travel took them to Iran, Karachi and Kenya, the family stayed in a Polish evacuee camp in Northern Rhodesia for a few months before leaving for the UK in 1948.

Not long after arriving in England, Josefa met and married Jan Mundziel in November 1948, who had been a mechanic in the army. With this knowledge, they set up a garage in a former abattoir in Fishponds and Ridgeway Road Auto Engineering became a successful business.

During the 1950s and 1960s, Josefa and Jan were at the centre of the Polish community's push to create a Polish parish at Arley Chapel on Cheltenham Road. They handmade the processional cross which is still in use in the church today. The Polish church, together with the old Polish Club in Clifton, formed the focus of the original post-war Polish community in and around Bristol. Which, in turn, a couple of generations later, enabled a new wave of post-communist Poles to have a central base from which to establish their lives in Bristol.

"She was quietly and strongly religious for her whole life, attributing her luck and success and happiness to God alone, not at all to her own resilience and strength," says Gabriela.

In 1961, Josefa became a UK citizen and, with Jan, she not only helped run the business but also raised their two children. Her vegetable garden was important to her and she spent her time cooking, pickling, baking and roasting enough vegetables to keep the whole family fed and healthy all year round. As her family grew, Josefa passed on her Polish recipes to her children and grandchildren to ensure the customs lived on. She also saved enough money to send her granddaughter to private school, because she saw how important education was for girls.

She and Jan celebrated their 60th wedding anniversary by renewing their vows and, after Jan died in 2009, Josefa spent her time as a widow by quietly doing jigsaws and cooking until her own death in June 2012. However, the family business continues and Ridgeway Road Auto Engineering in Fishponds is still run by Josefa's son Richard.[213]

ANN MURPHY
born c1830, COTTON FACTORY WORKER

By the end of 1850, business was so brisk at the Great Western Cotton Factory in Barton Hill that there weren't enough workers in Bristol to keep up with demand, so the manager John Ashworth brought in several young women from Northern Ireland. However, when the boom period ended, Ashworth (who has a well-documented history of not being the kindest boss) operated a last in, first out policy and the new recruits were out on their ear with insufficient remuneration to return home.

Ann Murphy from Belfast was one such unfortunate and, like many young women in her position left to fend for themselves

213 With thanks to Gabriela Staniszewska for the nomination of her 'babcia' (grandmother) Josefa Mundziel to this book.

in a strange city, was reduced to begging. Ann was arrested in February 1851 for petty theft and her case was heard in the Bristol Police Court. She admitted stealing a shawl which she had intended to pawn in order to raise a few pennies for food. The magistrate clearly took pity on her and, on learning that Ashworth had brought Ann and several other young women over from Belfast to work and then dismissed them, said that it was "cruel conduct" for him not to take care of them in Bristol. The result was that Ann's case was dismissed on the understanding that the shawl was returned to its owner. A surprising coda was that Ann was also given two shillings from the poor box to help her on her way.[214]

LILY NEWICK
dates unknown, TOBACCO FACTORY WORKER

In the 1920s, HO Wills added the concrete Canons Marsh Tobacco Bond Warehouse on the waterfront site that later became the headquarters of Lloyds Banking Group but was then known as the Eleven Bond. This was where tobacco leaf was bonded (stored) before being moved to the factories to be made into cigarettes. Lily Newick began work there in July 1941 at a time when the warehouse had been requisitioned for war work and this was where machinery was taken to be repaired and washed in paraffin. Lily recalled: "I was on the carburetor section assembling the carburetors which I didn't find particularly difficult but I used to be a dressmaker and it was a bit of a shock ... especially since I had to get my hands dirty!"

Lily explained that she worked six days a week, from 7.30am

---

214 'Bristol Police Court', *Bristol Times & Mirror*, 22 February 1851.

to 5.30pm. With no canteen on site, staff had to dash over to Electricity House for lunch and then rush back to pick up their shift, which led to a lot of afternoon indigestion. Being only 19, Lily was paid less than her colleagues who were over 21 "which annoyed me a lot".

Because of all the paraffin that had been used to clean machinery while the warehouse had been requisitioned during the war, the building couldn't go back to its previous use as a tobacco bond and it was demolished in 1988. Summing up her experiences, Lily concluded: "On the whole I enjoyed working there, especially because I was working with lots of people and it was quite good fun. From 3pm until half past we were allowed to listen to *Workers' Playtime* [a BBC radio variety show] so we heard all of the latest songs."[215]

MARY NEWTON
1748-1804, SISTER

When her younger brother – the child prodigy Thomas Chatterton – died in 1777, Mary Newton inherited all of his belongings and became the custodian of his archive. Living with her husband on Somerset Square, Mary was unwittingly conned into passing some of her brother's correspondence to the author Sir Herbert Croft, who then used it as the basis for his 1780 novel *Love and Madness*. It took 20 years before Croft's deception of Mary was uncovered, when the poet Robert Southey was preparing a book about Chatterton's writing. Although Croft protested his innocence, not many people believed him.[216]

215 bbc.co.uk/history/ww2peopleswar/stories/16/a4023316.shtml
216 With thanks to Dawn Dyer for the nomination of Mary Newton to this book.

GLADYS NOTT
1907-1935, MURDERED IN THE WOODS

Over to the east of Bristol sits Hanham, and it was in Hanham Woods that Bessie Gladys Nott (born Gladys Slocombe) was murdered in 1935: the case became known as the Hanham Woods Murder. Known to everyone as Gladys, she married her husband Henry Nott in 1926 and they had one son, Dennis, born around 1928. At this time, Hanham was considered a small village and for anything out of the ordinary to happen there was really unusual.

The Nott family lived as part of a small community of around 15 poor families in the Hencliffe Woods. Just down the path from them lived the Franklin brothers: Arthur and Frank. In November 1933, Gladys left her poultry farmer husband Henry and moved in with Arthur Franklin, a smallholder who kept pigs and was described as broad, stocky and with long fair hair. Although Gladys remained married to Henry, in court Arthur would call her his wife and said that his brother had conducted an informal marriage ceremony. Dennis stayed living with his father but, on Saturdays and Sundays, he would walk down the path to see his mother for the purpose of having a bath, his clothes mended and a hot meal.

Absolutely nobody involved in this story was living in any kind of luxury, in fact these were all single-storey shacks with no comforts. These were people who had been forced out of traditional housing due to poverty and forced to erect makeshift shacks in the woods that were made of mud, stone and timber. These people were seen as outsiders to more traditional communities and, as such, were subject to their own morals and policing. A newspaper photograph of the Notts' shack shows a shockingly simple dwelling made of wooden planks, with one door in the middle and two small windows on either side of it, this being the entire width of the single-room property. There is a bucket outside for water from the nearby river, which was the only form of sanitation for anybody.[217]

Local historian Dennis Gerrish later explained to a researcher how these families had come to live in the woods: "A lot of them had worked in the shoe trade and probably worked two hours a day in the factory. And so their wages at the end of the week was 10 or 12 shillings. So they were eventually turned out of where they were living for not paying the rent. They were in debt and they just went to the woods and built a shack and lived there. It was a common thing for shoemakers at that period to go to the factory at six o'clock in the morning and the foreman came out and said 'Nothing yet, come back at nine o'clock', and he said 'That's all for today'. So you did an hour and half during the day and that's all you got paid for. Of course everybody was in poverty. There were so many small shoe manufacturers in Kingswood, if you worked for those it was very poverty-stricken."[218]

Despite the tensions of living barely 100 yards down the road from Henry, Gladys and Arthur managed to make a go of their relationship for around 18 months… until 8 May 1935 when Gladys decided to pack her things and move back to live with her husband. Tensions simmered between Arthur and Henry while Gladys was negotiating the move back to her husband and son, and she briefly moved out of the woods altogether, taking a furnished room in Bristol. She did return to Arthur's shack but she never made it home to Henry.

Gladys managed to walk a few steps away from Arthur's home, heading towards Henry, when Arthur fatally shot her in the back with a single-barrelled gun. As she lay on the ground in front of him, Arthur shot her again. Gladys was just 28.

217 davidkiddhewitt.wordpress.com/2017/06/11/the-six-minute-murder-trial-of-love-triangle-killer/
218 weldgen.tripod.com/crime-and-punishment/id11.html

Drawn by the sound of gunfire and having heard Gladys scream, Henry quickly appeared with his own gun, meaning to shoot Arthur and cause him to stop. But Arthur got in first and shot Henry, leaving him in a critical condition and with the ultimate loss of one eye. Henry survived his injuries and later told the court that Arthur had said at the time: "I will play with you as a cat with a mouse."

Arthur was charged with the willful murder of Gladys. In his statement made at Staple Hill Police Court, Henry admitted: "I shot Mrs Nott twice in the head, and to make sure there was no feeling, I put another one into her head ... then I shot at [Arthur] but did not kill him. I hadn't another cartridge, otherwise there would have been two murders." When questioned as to why he had shot Gladys, Arthur simply confirmed that if he hadn't she would have left him.[219]

Following a trial of six minutes (the shortest murder trial in history at that time), Henry was sentenced to death and was hanged at Gloucester Prison on 25 June 1935.

KATHLEEN ORPEN
1886-1974, SOCIAL WORKER

Born in Cambridge into a religious household, Angela Mary Kathleen Orpen had a devout start to life, and an education at the University of Cambridge. During World War One, which claimed the life of her younger brother, Kathleen worked for the Volunteer Aid Detachment. She relocated to Bristol in the early 1920s. She studied for and completed her exams in the Social Science Testamur at the University of Bristol, before taking up

219 'Shots drama in a Glo'shire Wood', The Citizen, 24 May 1935.

employment at the Barton Hill University Settlement where she worked with young children.

Kathleen continued to study alongside her work, undertaking training to become the Head of School for Mothers at the Royal Sanitary Institute. When Hilda Cashmore[220] stepped down from her 15-year position as Honorary Warden of the University Settlement at Barton Hill, Kathleen was the obvious person to take her place. Hilda had been the first person to assume that role, so Kathleen was the second person to lead the Settlement when she was welcomed to Barton Hill in June 1926. During World War Two, Kathleen also worked as the secretary of the Bristol Council for Refugees.

GERTRUDE PARKER
1898-1969, MENTAL HEALTH PATIENT

Born in Stoke-sub-Hamdon, Somerset, Gertrude Elline Fursdon (as she was originally called) grew up in a loving family. However, her father, a commercial clerk, had been a widower when he married Gertrude's mother Ellen. It was said that he always carried a sadness with him, but his three children – of which Gertrude was the eldest – were a source of great happiness to him. By 1905 the family were living in a three-storey house in Florence Park, Redland, and Gertrude was a happy girl who enjoyed playing the piano and drawing pictures of animals.

In 1920, aged 22, Gertrude married a 45-year-old railway foreman named Edward Parker, moving to Dingle Close, Sea Mills, with him to be close to his work at Avonmouth Station. Their son Raymond was born in 1922, followed by Reginald

---

220 Hilda Cashmore is profiled in Volume One of *The Women Who Built Bristol*.

in 1924. But life as a young mother was difficult. Raymond was a sickly baby and Gertrude was constantly fearful that the mysterious condition that troubled him would take his life at any moment; he was later diagnosed with coeliac disease.

The stress of caring for a sick infant and looking after a new baby took its toll, and when Reginald was just 11 months old Gertrude, then 27, was admitted to the Bristol Lunatic Asylum in Fishponds, which would later be known as Glenside Hospital. Sadly, she would spend the rest of her life in mental health institutions and her care history has been documented at Glenside Hospital Museum, along with photographs of Gertrude and items connected to her. These provide an interesting and valuable case study of an 'ordinary' Edwardian woman for whom circumstances became overwhelming.

Her admission record stated that Gertrude was suffering from 'chronic mania' following the births of her children and the prolonged stress of worrying about Raymond's health. An entry in her case notes from July 1925 noted that: "She is very restless, dishevelled and uncontrolled. Talks antics and asks conundrums, eg why did Jonah swallow the whale? Often kneeling in a praying attitude and says, 'I have blasphemed against the Holy Ghost.'"

In 1928, Gertrude was moved to the Ashley Grange Care Home in Shirehampton, which suggests that perhaps her condition was improving. But in 1934, she was returned to Glenside where she remained until her death in 1969. On the 1939 Register, Gertrude is listed as living at the 'Mental Hospital, Fishponds' where her occupation is given as book binder.

Edward visited Gertrude every other Sunday until his death in 1945, and he would be her main link with her family. Hospital records suggest that Gertrude's mother Ellen never came to visit, which may have been to do with the social stigma of mental health at the time which was very poorly understood. Further,

Gertrude's sons Raymond and Reginald were not allowed to visit their mother until they reached the age of 16, by which time neither mother nor children knew each other at all.

Reginald later described the experience of visiting his mother saying: "When I visited my mother at the age of 16 she could not recognise me, whether she later had any understanding I do not know. Even though my grandmother and my aunt sought to 'mother' me, I have never thought of anyone else as my mother. I look forward to meeting her in a more radiant form in another world."

By the time of her death, Gertrude had spent 44 years within the mental health system, and her death certificate states that she died of 'bronchopneumonia and chronic schizophrenia'. Gertrude was buried in Canford Cemetery, but at the time of her death her name was never added to her gravestone, something that her grandchildren sought to rectify many decades later.[221]

LOUISA PARKER
1829-1894, SHOE BINDER

A shoe binder from St Pauls, Louisa Blackmore married a former enslaved man called Henry Parker. With Louisa being a white woman, this mixed–race marriage was seen as a bold move for a woman in 1854.

Henry had been born in Florida in 1826 and sold to a plantation owner when he was a child; slavery was not abolished in the US until 1865. When he was about 15, assisted by a family of Quakers, Henry escaped from slavery and boarded a ship headed to the UK where slavery had been abolished in 1833. This was how he came

221   With thanks to Glenside Hospital Museum.

to Bristol, where he first lived in Stapleton and appears on UK census reports as early as 1841. By the 1851 census, he was living as a lodger in St Mary Redcliffe.

Louisa and Henry married on 18 September 1854 in St Pauls and, once they had set up home together, Louisa helped Henry learn to read and write. He then worked as a Lay Preacher at the Hook's Mill Church (now the Ivy Church) and as a Stonemason. Louisa gave up her work as a Shoe Binder after their marriage and, given the couple had seven children, it's doubtful she would have had much time to work as well as be a mother.

The family lived at 2 Paradise Cottages in St Pauls, which has since been demolished.[222]

ETHEL PARR
1868-1957, SOCIALITE

Being a woman and a journalist in the late-Victorian and early-Edwardian era was no picnic but Clifton's Ethel Parr did a damn fine job of holding her ground. Born into a comfortable family living at 3 Royal Park, life for the Parrs was fairly smooth given Ethel's father Thomas was an attorney and therefore would have earned a respectable income; indeed, in the 1871 census the family are listed as having four servants.

By the time of the 1911 census, 42-year-old Ethel was living at 12 Worcester Terrace, Clifton, with her sister Alice and their widowed mother Henriette. Ethel's job is listed as Secretary and Journalist. And the fact that the family of three still has two servants to look after them suggests Thomas has left them in a comfortable situation.

222 discoveringbristol.org.uk/browse/slavery/emma–head/

In terms of Ethel's journalism, this may have been a stretch. A hunt in the British Newspaper Archives brings up many stories reporting on Ethel's involvement in all manner of charitable and entertainment events, but very little written by her. Those stories she did write tended to be confined to the women's pages of the Bristol newspapers and related to the standard ladies' fare of fashion, health tips and gardening.

Ethel's work involved lots of good deeds for local charities, as well as taking part in amateur theatrical productions and music performances. She sounds like she had an enjoyable life, and that was certainly the case when she helped arrange a 'ladies' musical bicycle ride' at a charity fete in Clifton in July 1903. If you're wondering what such an event might look like, imagine a version of synchronised swimming... but on bicycle. And this curious event seems to have been typical of the sort of entertainment that Ethel was no stranger to putting on.

By the 1920s, Ethel had joined the Bristol Venture Club which would later become the Bristol branch of the Soroptimists. She attended, and often chaired, meetings at Charlotte Street. In 1920, Ethel wrote in the *Bristol Times and Mirror* about the frustration of professional women at being denied entry to the Rotary Club, which saw businessmen gather to do charitable work. Ethel wrote: "Why should women not follow the admirable example set by their male relations and friends and start a club on Rotary principles, or join a club already in existence run on these lines?"[223] Ethel would ultimately be one of the women who would help set up the Bristol Venture Club for professional women and, as such, she was one of the leading lights behind the Bristol branch of the Soroptimist movement and became the group's fourth President when she was voted in to that role from 1923-1924.

223 'Barbara's Budget', *Bristol Times and Mirror*, 17 April 1920.

In 1926, when she was 56, Ethel married Charles Budgett, who was the chairman of a food manufacturing company and a respected city councillor, and the couple remained living in Clifton. This was the year after Ethel's sister Alice had died, and Henriette had also likely died by this time, so perhaps Ethel's decision to marry later in life was prompted by her change in circumstances and need for companionship. I also wonder whether Charles was the brother of Georgina Budgett[224], who was the grocers' wife who established the sending of Red Cross parcels to servicemen during World War Two, but have been unable to confirm this.

MARY PELOQUIN
died 1778, ABOLITIONIST

Fiery women such as Mary Ann Peloquin bring hope to my heart. Frustrated (perhaps disgusted) by the dealings of her brother David Peloquin, Mary took matters into her own hands. But what had David done that was so terrible? Well, in 1751, David was the Mayor of Bristol, which meant that he was a respected, admired and powerful man. But he didn't always use his power for good. David had amassed great wealth as a sugar merchant and, as we know, merchants often depended upon the work of enslaved people to run their businesses. Yet Mary was an abolitionist.

Mary and David's father Stephen Peloquin, a Hugenot, had arrived in Bristol in the 1680s after fleeing France, bringing a lot of family wealth with him. Stephen further increased this money through his dealings with the tobacco trade, which relied on the labour of enslaved people. On Stephen's death, this wealth passed

---

224 Georgina Budgett is profiled in Volume One of *The Women Who Built Bristol*.

to David, and then to Mary after David's death in 1766.

With all this accumulated money now in her command, and no pesky men to tell her what she should do with it, Mary established the Mary Ann Peloquin Charity, leaving £19,000 in trust to the Court of Aldermen. Interest generated from this considerable sum of money was to be paid to 40 poor women and 40 poor men who lived in the ward of St Stephen (the ward in which many merchants lived) to enable them to live comfortably. Mary left further money to benefit another 66 poor women and men from 11 other wards across Bristol, as well as another pot of money to support 50 poor women each year who had recently had babies.

Mary also inherited the deeds to the family's lavish home on Queen Square. With the men out of the picture, Mary moved herself out of this house and loaned the property to Josiah Tucker, an anti-slavery campaigner. And in her will, Mary left the house to the parish of St Stephen.

However, as society would have expected, Mary did pay tribute to her father and brother. She erected a marble wall monument at St Stephen's Parish Church, which can still be seen. And at the base of that monument has been added a bronze panel which honours Mary herself: she was the final member of the Peloquin family left in Bristol at that time.

After her death, the Mary Ann Peloquin Charity was managed by the Court of Aldermen in Bristol, before being taken over by Bristol Charities when it was formed in 1836. The charity continued to function until 1997.

OLIVE PERRY
1925-1990, TOBACCO FACTORY WORKER

In 1939, when she was 14, Olive Lillian Perry of 10 Charlton Street, St Phillips, attended an interview for what would be her first job: as a worker at the HO Wills tobacco factory on Redcliffe Street, where her older sister Daphne already worked. Looking back, Olive recalled the busy office, bustling with people coming and going, accompanied by the strong and spicy smell of fresh tobacco. When she was called to walk down a long corridor for her interview, Olive remembers a man sitting behind a big desk and puffing on a cigar while he looked at her. "I noticed how well kept his hands were and thinking that he wasn't used to hard work like my dad," Olive said. After reading character references for Olive from a policeman, a businessman and her Sunday school teacher, the interviewer then looked at Olive and asked her who she thought was responsible for the outbreak of World War Two, which was quite a question to spring on a nervous young teenager. But evidently her answer of 'Poland' seemed to be what he wanted to hear and Olive was given a job in the stripping room.

This was located at the back of the factory where Olive joined a small group of girls who were also fresh out of school. Their supervisor was Georgina Black and, Olive recalls, "the expression on her face was more like a sly grin than a smile, her pointed nose and small beady eyes didn't endear her to me". After pulling on her standard issue cotton overall and hat, Olive took up her post beside a large wooden table, which had about 50 girls facing one way and another 50 girls facing the opposite way, and began work stripping the tobacco: with the expectation being that each girl would strip between seven to nine pounds of tobacco every hour with a small sharp knife. Every so often, Georgina would come down from her high stool at the end of the room and walk among the girls, reprimanding them for slow or shoddy work, with absolutely no tolerance for even a moment of idleness. Singing, talking or chewing were cardinal sins in Georgina's eyes. Olive was paid ten shillings and sixpence a week, and twice a year she received a bonus of £5.

Olive never loved her time at the tobacco factory, saying: "Those autumn mornings walking from the bus stop to work I wished I could just wander off somewhere and not have to go into the factory, with all its heats and smells, which got into your hair and clothes." Sometimes the working day would be punctuated by change, though: whether that be something fun, such as a shared bar of chocolate for a colleague's birthday, or something less fun such as an air raid drill in the early days of the war.

After making friends with some of her colleagues, Olive would enjoy walking around the docks on her lunch break where, if she was lucky, a workman unloading goods from the ships might throw her an orange.

When there was less tobacco available to be stripped, the girls from the stripping room would be put to work in the packaging department, glueing together boxes or advertising signs. A more preferable alternative was time spent in the packing room, putting cigarettes into tin boxes.

The war eventually offered Olive the chance to escape the tobacco factory in 1941 when she was 16. She gave her week's notice and enlisted to join the Bristol Aeroplane Company in Filton who were recruiting girls to take on the jobs made vacant by the men sent to war. However, Olive's father was furious that she had quit what he deemed to be a good job with Wills, caned her and turned her out of her house, so she moved in with her grandmother in Barton Hill. Two years later in 1943, aged 18, Olive joined the Auxiliary Territorial Service and moved out of Bristol permanently.

In 1946, Olive married a man called Walter Evans with whom she had one son.[225]

EILEEN PHILLIMORE
dates unknown, TELEGRAPHIST

When World War Two broke out, 16-year-old Eileen Phillimore was required to leave her job at a paint factory and go and work for the Great Western Railway as a Telegraphist, sending secret messages in Morse Code. During the war, the Telegraph Office was moved to the caverns beneath Bristol Temple Meads train station to protect the staff from bomb blasts... although Eileen and the other 'telegraph girls' were afraid of the rats that lurked down there and knew that Temple Meads was an obvious target for the bombers. However, because of the importance of the work the telegraphists did and the need for secrecy, armed soldiers were positioned at the doors. Eileen's daughter later recounted: "On many occasions, when my father went to meet Eileen so that she would not have to walk home through the darkness alone, he was stopped with a gun in his chest, being challenged, 'Halt, who goes there?'"[226]

ELEANOR ADDISON PHILLIPS
1874-1952, EDUCATOR

She may have been the headmistress of Clifton High School from 1908 to 1933, but Eleanor Addison Phillips was more than an educator. This London-born woman was also the co-founder of

225 Olive Perry, 1988, 'Bristol Factory Lives 1939' in *More Bristol Lives*, Bristol Broadsides, p207-212.
226 bbc.co.uk/history/ww2peopleswar/stories/61/a1961561.shtml

a global movement for professional women.

Born into a wealthy family, Eleanor was the third of nine children and she trained to become a teacher before studying history at the University of Oxford. On the suggestion of one of her professors, Eleanor successfully applied for the post at Clifton High School and made her move to Bristol.

Her home for the first decade or so was at 1 Clifton Park, and under Eleanor's watch Clifton High School expanded into a greater area of Clifton, the number of students doubled, and more than 60% of pupils were successful in gaining places at university once they left the school.

At the same time, Eleanor played a key role in the founding of the Venture Club movement, which later evolved into the UK wing of the global Soroptimist movement. The Venture Club and Soroptimist movement had similar goals, both being volunteer-led women's organisations advocating for human rights and gender equality in a peaceful manner. Under Eleanor's guidance, the Venture Club worked on various service initiatives that were later taken over by Social Services or the National Health Service.

On 10 May 1920, Eleanor was unanimously elected as President of The Venture Club at a ceremony held at Bristol's Royal Hotel on College Green (now the Marriott Royal Hotel). By 1928, there were seven branches of the Venture Club around the UK and, by 1930, the scheme had merged with the existing Soroptimist movement, with Eleanor being voted in as Vice-President of Britain's Union of Soroptimists.

Eleanor retired in June 1933 and, to mark all that she had achieved in her career, she was appointed as an Honorary Member of all Soroptimist Clubs in recognition of her outstanding services. To date, Eleanor is the only woman to have ever received this honour.

Following her retirement, Eleanor remained in Bristol until

1941, at which point she returned to Oxford for a few years before settling in London until her death in 1952. A portrait of Eleanor is stored at the National Portrait Gallery in London, and while she looks rather stern in this and other photos, those who knew Eleanor insisted she had a good sense of fun. In 2021, a blue plaque was unveiled in her honour at Clifton High School.

JEAN PICKWELL
1939-2018, NURSE, CATERING ASSISTANT

Known to her friends as Pixie, Jean Pickwell was a long-standing team member at the University of Bristol, working as a catering assistant at Wills Hall from 1982 until well beyond retirement age. Before joining the university, Jean had been living in Australia where she worked as a nurse and midwife before returning to the UK. Remembering his colleague, her manager Peter Grindon said: "She would never say an unkind word or complain about her job even when faced with a mountain of pots and pans to clean every day."[227]

MURIEL PIEROTTI
1897-1982, SUFFRAGIST, TRADE UNIONIST

Although she was born in Clifton, Muriel Pierotti only lived in Bristol for the first ten years of her life, after which time her family moved to London. However, she is worthy of mention given the extraordinary life she lived, and the fact that Muriel was born in Bristol means we can lay a claim to her.

227 bristol.ac.uk/news/2018/april/jean-pickwell.html

When Muriel and her sisters were young, their mother Laura joined the Women's Freedom League because she was adamant that she wanted a better future for her daughters. Laura was a very active member of the organisation and she kept her daughters involved with the League's activities all the way through the 1920s.

After leaving school at 18, Muriel worked as a secretary before working at a hospital school run by Kate Hervey, who was a friend of Charlotte Despard, the founder of the Women's Freedom League. Charlotte had become a family friend by this point.

By 1925, Muriel had moved to work as a secretary at the National Union of Women Teachers (NUWT), and in the same year she wrote a suffrage pamphlet called 'What We Want and What We Have!' which continued to call for votes for women. Muriel was also a frequent contributor to *Vote*, the campaigning newspaper of the Women's Freedom League. Within her job, Muriel lobbied with the Equal Pay Campaign during the 1940s and 1950s, and hers was the very first signature on a 1954 petition calling for equal pay for women and men in public services.

At one point, Muriel remarked on the irony of the fact that the government was cajoling women to train and work as teachers but it failed to incentivise women to do so by continuing to pay them less than their male counterparts. She pointed out how many trained women had already left the teaching profession because they could find better paid work elsewhere. Muriel also criticised the government for failing to support married women to remain in work as teachers, or anything else.

Muriel continued to progress through the ranks at the NUWT and remained with the organisation until it disbanded in 1961. In 1963, she published a history of the trade union. Other organisations she had been involved with included the Joint Standing Committee of Women's Organisations and the Status of Women Committee.

JANE PINNEY
1752–1821, MERCHANT'S WIFE

Born Jane Weekes in Nevis in the West Indies, upon marrying the wealthy English merchant Sheriff John Pinney, Jane also gained a new name and a lot of wealth. Her husband had inherited a great deal of land in Dorset, and he owned a number of highly profitable sugar plantations in Nevis. However, Pinney used the labour of enslaved people to further his riches. Between January 1765 and July 1768, Pinney bought more than 60 Africans, a figure that would grow to 210 enslaved Africans by the height of Pinney's career.[228] By the time slavery was abolished in the British Empire in 1883, the Pinney family had more than 1,220 enslaved people working on their land.

Jane met and married Pinney in Nevis on 14 June 1772, but the couple decided to relocate to the UK in 1783, settling on Bristol the following year. With the help of managers, Pinney continued to run his sugar plantations from Bristol. It is thought that at the time of the marriage Pinney was worth the equivalent of £8.5 million in contemporary money, so they were not a family to be messed with. By the time of Pinney's death in 1818, he would be worth five times that amount.

The family, who had seven children, settled at 7 Great George Street (now a museum dedicated to the family's history) and had six servants to help them run the home, just as they had done in Nevis. Two of the servants were people whom the Pinneys brought with them from the West Indies: an enslaved servant named Pero (for whom Pero's Bridge outside Arnolfini is named) and a freed servant who worked for Jane called Fanny Coker.[229]

---

228 Madge Dresser, 2007, *Slavery Obscured: The Social History of the Slave Trade in Bristol*, Redcliffe Press.
229 Fanny Coker is profiled in Volume One of *The Women Who Built Bristol*.

Pinney was pro-slavery, as you will have deduced, and in Bristol he teamed up with James Tobin who shared Pinney's views on enslaved people. Between them, they owned a number of ships that sailed back and forth between Bristol and the West Indies, moving not just sugar and other consumables but also a large number of enslaved people.

ELIZABETH PIPER
died 1932, ARTIST

Although she ultimately settled in London's Chelsea, the etcher and painter Elizabeth Piper was a student at the Clifton School of Art, part of the Royal West of England Academy on Queen's Road, of which she was a member. Elizabeth completed further studies in Belgium and Paris, before becoming an Associate of the Royal Engravers in 1892. Elizabeth's highly detailed etchings and paintings of churches were well respected during her lifetime and she exhibited at numerous prestigious venues including the Royal Academy and Royal Engravers in London. Queen Victoria even purchased one of Elizabeth's pictures for her private collection. In Bristol in 1910, Elizabeth published a series of around 40 etchings depicting churches, which all show her talent for reflecting architecture and the nearby landscapes.[230]

230 With thanks to Dawn Dyer for the nomination of Elizabeth Piper to this book.

ROSE POCOCK
1810-1879, LITHOGRAPHER

Lithography is a form of printing that really came into its own in the 19th century. One Bristolian lithographer of note is Rachel Rose Pocock of Clifton, who was admired from the 1840s for her talent at capturing views of grand houses. The prints were sold through the Lithographic Press on Broad Street, which was run by Rose's brother Alfred Pocock. Writing in appreciation of Rose's work, the *Bristol Times & Mirror* stated: "Some years ago, a Bristol lady, Mrs Rose Pocock, skillfully succeeded in reproducing, as it were, the ancient air of the modern city. In a series of large folio lithographic drawings the chief beauties in the architecture of Bristol were represented – houses, gates, streets etc, still existing but with the personages in the costume of the olden time. This, perhaps, is as ingenious a way as could be contrived whereby to convey the truest idea of what the old city looked like."[231]

Rose was much admired for her lithographic views and landscapes, which were far ranging in subject and included numerous images of Longleat House. With her husband, she was also highly respected for her work in lithographic printing and for lithographing the work of other artists. For instance, in 1840 Rose and Alfred reproduced six views of colonial South Australia that had been drawn by the Bristol-born Edward Castle, which stand as rare instances of the lithographs created to show prospective British emigrants and investors what rural Australia was like.

Rose was married twice. Her first wedding was in 1835 to her cousin George Pocock, and their daughter, also called Rose, was born in 1837. Rose's second marriage was to George Gilbert in 1848, and with him she had two sons, one of whom died in

---

231 'The aspect of Bristol', *Bristol Times & Mirror*, 28 September 1869.

infancy. Here's a bonus fact: Rose and Alfred Pocock's younger sister was Martha Pocock[232], who was the mother of cricketing legend WG Grace. Alfred used to play cricket with William when he was simply an enthusiastic child.[233]

MARIA POLICELLA
1880-1947, ICE CREAM VENDOR

Originating from Atina in southern Italy, Maria and Luigi Policella came to the UK in 1909 in search of a better life, along with many of their compatriots, and – after Luigi had served in World War One – they settled in Bristol in 1919. The couple lived and worked at 26 Marlborough Street, Stokes Croft[234], and sold ice cream made by Luigi from the shop on the ground floor of their home. They would also walk the streets of Bristol, selling ice cream from a handcart that they had tightly packed with ice to keep it cold. The Policellas would take their ice cream to places such as the Park Picture House in St George, an arrangement that only came to an end when the cinema invested in its own freezer around 1930. In subsequent years, Policella ice cream was sold from the cart in other areas of Bristol including around the Tramway Centre. The ornate shawl that Maria wore while selling ice cream has been donated to Bristol Museums and can be viewed on the website. On the 1939 Register, Luigi is listed as a shopkeeper and Maria as an unpaid domestic, although both descriptions grossly underestimate what this couple actually did. Maria and Luigi had three children born in Bristol: sons Carmine and Antonio, and daughter Matilda.

232 Martha Pocock is profiled in Volume Two of *The Women Who Built Bristol*.
233 With thanks to Dawn Dyer for the nomination of Rose Pocock to this book.
234 There were other Italian immigrants who lived and worked on Marlborough Street at this time, including the Capaldi family who ran a fruit and vegetable shop.

DOROTHY PORTEOUS
1889-1977, WELFARE WORKER

Born in Newport, Dorothy Armstrong Porteous had made her way to Bristol by 1911 where she was living and working at the Collegiate School in Redland. After leaving work as a teacher, Dorothy moved further south in the city and joined the staff at the ES&A Robinson paper bag factory in Bedminster where she was responsible for the welfare of employees. She was awarded an MBE in recognition of her contribution to looking after others.

Dorothy was elected the seventh President of the Bristol Soroptimist organisation of professional women for the years 1926-1927. As a Christian, she was also a member of the Old King Street Baptist Chapel for which she acted as Secretary. Later in the 1930s, she travelled to Indonesia, Italy and New York to undertake missionary work. Dorothy's role with the mission was primarily concerned with its women's committee and with improving the lot of unmarried women in less privileged countries. In her later years, Dorothy was a committed member of the Tynedale Baptist Church on Whiteladies Road where, true to form, she also led the women's committee..

By the time of her death in 1977, Dorothy was living in Redland with two of her sisters and their brother. The Dorothy Porteous Charitable Trust still exists in Bristol and makes small grants to individuals for educational purposes. This ties in with the fact that Dorothy founded the Old Girls' Scholarship Fund at the Collegiate School to enable girls from a less fortunate background to attend the school.

DIANA PORTER
1942–2021, JEWELLER

Anyone who has travelled up or down Park Street in recent years will have noticed the shopfront for Diana Porter Jewellery at No 33. It's still there and still in business, despite the death of its founder in 2021.

Although born in Weston-super-Mare, Diana Porter spent almost her entire life in Bristol. She first went to school at La Retraite in Clifton, and then she attended Clifton High School. And she remained in education by starting her career as a primary school teacher in Bristol.

Her first marriage was to Chris Smailes in 1962 and saw her leave work to concentrate on bringing up their two children. But following her divorce in 1970, Diana returned to work and began a 20-year career in arts administration, as well as setting up the Birmingham Women's Festival. Always ethically minded, Diana campaigned for more money for the arts, for equal opportunities for women in the arts, as well as equal opportunities for Disabled people and those from minority backgrounds. She also campaigned against nuclear armaments.

In 1973, Diana met her new partner, Jeremy Dain, while they were working on a production of *A Doll's House* at the Bristol Arts Centre. A long and happy relationship followed that finally, after 46 years, saw them marry in 2019.

It wasn't until 1990 that Diana decided to follow a new direction and pursue a career in jewellery making. She studied for a three-year degree in jewellery and silversmithing at the University of Central England in Birmingham, before setting up her own studio and shop in Bristol. Talking about what the change in direction meant to her, Diana said: "I loved the way that working with metal centred and concentrated my mind; I learnt about design and form and my teachers pushed me to develop my design ideas which I now thank them for; I loved the History of Art part of the course and became passionate about investigating the history of the involvement by women in the arts and crafts. This was three years to take stock and to create, it was a gift and the jewellery is an outcome of that."[235]

With a clear commitment to maintaining ethical standards, Diana was one of the first jewellery designers in the UK to produce a collection made from Fairtrade gold. In 1999, nine years after she started her new venture, Diana was named UK Jewellery Designer of the Year by a leading industry magazine, *Retail Jeweller*.

MARGARET POTTER
1915-2010, CODE BREAKER

During World War Two, Margaret Blanche Potter undertook top secret work for the government as a highly skilled code breaker. Margaret worked at Flowerdown near Winchester, intercepting enemy signals. She later moved to a small RAF station in Scarborough where she continued to intercept enemy signals. But how did she get there?

Margaret was a bright child but her parents were of the Victorian opinion that girls did not need a full education, which would just be wasted on someone who's destiny was to be a wife and mother. Being unmarried when World War Two was declared, Margaret enlisted with the Women's Royal Naval Service and she was there from 1940-1945, working at HMS Raleigh in Plymouth dealing with the paperwork involved

---

235 dianaporter.co.uk/pages/about–diana–porter

with enlisting new servicemen: work she found boring. After convincing her superiors that she was capable of more, Margaret became a Wireless Telegraph Special Operator and this was how she became a crucial code breaker: she even learned Japanese Morse Code so that she could better perform her role. In 2009, Margaret received a gold commemorative medal in recognition for the part she had played in the national war effort.

After the war ended, Margaret stayed in the South West and worked for the civil service, assigning foster parents to children who had been orphaned by the war. She helped around 500 children and her commitment was such that, even on her days off, she would take some of the children on day trips, such as to the seaside. Margaret ended her career as the Chief Officer for the War Victims and Pensions Department: a role for which she received an MBE from the Queen Mother in 1970.

During her retirement, in 1964 Margaret became a member of the Bristol Soroptimists and acted first as Secretary and later as President, assuming that role from 1974-1975. Such was her belief in the organisation that Margaret later helped found sister branches in St Austell and Guernsey.

ALICE PRICE
born 1899, COTTON FACTORY WORKER

Young Alice Price had an awful start to life. Her father was driven mad by lead poisoning from his job as a Smelter and tried to take his own life numerous times, as well as threatening to slash the throat of Alice's older sister. In addition, several of her siblings died in infancy, and her mother died when Alice was 13. Consequently, Alice was removed from school in 1911 and told to seek work by her father, who then threatened to kill her in one of his rages so Alice ran away from home. Having no money, the 13-year-old slept rough in some washhouses backing onto the Feeder Canal waiting for Monday morning, when she could present herself at the Great Western Cotton Factory in Barton Hill as looking for work.

Alice recounted: "To my surprise I was taken on, mainly for the cheek I think, at the princely sum of three shillings and sixpence … But the clothes I was wearing were my entire wardrobe until I could sneak back and get some more. I had not eaten since Saturday, except for bread thrown out for the birds; payday was a long way off and I was homeless."

Alice continued to sleep out in the washhouses until her first payday. During this time some of the sympathetic loom women gave her leftover food and tea to keep her from starving. But despite all this, when she finally received her first pay packet, Alice's furious father found her and demanded she hand over the money. Thanks to the sisterhood of older women from the factory, Alice was saved: "I shouted and screamed for help – and it came. A solid body of women from the looms bore down on us, pulled me out of his grasp, and tore into him in a combined fury, which matched anything he could muster. He retreated, shouting, cursing, threatening – but he went. I never saw him again until his death in 1918." One of the women who saved Alice was Mary Ann Fry and she took young Alice home to live with her.[236]

236 Alice Price, 1987, in *Bristol Lives*, Bristol Broadsides, p5–9.

FRANCES PRIDEAUX
1858-1885, SURGEON

Frances Helen Prideaux had a short life but an important one. Born in Clifton to Frances and Francis Prideaux (a couple who not only shared the same first name but also saw fit to impart it on their first born), Frances may have died before she reached the age of 30 but she certainly made an impact on the world.

With a natural intelligence and supportive parents, young Frances enjoyed a good schooling at Queens' College in Westminster, London, at a time when young ladies of her class were not expected to work for a living and therefore not to be in need of an education beyond the bare essentials.

However, Frances later earned a place at the London School of Medicine for Women, despite a certain degree of resistance from some of her academic superiors to the notion of women in the medical profession.

The London School of Medicine for Women, established in 1874 as part of the University of London, was the first medical school in the UK to train women to be doctors, and in 1877 France's signature was noted on a letter to the University of London thanking them for taking steps towards granting medical degrees to women. She qualified in 1878 after passing the General Examination for Women: this was not a full degree but a certificate of proficiency, and the best that women could expect at a time when they were not entitled to graduate. By 1884, Frances had achieved Bachelor of Medicine and Bachelor of Science degrees from the London School of Medicine for Women, and was graded first in her class for anatomy.

Posts in London followed at the school where she had trained, as well as at Bethlem Hospital and Elizabeth Garrett Anderson Hospital. And four weeks before her death, Frances made history as the first woman to be appointed – ahead of male candidates – to the role of House Surgeon, which was at the Paddington Green Children's Hospital.

Her career was cut tragically short when Frances contracted diphtheria, possibly from a patient. She underwent a tracheotomy and laryngotomy, both of which she assisted with despite being the patient, but Frances died from the disease. She had refused to allow family or friends to visit her bedside in case they also contracted the infectious illness.

Following her death, Frances was publicly mourned in the national medical press and her death was cited as an example of the dangers doctors faced in their profession. A memorial fund was set up in Frances' name, for which one of the sponsors was Sir William Gull: a man who had initially been opposed to women working in medicine but who had his opinion radically changed thanks to Frances' many accomplishments.

ANGELA REDGRAVE
1917–2024, DANCER

When she was just ten, Angela Redgrave began attending dancing lessons, although that was considered a late start for this particular artform. However, Angela would carry on dancing for the rest of her life becoming, in 2022 at the age of 104, a recipient of the British Empire Medal, in recognition of her life's commitment to dancing.

Born in London, Angela (who is connected to the theatrical Redgrave family) demonstrated a passion for performing from a very young age and attending dance classes as well as performing arts school. Angela trained in classical ballet but she also experimented with musical comedy and tap dancing. She went on to perform in a number of shows in London's West End, an experience of which she recalled in 2022: "It was a wonderful time. We had some of the most prestigious singers appear in the production. If I close my eyes, I can still hear them singing."[237] Angela performed in a production of *Hiawatha* at the Royal Albert Hall where the principal dancer was Bristol's beloved Phyllis Bedells, with whom Angela would keep crossing paths one way or another.[238]

During World War Two, Angela kept performing in London as far as was possible in the circumstances, remembering: "I worked and danced through some pretty hair-raising experiences as I was living in London and had to regularly dodge air raids, running as fast as I could into the nearest underground station."[239]

After the war, Angela moved to Somerset where she began training to be a teacher at the Maddox School in Bristol, which was the only Royal Academy of Dance school in the area. She opened a dance school in Nailsea but, when she heard that the Bristol School of Dancing (founded by Mary Hoskyn and Muriel Carpenter in 1947) had come up for sale in 1970, Angela knew she had to buy it. The school had already sold its original premises so Angela set about hunting for new ones, and found the ideal place on Lansdown Road in Clifton, which is where the School remains today. When she found the new property, Angela didn't realise that she had chosen the site of the former West of England Academy, which had been the dance school set up by Phyllis Bedells. In fact, the barres that Phyllis installed in the dance studio still remain in place for students to use today.

Speaking about the advantages of teaching young people to dance, Angela said: "We need to encourage more children to

237 thebristolmag.co.uk/royal-honour-in-conversation-with-principal-of-the-bristol-school-of-dancing-angela-redgrave/
238 Phyllis Beddells is profiled in Volume Two of *The Women Who Built Bristol*.
239 royalacademyofdance.org/people/rad-voices-angela-redgrave

dance. It does give confidence and it does give happiness. I've had parents say to me, especially the father of one child who had a disability, 'You have made her life'. What more could you ask for?"[240]

When the Covid pandemic struck in 2020, Angela was not one to be stopped and simply switched from teaching in-person dance classes to teaching online. However, by the end of March 2020 she had decided – at the age of 102 – to stop teaching, although she continued to help her daughter Felicity Redgrave with the running of the School of Dancing. Reflecting on their founder, the School's website notes: "Angela Redgrave's journey reflects resilience and success in the face of challenges, shaping a lasting impact on the world of dance education."[241]

ELIZABETH REES
1801-1854, TEACHER

Elizabeth Pocock (as she was born) ran a school for young ladies called the Cleve Wood Establishment with her widowed mother. However, this was before Elizabeth married an eminent surgeon called James Rees in August 1825 at St Michaels in Bristol. Sadly, James died in 1840 so, to support herself and their young son, Elizabeth returned to life as a teacher and established the Overn Lodge school in Downend. However, in 1851, Elizabeth and her son William emigrated to Melbourne where he became a minister. Cricket was always a strong feature in the Pocock/Rees household, indeed Elizabeth's sister Martha[242] married Henry Grace, and their son William 'WG' Grace went

---

240 thebristolmag.co.uk/royal–honour–in–conversation–with–principal–of–the–bristol–school–of–dancing–angela–redgrave
241 thebristolschoolofdancing.co.uk/ourpeople
242 Martha Pocock is profiled in Volume Two of *The Women Who Built Bristol*.

on to be a highly acclaimed cricket superstar. William Rees also became a first-class cricketer in both Australia and New Zealand, where he later settled.[243]

MARGARET REYNOLDS
1927-2012, ADMINISTRATOR

I've been saying it for years, and doubtless will keep saying it: the work of administrators should never be understated. Often dismissed as 'just' a secretary, or 'just' an assistant, these are the people who quietly keep everything going. These are the people who know a business inside out, who know what needs to be done to keep it going, and who know everyone everywhere in that business. In this capacity, we welcome Margaret Reynolds who was a Senior Secretary and Administrator at the University of Bristol for more than 25 years.

Bristolian through and through, as Margaret Callaghan she attended school in Sea Mills before leaving at 14 and training to be a secretary. During World War Two, Margaret worked for the Ministry of Food in North Devon and then for the War Office in London. In these roles she really honed her skills in shorthand, dictation and unparalleled organisation. All of which were assets she would really need when she joined the university, where her older sister already worked in the chemistry department.

Following the death of her husband when Margaret was in her early 30s, she returned to Bristol with her daughter Catherine and joined the University's geography department in 1964. She stayed in this role for the next quarter of a century until her retirement in 1989. Margaret worked through an era of massive

243 With thanks to Dawn Dyer for the nomination of Elizabeth Rees to this book.

change in the way an office functioned: the switch from manual typewriters to computers, from shorthand to transcription and much more. However, she was admired by her colleagues for her calm approach to life, and for always coming up with a solution to whatever problem she was presented with. Which, after all, is what administrators do.

POLLY REYNOLDS
dates unknown, CLOTHES SELLER

In the olden days, second-hand shops were places where people on low incomes could buy donated essentials for a low price. However, these days, charity shops, as they are largely known, usually function in a different way, where donated items are sold to raise money for a particular good cause.

Operating from her shop on West Street, Bedminster, from the 1910s to the 1930s, Polly Reynolds bought and sold second-hand clothes, providing a lifeline for the hard-working but lowly-paid folks who lived nearby.

By buying and selling people's unwanted clothing, she not only provided a source of income for sellers but also a source of good clothing for buyers. South Bristol resident Pat Ellwood remembered: "We knew she would give us a fair price, a penny or tuppence for our goods, and always a [religious] text, as Polly belonged to the Salvation Army and was a good living lady."[244] Polly was presumably a member of the Salvation Army that was based on Dean Lane, where a specially constructed church and hall was opened in 1909: sadly this is now awaiting conversion to flats.[245]

244 Pat Ellwood, 1988, 'Recollections of Bedminster in the 20s and 30s' in *Bristol Reflections*, Bristol Broadsides, p37–39.
245 Mary Ridsel, who was heavily linked to the Salvation Army in Bristol, is profiled in Volume Two of *The Women Who Built Bristol*.

Before it became the gentrified suburb that it is today, where mid-terrace properties with tiny gardens and no parking sell for extraordinarily high amounts, Bedminster had a very different type of resident and therefore a different type of community. David Harrison reminisced in 1981: "In the years between the wars it was a tightly knit, almost village community – a community which started to drift apart as the slums came down ... Much of the community spirit came through sharing adversity, for many parts of Bedminster were still squalid slums in the 1920s, with shared water and toilets." He adds: "It was a time when ... Polly Reynolds sold religion with second-hand clothes on West Street."[246]

Caroline Dallimore, who grew up in Knowle, remembered going to Polly's shop to treat herself after receiving a £6 bonus from her job at the Wills No 3 Factory: "I went down to Polly Reynolds. She lived in West Street and kept a second-hand shop. I would keep myself tidy from the things I did buy down there. She was a good woman and when she died she was missed by the people."[247]

Another person who remembered Polly was JL Potter, who wrote to the nostalgia page of the *Bristol Evening Post* in 1975 about what it was like to grow up in poverty in Bedminster: "Hard work and poverty were the lot of most folk residing in Bedminster ... Cloggy Davies [the clog maker] and Polly Reynolds were household names. ... You name it, it was all in Bedminster."[248]

Following Polly's death, her daughter continued to run her business.

---

246 David Harrison, 'A social spirit that vanished with the slums', *Bristol Evening Post*, 10 December 1981. When the slums came down, many of the displaced families were rehoused in the new council estate at
Knowle West.
247 Caroline Dallimore, 1977, 'A Wills Lady', in *Up Knowle West*, Bristol Broadsides, p16-22.
248 JL Potter, 'Thrills of the paper chase', *Bristol Evening Post*, 12 December 1975.

YDA RICHARDSON
1856-1936, PHILANTHROPIST

With a name like Yda Emily Margaretha Stancomb-Wills, this woman was going to go far. But it wasn't always easy for her.

Born in Trowbridge, Wiltshire, to a wool agent called George Perkins Stancomb and his wife Catherine Lobb, Yda and her elder sister Janet Stancomb (1854-1932) were adopted by their maternal aunt Elizabeth and her husband Sir William Wills, who had no children of their own, despite both of their parents still being alive. The sisters were 15 and 17 at the time of the 1871 census, which shows them living with Elizabeth and William at Hawthornden House, Clifton. Their father George died in 1873 at the age of 49, and their mother lived until 1897, so it is unclear why they were adopted at the time they were. Nor why it took them until June 1893 to jointly write a formal letter to *The Times* declaring that they had officially changed their names to include 'Wills' in respect of William.[249]

And, yes, the name Wills is familiar to Bristolians, and yes, William was related to the tobacco manufacturing Wills family in Bristol, in fact he was the son of WD Wills of 'WD & HO Wills' fame. William had joined the family business at a young age and, in 1858, went into partnership with two of his cousins to take over WD & HO Wills, which became Imperial Tobacco and for which William was the first Chairman; in this way, he was seen as the head of the British tobacco industry. Among his many accomplishments, William was also Sheriff of Bristol from 1877 to 1878, a Liberal MP, and the High Sheriff of Somerset in 1905. Phew.

In London in 1900, Yda married a ship builder called Joseph

---

249 Letter, *The Times*, 8 June 1893.

Richardson and the two set up home in Yorkshire. But it was to be a short marriage: Joseph, almost 30 years Yda's senior, died in September 1902 just 14 months after the wedding. Aged 46, Yda was left a widow and she and Janet, who never married, set up home together in London, where the 1911 census has them living so comfortably off their own means that they employed six servants between the two of them. By 1921, Yda and Janet had returned to Bristol where they settled at the Manor House in Abbots Leigh.

In 1904, William gave the Bristol City Museum & Art Gallery at the top of Park Street to the people of Bristol, and he remained the President of the organisation (which still exists) until his death in 1911. The sisters clearly took inspiration from their adopted uncle's passion for the arts. For instance, Janet became President of the Bristol City Museum & Art Gallery immediately following William's death and held the post until her own death in 1932, at which point Yda assumed the role until she died in 1936. It is worth pointing out that Yda and Janet's appointments were decades before any other British gallery even permitted women to be full members, never mind the president of the organisation. However, both Yda and Janet had been involved with the Bristol City Museum & Art Gallery for many years prior to their appointments as President.

The Bristol newspapers were full of reports of Yda doing one good deed after another and making endless financial donations to good causes. By the time of her death, Yda had an estate worth a staggering £374,000 (approximately £22 million in contemporary money). In her will, Yda left £7,850 to the Colston Hall[250] to enable it to restore the ailing organ as part of wider refurbishments.

---

250 While I acknowledge the Colston Hall has now rightly been renamed and is now called the Bristol Beacon, I am referring to it by its original name in this book because that is the name it was known by when the events in the book happened.

When the Hall re-opened in December 1936, it had an all-electric console separate from the main organ for the first time. Yda was also committed to the Abbots Leigh area where she lived and, with no children to leave her estate to, she bequeathed the Abbots Leigh Village Hall on Church Road to the community. The Hall remains in use today and is maintained by the parish council.[251]

ANTONIA RIDGE
1895-1981, WRITER

Born in Amsterdam, Antonia Florence James (as she was originally called) had moved with her family to 9 Whiteway Road, St George, by the time she was a toddler. Aged 13, Antonia earned a scholarship from the Bristol Educational Committee, before becoming a teacher in her own right and working at Whitehall Girls' School. Antonia was also a regular fixture at St George Library, where she indulged her passion for literature.

In 1926, Antonia married a man called James Ridge in Hanham and the couple moved to Cardiff where they had three children. It wasn't until the family had grown up and World War Two had come to its end, that Antonia's talent for writing began to emerge. She started out as a children's author, before extending this to writing and reading plays and stories for children on the BBC radio show *Children's Hour*. She was also a contributor to *Woman's Hour*.

In time, Antonia also began writing for adults and her novels include *Family Album* (1953) and *Cousin Jan* (1956), both of which were anti-war novels with a strong theme of European unity. Her 1965 biographical novel *For the Love of a Rose* tells the story about

251   With thanks to Eugene Byrne for the nomination of Yda Richardson to this book.

the peace rose and led to a rose being named in Antonia's honour at the Chelsea Flower Show in 1975.[252]

MARTHA ROBERTS
1857-1948, MARKET GARDENER

Once upon a time, Bristol had a thriving community of market gardeners. This trade has all but vanished from the city, and the Roberts were the last prominent family of market gardeners in Bristol with their premises at Frenchay and Stapleton.

Former butcher George Tyler founded Roberts Bros in 1829 and set about growing a range of crops for the Bristol Market, employing colliers from the nearby mines when he needed extra help. When George died in 1880, Martha's father (also called George) took over the business and then, when he died in 1900, the market garden was put up for auction and Martha Roberts (George's granddaughter) arranged to buy the business with the help of a mortgage. It took her until 1916 but eventually Martha paid off the mortgage and owned her business outright.

Martha had married baker George Roberts in November 1877 and, because it was fairly acceptable at this time for women to run a market gardening business, he left her to it and carried on with his baking business. George died at the age of 55 in 1910 leaving Martha as a widow with six children (a seventh child had died in infancy) to look after, so she had no choice but to work hard.

Martha was described as a "formidable woman" who supplemented her income from the market by also selling fragrant herbs and flowers at St Nicholas Market. Martha would take her children to work with her, both as a free source of extra labour

252 With thanks to Dave Stephenson for his research. And to Eugene Byrne for the nomination of Antonia Ridge to this book.

and to avoid having to find someone to mind her children. While Martha and the kids were at work selling in the markets, other members of her family were helping to run the smallholding where the crops grew at Croft End Road, St George.

Martha and her children lived near the smallholding in a house that her grandfather George had built. When the house and the smallholding were compulsorily purchased by Bristol Corporation in 1936, Matha was allowed to stay there until her death in 1948. However, by this time she was living amid a sea of post-war prefabs. Despite this, Roberts Bros continued after Martha's death, with two of her grandsons buying land in Stapleton to continue the business into the 21st century.

PAT ROBERTS
died 2018, COUNCILLOR, SOCIAL WORKER

Between the 1980s and 2005, Alderman Pat Roberts served as the Labour Councillor for Knowle and then for Avonmouth. During that time, she also served on the Women's Committee at Bristol City Council, chaired the council's Arts Committee and Bristol's Tourist Forum, among other posts. Alongside her council work, Pat was a Social Worker at Manor Park Hospital.

She was an advocate for the underdog, be they mothers, Disabled people, dock workers (Pat campaigned against privatising the docks) and many others. In 1992, in the face of resistance from some who felt lesbians were a niche group, Pat lobbied for funds for Evening Out, a lesbian nightclub. She told the *Bristol Evening Post*: "It's an opportunity for [lesbian women] to see lesbian cabaret items, and to allow women to experience using the disco equipment. Lesbian women comprise 10% of the female population of this city, but they only get 1% of the Women's

Committee budget each year."[253] Pat was also an early supporter of the council giving funding to bring the Pride festival to Bristol back in 1995.

At the time of her death, the council's Cabinet Member for Housing, Paul Smith, said: "Pat was a great promoter of the city, she was an amazing advocate. She was someone who was very feisty, she spoke with great passion within this chamber. She was dedicated to all that she did. She is someone we will all miss a great deal."[254]

DAPHNE ROBINSON
1916-2017, PILOT

Before the outbreak of World War Two, Daphne Elizabeth Abrahams (as she was born) worked as a Stenographer for Imperial Airways in Filton. At the time of the 1939 Register, she was lodging at Sutherland House on Clifton Down. Daphne became an ambulance driver in the early war years but her role as one of the first women pilots is what most interests us today.

Daphne was raised in Portsmouth, and was living at 95a Coombe Lane, Westbury-on-Trym, in 1942 when she signed up as a Pilot with the Air Transport Auxiliary (ATA), a branch of the British Overseas Air Corporation for whom she would serve as a Second Officer from 23 September 1942 until 13 February 1944. She had earned her pilot's licence in Southampton in 1935 after learning to fly at the Portsmouth Aero Club, and applied herself hard as an ATA girl. A senior noted: "This pilot came to ATA with very little experience. She worked hard in Class I flying and

253 'Gay row', Bristol Evening Post, 31 January 1992.
254 bristolpost.co.uk/news/bristol-news/livefull-council-meeting-discuss-ashton-1993548. With thanks to Andrew Kelly for the nomination of Pat Roberts to this book.

reached a good standard. She should make a useful ferry pilot and a good officer."

However, 1943 would prove to be a turbulent year for Daphne. On the negative side, she was involved in an accident that May when the Spitfire she was flying landed upside down, causing serious damage to the plane. On the positive side, she married a former Theatrical Producer called Philip Lester, who was now a Flight Sergeant. However, Daphne was also recorded as going on sick leave from September 1943 until her contract was terminated in February 1944. One wonders if the cause of Daphne's poor health was related to the accident or to her marriage. Because while she and Philip had two children fairly soon after the wedding (son Phillip in 1944 and daughter Taniya in 1946), the marriage was dissolved in 1946. In order for a marriage to be dissolved, rather than for the couple to divorce, it generally needs to be proved that the marriage was never legal in the first place... What had happened?

In 1956, Daphne married again, this time to Philip Robinson whom she met while they were working for De Havilland aircraft manufacturers in Christchurch. Following Philip's death in 1967, Daphne lived in the Wiltshire village of Seend for 30 years, becoming a much-loved part of the community: driving people to hospital appointments, arranging church flowers and volunteering at the local museum. For many years, she was a member of the Aviation History Group of Devizes U3A. Daphne went on to live a long life, reaching the age of 101. For her 100th birthday, Astronaut Tim Peake was among those to send their good wishes to Daphne.

At the time of Daphne's death, her daughter Taniya Lester said: "In the early years of the Second World War, Daphne worked as an ambulance driver in the blackouts in Bristol, before becoming one of the wartime ATA girls, flying Spitfires and other single-engine aircraft for the Air Transport Auxiliary. Despite her adventurous and brave spirit, Daphne remained extraordinarily humble throughout her life and many who knew her through her life were unaware of these remarkable achievements."[255]

As a side note, Daphne's daughter Taniya Lester was named after the ATA Pilot Taniya Whittall, who had been killed in 1944 at the age of 24 following an aeroplane crash. Many years later, Taniya Lester's daughter was named Taniya Morris and she also served as a military Pilot. Showing that there is definitely something in a name.[256]

RICHENDA ROBINSON
1889-1950, WAR SHERO

If you've ever been along East Street in Bedminster, the chances are you have noticed the prominent signage outside the former ES&A Robinson paper bag factory down there. This is where you would also have found Richenda Robinson.

As you have probably deduced from her surname, Richenda was linked to the family business. But it wasn't always that way. Born Richenda Abbott in Sneyd Park, her father was a solicitor and the family lived a comfortable life. In 1911, aged 22, Richenda married Harold Robinson, whose grandfather had established the paper merchants in Bedminster, and she carried on living a life of great comfort at Cote House in Westbury-on-Trym, aided by a large number of servants.

By the time of World War Two, Richenda had become a committed member of the Bristol Soroptimists, working alongside other prominent Bristol businesswomen to do charitable work.

255 'Much loved aviator dies', *Gazette and Herald*, 25 August 2017.
256 ata-ferry-pilots.org/index.php/category-blog-1942/769-abrams-daphne-elizabeth-w-100

Keen to support the war effort, the group established a residential club and canteen for servicewomen with the aim of providing short-term hostel accommodation for women. Called the Soroptimist Venture Club for Service Girls, it was located at 15 Upper Belgrave Road, Clifton, and opened in December 1941.

Richenda was the President of Bristol Soroptimists during this time and oversaw the running of the club, which was officially recognised by the government's war office. As a well-connected local figure, Richenda was ideally placed to lead this enterprise and called in many favours to secure donations of everything from cutlery to beds. The facility operated for three years. During the course of the war, around 10,000 women enjoyed hospitality there, whether in the form of accommodation, meals or both. The hostel was also the location for the Soroptimists' Christmas party in 1943 and, in acknowledgement of what their Bristol sisters were doing for the war effort, Soroptimist groups in the US sent generous gifts to be donated to the servicewomen staying there. Richenda also offered use of the grand Cote House as a space to hold fundraising events.

When she died in 1950, Richenda left a considerable legacy in her will and she stipulated that the sum of £1,000 should be divided up between the servants at her home in gratitude for their work.

MABEL ST CLAIR(E)
1894-1975, MATRIARCH

The St Clair (sometimes spelled as St Claire) family lived in St Pauls from the 1910s and included wife Mabel and husband Joseph. They were unusual in being a Black family living in St Pauls prior to the Windrush generation of the 1950s.

Joseph had been born in Barbados around 1876 and subsequently travelled to Bristol as a stowaway on a ship. Once here, he found work as a dentist on Bristol Bridge, and also worked as a herbalist and was a lay preacher at both the Ivy Church and City Road Baptist Chapel.

Joseph met his Bristol-born wife Mabel Emily Stallard while out walking in Victoria Park, Bedminster. At the time that Joseph met her, 18-year-old Mabel was broken-hearted because her parents would not allow her to marry the man with whom she had fallen in love because he was an Orthodox Jew. It was in this lovelorn way that Joseph found her crying on a bench in the park. He sat beside her and asked, "What's the matter, pretty lady?" and the rest, as they say, is history.

The couple were married in 1913 and set up home at 10 Ashley Parade, St Werburghs, where they had four children. However, a newspaper report from 1925 indicates that the marriage was not entirely without troubles because Mabel called the police to complain that Joseph had struck her and threatened to throw her down the stairs. The Bristol Police Court dismissed the claims saying Joseph was merely trying to stop her getting at this wallet.[257]

After Joseph died in 1935, Mabel moved the family to Henleaze where her sons founded Westbury Upholstery, where they worked for the entirety of their careers. Mabel's daughter Naomi, known within the family as Sissy, became a celebrated singer, performing under the stage name of Eve.

257 · 'Wife's Summons Dismissed', *Western Daily Press*, 12 September 1925.

FLORENCE SAGE
1893-1988, TOBACCO FACTORY WORKER

In a few pages, we will meet Florence's grandmother Rebecca Sanders and, when you get there, you will have an 'Ohh, I see' moment of why Florence Sage was such a fun and feisty woman. But for now, let's focus on Florence, or Flossy as she was known.

Florence Kate Kington (as she was born) was the fifth child to Agnes and Alfred Kington from Bedminster. Right from childhood, she was known to be an imaginative girl who treated every day like an adventure. The family may not have had much money but that was no obstacle to Flossy's imagination. As a child, she was known to enjoy 'mooching' and, one afternoon, while on an unofficial holiday from school she took herself to Victoria Park where she was enjoying playing on the swings... until she fell off and cut her head.

After leaving school, like many in her family, Flossy was a cigarette machine operator for the Wills tobacco factory. Staff did not have a uniform to wear so they wore their own clothes, and Flossy was delighted one day when a member of the Wills family passed her station and commented that her green blouse made her look like a mermaid. Flossy lived to be 93 and maintained a lifelong friendship with women she had met in the Wills workroom all those decades before.

With those friends from the factory, Flossy enjoyed visiting the shops in central Bristol and going on dates with men, often in defiance of her father Arthur's curfew. But if she ever came home late, Flossy would call on her colourful imagination and tell him a convoluted story about a broken-down tram or how she had rushed to help someone who had been in distress.

During World War One, Flossy worked as an assistant to her sister Violet in a church project to entertain wounded soldiers who were convalescing in hospital. Her effervescent personality suggests this is a role she would have excelled at. Flossy and Violet would provide tea to the soldiers and then sometimes accompany them to the evening service at St Mary Redcliffe before helping them back to the hospital. Flossy also enjoyed reading tea leaves, so perhaps she attempted to predict the fortunes of the soldiers she supported.

Flossy finally settled down in 1930 and married Albert Sage and, while they had no children of their own, Flossy was remembered for being fond of her many nieces and nephews and for making up elaborate stories to keep them entertained.[258]

'SALLY ON THE BARN'
SHROUDED IN MYSTERY

There's a barn (you didn't expect that, did you?) at the 18th century Hanham Court Farm on what is now Court Farm Road. And that barn has the unusual name of 'Sally On the Barn'. But why? A stone statue of 'Sally' was placed on the roof of the barn at Hanham Court Farm on 5 January 1839 and there are at least four stories about who Sally is and why she is there.

One story is that the statue came from the ruins of the nearby Keynsham Abbey and that Sally represents Ceros, the Goddess of Harvest, which would make sense for a farm. The barn was initially a 15th century tithe barn used by the monks in Keynsham and, although the property has now been converted into a private home, it remains a listed building.

Another story is that Sally was a serving girl to the family who ran the farm during the Civil War, and that she was killed by

258 Ivy Herwig, Winifred Harris, 1992, *A Tree Grew in Bedminster: An Anthology Based on a Family Tree*, p23–24.

the Roundheads after refusing to give away the whereabouts of some Cavaliers. Apparently, Sally tried to escape the Roundheads by squeezing through the trapdoor onto the barn roof and that, according to some sources, explains why you sometimes see the ghost of a young woman on the barn roof.

A third story is that Sally was the daughter of an earlier farmer at Hanham Court Farm. This tale claims that when Sally realised the barn was on fire, she rushed inside to rescue the horses that were trapped indoors but met her own fate instead. And that her father erected a stone statue in her memory and rebuilt the barn.

Yet another story asserts that there was a young woman named Sally who lived at the farm and had a beautiful singing voice. She was in the habit of standing on top of the barn and singing to the moon, and the sound of her voice carried through Hanham which, at that point, would not have been as built up as it is now. Neighbours were drawn to the barn to listen to Sally sing. And, it is claimed, when the moon is bright Sally's figure can still sometimes be seen on the roof.

Which, if any, of these stories is true? Nobody knows for sure.

HONOR SALMON
1912-1943, PILOT

Honor Isabel Pitman (as she was originally called) was 31 when she was killed after crashing her plane above Devizes when she was flying for the Air Transport Auxiliary.

The granddaughter of the man who invented shorthand note taking[259], Honor was just 14 when she learned to fly in 1927 at the Bristol and Wessex Aero Club. Understandably, "because of my

---

259 Sir Isaac Pitman (1813-1897) lived much of his adult life in Bath, not a million miles from Bristol.

age, I always had to fly with someone and could never go to other aerodromes to land". However, by the time she was 24 in 1936, Honor had passed her Royal Aero Club certificate and amassed 120 hours of solo flight time. This achievement stood her in good stead to join the Air Transport Auxiliary (ATA) when World War Two was declared.

Honor, who had been briefly living in Australia, worked as a driver for the war effort in the UK but, when she heard that they were seeking people with flying experience, she immediately wrote to them: "I would very much like to know if there is the possibility of my joining your section of the service? I am an 'A' pilot and have only done about 120 hrs flying in small club planes – Swallows, Cadets and Aroncas, but I am prepared to take any training in any line if I could help you. Four years ago I joined the FANY [First Aid Nursing Yeomanry] in hopes of a flying section being started, but this never materialised... I had been hoping on my return from Australia last year to have my own plane and work for my 'B' licence but instead I have had to content myself with reading textbooks."

In March 1941, Honor finally joined the ATA, three months before her marriage to Major Henry Salmon. However, she was an accident-prone pilot and her ATA records note a number of mishaps, including two in two days. The report states: "This pilot needed a refresher and has benefitted by being returned to school. Her chief fault is her attitude towards her job. If she can be persuaded that flying is, after all, a very ordinary occupation, with common sense the main ingredient and that an ordinary sensible woman makes a better ferry pilot than a temperamental prima donna, she will do better and inspire greater confidence."

In April 1943, Honor met her fate when her plane crashed in bad weather and she was killed in the impact. Pauline Gower, who had established the ATA, said: "Honor will be very much missed not only as an excellent pilot but as a friend. She was a charming and gallant person."[260]

GLADYS SALT
1925-2011, TECHNICIAN

A true, ahem, salt of the earth type, Clifton's Gladys Salt joined the department of biochemistry at the University of Bristol in 1980, where she primarily assisted two biochemists and was largely responsible for glassware washing in the laboratory. However, Gladys was no stranger to the university having previously been employed there as a cleaner. Her colleagues were so impressed by Gladys' ability to keep everything spick and span that when an opportunity arose for a laboratory technician they encouraged her to apply.

But Gladys did more than keep the laboratory's glassware spotless. She was also known for providing a listening ear to any students or staff who needed someone to talk to – dishing out cups of tea and Kit-Kat biscuits to anyone who needed them. Gladys took compulsory retirement in 1992 due to her age, although she made it clear she would much rather have stayed in post.

REBECCA SANDERS
1841–1927, MATRIARCH

This redoubtable woman witnessed many extraordinary social changes in South Bristol during her decades living in Bedminster. Born Rebecca Caddick, her father William Caddick was an anchor

---

260 ata-ferry-pilots.org/index.php/category-blog-1941/399-pitman-honor-isabel

maker, presumably working at the nearby Bristol Docks. It must have been a tough job because he died in 1859, aged 54, leaving his widow Mary to care for their ten children on her own.

One experience that stood out to Rebecca was, when she was eight, watching the last ever public hanging of a woman in Bristol, which took place from the roof of the old Cumberland Road Gaol (a site which is now luxury flats). This was the execution of a servant called Sarah Thomas, who was found guilty of having poisoned her unkind mistress.[261] The episode was so terrifying to young Rebecca that she had a fit of hysterics, which is not entirely surprising.

A less traumatic experience was her marriage to John Sanders in 1861, when she was 21. John worked as a flax dresser and, with Rebecca, had six children. The family lived on Stillhouse Lane, off Phillip Street, in a house with a kitchen/living–room with a flagstone floor and a rag rug in front of the coal fire. Rebecca was house proud and kept the wooden stairs scrubbed "as white as houndstooth", and the floors generally were clean enough to eat off if you really wanted to. The house had a front room that was kept for special occasions and housed a piano that Rebecca's granddaughter Lily would play hymns on.

John died in 1881 aged 56, leaving Rebecca to care for the family. However, her younger brother Sam had also been widowed so he and Rebecca set up home together, leading some neighbours to believe that they were wife and husband rather than sister and brother.

The many grandchildren were always welcome and Rebecca would put a pan of potatoes on to boil every morning, so that whenever a grandchild popped in they could be given a hot potato to eat. In a book about the family's history, Rebecca's relatives Ivy

---

261 Sarah Thomas is profiled in Volume Two of *The Women Who Built Bristol*.

Herwig and Winifred Harris said: "This homely cottage was the haven of refuge to which children were sent to be cared for in time of need. During the early part of World War One, Nora, her eldest and then only grand-child, was taken to Gran [Rebecca] each morning to enable her mother to work at the Wills Factory. Winifred remembers being sent there to stay at the time when her brother Norman was born."

Rebecca never properly healed from an accident in which she broke her leg, and she subsequently found it difficult to bend down. For this reason, even after her adult children had moved out and started their own families, one granddaughter or another would live with Rebecca to help her. In 1909, Rebecca was one of the first people to benefit from the newly introduced state pension of 5 shillings, which had been set up by Prime Minister David Lloyd–George.

Remembering Rebecca with fondness, Ivy and Winifred wrote: "Gran [Rebecca] was a strict disciplinarian where her children were concerned, especially when it came to being in early at night. She hated her name 'Rebecca' and made it plain that her family were forbidden to call any of their daughters after her. Things had to be what she thought 'proper', like strict adherence to periods of mourning. Even towards the end of her life, when [daughter] Elvena's husband Tom died, she looked at three-year-old Norman playing on the hearth rug and said, 'Violet, don't you think you ought to make a black hat for that child?'"[262]

262 Ivy Herwig, Winifred Harris, 1992, *A Tree Grew in Bedminster: An Anthology Based on a Family Tree*, p7.

ELL SHADDICK
dates unknown, QUEEN'S NURSE

Working in Almondsbury and Patchway since 1946, Ell Shadwick was no stranger to the medical profession and had variously worked in psychiatric and general wards, and was known as a Queen's Nurse. A Queen's Nurse, by the way, is not a nurse who tends to royalty but a prestigious title given to those in the nursing profession who have demonstrated a particularly high level of patient care. The Queen's Nursing Institute still exists today.

As a Queen's Nurse, Ell was used to being on call for 24 hours a day and only having a day off once in a blue moon. But with low salaries, there was little spare money to spend on that rare day off anyway.

Ell began nursing in 1946, two years before the formation of the National Health Service. Even back then, there were budgetary constraints in the profession and Ell and her colleagues were tasked with reducing their daily mileage by 20% – no easy feat when these nurses, who were effectively district nurses, needed to drive to wherever their patients happened to be.

Ell worked hard to plan her days to ensure that patients were visited in order of priority: pregnant women were seen first, and then patients whose surgical dressings needed changing in order to avoid infections. Third in order of priority were new patients, who might be feeling anxious. And then Ell would see those patients who needed injections every 12 hours, otherwise there wouldn't be time to get the second injection of the day in. Fifth on the list were diabetics, who required their insulin shot before they had breakfast, and then there were the children who needed to be seen before they set off for school. Last, but not least, were incontinent patients who couldn't be left in unhygienic conditions. As you'll have noticed, all of these patients had requirements that meant they needed to be seen first thing in the morning, which meant that Ell's day often began at around 4am. Her meals, if you could call them that, were eaten in the car as and when there was a scrap of time.

In the 1940s, most babies were delivered at home and rarely by a doctor, instead a midwife usually handled things on her own. This made it hard for nurses to make plans and, however tired they might be, their hope of finishing work for the day could be dashed in an instant following a call that a woman had gone into labour and Ell would need to rush around to take control of the situation. With a bit of luck, she might be able to grab a few hours of sleep before getting up at 4am the next day to start all over again. However, looking back on those long hard days, Ell said: "Such lovely memories."[263]

BECKY SHARPE
born 1910, PILOT

Born in Bristol but living in India until 1928, First Officer Roy Mary Sharpe (known to all as Becky) served with the Air Transport Auxiliary (ATA) from September 1941 to September 1945. She had been based in Thornbury at the time of the 1939 Register, where she lived in squadron lodgings and her job title was listed as 'Airwoman'. Prior to this, motorcycles had been Becky's passion and she had worked as a Secretary and Saleswoman for a motorcycle company in Cheltenham and was described as "an accomplished and daring motorcyclist"[264]. Before joining the ATA, Becky had a mere 10 hours of flying experience with the Civil Air Guard, but in time she became an accomplished and respected

263 Ell Shaddick, 1988, 'I Remember' in *More Bristol Lives*, Bristol Broadsides, p66–69.
264 ata-ferry-pilots.org/index.php/category-blog-1941/663-sharpe-roy-mary

wartime Pilot. After peace was declared, Becky received an MBE in the New Year's Honours list of 1946 and continued to work in aviation as an Aeroplane Demonstrator and Saleswoman, and she competed in many flying races.

NELLIE SHELLARD
1900-1965, GAS GIRL

When World War One broke out, Nellie Jeffries (as she was born) was 14 and living with her family at 2 Heber Street, Redfield, where she was the youngest of 15 children. Her young age didn't stop Nellie from playing her part in the war effort, and by 1918 she was working in the mustard gas factory at Chittening, Avonmouth, where she was filling the containers with this toxic substance. The factory was established in 1917 to make mustard gas in response to the Germans' use of the same in Ypres, and as such all employees had to sign the Official Secrets Act.[265]

For those women and girls working in National Filling Factory No 23, as the Chittening factory was officially known, every day was dangerous. Mustard gas was as lethal as it comes and caused severe burning to the skin, eyes and respiratory tract. Between June 1918 and the end of the war in November 1918, three workers died at the Chittening factory and a further 710 out of 1,100 employees endured injuries. Things were so bad that the factory had its own hospital. A report noted that the safety of the staff was a secondary concern to the manufacturer of the wartime weapon. Nellie received her share of injuries, although hers were limited to scars on her arms that she downplayed in later years, simply saying that she "had been doing something stupid" when

265 Maud Isaacs, who also worked at Chitterning, is profiled in Volume One of *The Women Who Built Bristol*.

asked about the marks years later.

However, one thing that Nellie did at the factory which wasn't stupid was meet her future husband, Fred Shellard, with whom she would have two daughters. Fred had been discharged from the army in 1917 aged 22 having experienced debilitating injuries. They married in August 1920, which was the same year that Nellie received a letter from the Home Office saying the King would like to offer her an OBE in recognition of the work she had done for the war effort. The OBE medal and its case remains with her family.

In later years, Nellie was remembered by family members for having a keen interest in politics and for being a strong woman who would keep an eye out for anyone in need. She passed away at the relatively young age of 65, possibly as a result of her lengthy exposure to mustard gas.[266]

LILLIAN SHELMERDINE
1878-1956, LOCAL GIRL DOES WELL

This entry reads rather like the synopsis for a film written by Julian 'Downton Abbey' Fellowes. Lillian Haskins, daughter of a grocer in Warmley, had done very well for herself by the time of her third marriage, becoming Lady Shelmerdine in the process. But she had worked bloody hard to get there.

The Haskins family was a prominent one in Warmley having made its name in pottery and pipe manufacture, and the family is linked to Warmley Towers: a grand house that looked very comfortable and desirable. Alas, Lillian's branch of the family never grew up in it, with her father James instead taking on the

---

266 With thanks to Sue Haskins for the nomination of her grandmother Nellie Shellard to this book.

Haskins' grocery business after his father died.[267]

When she was 17, Lillian requested her father's permission to get married... to Joseph Hanham, a farmer in Bath and a widow 19 years her senior. This decision may have been prompted by James' decision to move the family to South Africa and Lillian's reluctance to emigrate. Instead, she set up home with Joseph in Kingswood. The marriage was not a happy one, and Lillian was infected with a sexually transmitted disease within four months of the wedding. She also reported Joseph as being a drunk and cruel man who, on one occasion, threatened to shoot her. Their daughter Irene was born in 1897 and, in February 1899, exhausted by Joseph's abuse, Lillian took Irene and left. She settled in Reading and filed for divorce in 1901, which was granted in 1904.

Soon afterwards, Lillian married her second husband, hotelier Somerset Playne, and she moved to South Africa to live with him in Durban, close to where the other members of her family had settled a decade or so previously. Her daughter Irene didn't make the trip and was placed in an English boarding school. Lillian began an affair with a married naval captain.... with whom she set up home in 1912 and Somerset filed for divorce the following year. However, by the time the divorce came through, Lillian's naval captain had died of heart problems and she was left alone while Somerset promptly remarried.

Lillian remained in Durban and it is likely that this is where she met Francis Shelmerdine of the Royal Flying Corps... whose wife Mary was very much alive. However, Francis and Mary had been separated since 1912 owing to his cocaine habit. Mary also wanted to divorce Francis for infidelity but this was not permissible as he had not been physically cruel towards her.

Here things get a little confusing. Lillian's teenage daughter

267 Lillian is a second-cousin of the poet Minnie Haskins, who is profiled in Volume One of *The Women Who Built Bristol*.

Irene applied for her own marriage licence but, being only 17, she needed parental approval. Claiming that her father Joseph was dead (he didn't die until 1926), Irene instead said that her mother was Mrs Sheldermine, to give Lillian more respectability than a twice-divorced and unmarried woman would otherwise have had. To further confuse matters, and to circumvent the societal embarrassment of being single, Lillian would sometimes go by the name of Sylvanie on legal documents in an effort to hide her real identity.

Lillian and Francis finally married in London in 1925, after the Matrimonial Causes Act of 1923 enabled Mary to divorce her husband. Francis had left the army in 1919 and taken up a role at the Civil Aviation Department of the Air Ministry, later becoming Controller of Aerodromes and Licences. As his glamorous wife, Lillian was regularly photographed on his arm at events and she travelled the world with him. The couple settled in India, where Francis spent four years as Director General of Civil Aviation, while maintaining a home in a fashionable area of London to which they returned in 1931. The couple then moved to Bristol before the start of World War Two.

Lillian pursued her own interest in aviation and became an advocate for the industry, presenting trophies to women pilots after races and attending meetings with women aviators: on one occasion, Lillian was complemented by the acclaimed Aviator Amy Johnson for all that she had done to further women's flying. Lillian was also the chair of the Aviation Group of the Forum Club, entertaining overseas aviators who visited England. Following a premonition, Lillian refused to allow her husband Francis to board the ill-fated R101 airship in 1930... Prudently, as it happened, because the airship crashed and there were no survivors. One of the men who had been aboard the R101 was the Director of Civil Aviation and, with that post now vacant, Francis was promoted yet again. In 1936, he was knighted, meaning that Lillian became Lady Shelmerdine.

Francis died in 1945 and Lillian spent her widowed years travelling between South Africa and England. She died of a stroke in 1956 while on a visit to South Africa.[268]

SISTER AMY
1830s-1890s, NUN

Between 1851 and 1943, the building now known as Arnos Court House in Brislington was the home of the Good Shepherd Convent. The Good Shepherd Sisters had arrived in England from France in 1841 and, as you can see, quickly spread from London to Bristol and elsewhere in the UK. The order worked to support women and girls who were living on the streets or otherwise struggling to survive, and aimed to help them find a safer and more comfortable way of life. There have been stories that some of the convents associated with the Good Shepherds exploited the women they claimed to care for by making them work unpaid in laundries, but it is not clear whether the Bristol convent is linked to those claims.

By the 1860s, the Bristol convent was being led by Sister Amy. She had been born into a large Catholic family in the 1830s and, along with her twin sister, was the youngest child. While all of the sons went on to marry and have their own families, none of the sisters did and they all became nuns. Amy became the most prominent of her sisters. She was initially the Superintendent of a convent in Essex that was largely a refuge for penitent women, and then she relocated to Bristol.

268 Huge thanks to Lucy Whitfield of The Women Who Made Me project: thewomenwhomademe. wordpress.com/2019/10/20/lillian-hs-story/

The Good Shepherd Convent in Bristol was essentially a reform school, just as the convent in Essex had been, except on a larger scale: accommodating up to 127 women and girls who were expected to undertake needlework and laundry. The intention was that by doing this work, the women would be serving penance for their past 'bad behaviour'. Amy was supported in her work by an assistant, a huddle of 12 nuns and 12 lay sisters.

During the mid-1880s, Amy relocated again, this time to London and another branch of the Good Shepherd Convent, before moving to Manchester and then to her final posting in Lancashire, which is where she died.

The Good Shepherd Convent remained in Bristol until 1986, although it had moved from Arnos Court House in 1943 following extensive damage to the building caused during the Blitz.[269]

POLLY SKYRME and AGNES SKYRME
1870-1940 and 1910-2006, BAKERS

In the early 1890s, Mary Ann Crockford (known as Polly) was a sales assistant at a bakery called the Coffee Tavern on Passage Road, Westbury-on-Trym, when she met an entrepreneurial baker called Arthur Skyme. The two married and, when Polly's aunt (who ran the bakery) retired, Arthur bought the Coffee Tavern for them to run together. However, Arthur developed 'baker's asthma'[270] so he instead went to work at the Bristol Lawn Tennis Club, leaving the Coffee Tavern entirely in Polly's capable hands. A trained cook, Polly used her experience to build up the bakery, which also offered dried fruits, local eggs and cheeses, and freshly

269 Huge thanks to Lucy Whitfield of The Women Who Made Me project: thewomenwhomademe. wordpress.com/2017/11/13/amy-ws-story/
270 'Baker's asthma' is the term for an allergy linked to breathing in flour dust.

made soft drinks. All of the shop's cakes, pies and pastries were handmade by Polly.

Polly and Arthur's daughter Agnes Florence Skyrme was born in 1910 but, when Agnes was four, Arthur was called up to serve in World War One despite being 47. He was stationed in Ireland and Polly would send parcels of homemade food to Arthur and his fellow soldiers to try and bolster their rations. Back in Bristol, Polly enlisted the help of her sister-in-law Ethel who moved in until Arthur returned home.

After leaving Redland Collegiate School, Agnes joined her mother in the bakery, which had become a central part of the Westbury-on-Trym community. In a local history book, Agnes recalled how she and her mother were required to supply provisions to prisoners at the local police station, which was something Agnes found rather intimidating: "Agnes learnt all about the business from her mother and by working in the shop learnt about other aspects of village life. Whenever a prisoner was lodged at Westbury Police Station, the Skyrmes were 'privileged' to provide a supper for him. This consisted of a billycan of tea and a hunk of bread; for this they were paid sixpence. Agnes was given the task of taking the supper up to the police station. She went in 'fear and trembling', not so much of the prisoner but of the policeman, who in those days was a figure of awe."

Running the bakery meant that the Skyrmes family had ready access to food and never went hungry, and they shared this privilege with those in need. For instance, Polly would always send a hearty meal of gruel and stew to local women who had just had babies, knowing they wouldn't be up to cooking. Polly was also known to sometimes add in a few treats for her customers who came in with Parish Relief food vouchers, knowing that a sweet treat would be a rare thing for those people. But this act of kindness meant that Polly had to fiddle her books so that when the Parish Relief officer made his weekly inspection, he didn't discover that she had been giving food away.

Polly died in 1940 but even on her dying day she retained a stoic attitude. Agnes recalled: "The day she died she continued in her no-nonsense way, calling [Arthur] upstairs and saying, 'I'm dying and you must make the business over to Agnes who has given up her life to helping us. If you don't, I'll come back and haunt you.' Agnes had run the business for some time as her mother had been crippled with arthritis and Dad wasn't really a businessman."

Arthur obeyed Polly's wishes and the bakery was signed over to Agnes who continued to run it in the way her mother had. When the newsagent next door went up for sale in 1966, Agnes purchased it and opened Westbury Health Foods in response to a gap in the market that she had identified. A few years after opening, Agnes told the *Bristol Evening Post*: "The shop seems to be popular with both the older residents of Westbury and the newcomers alike. We felt that as a health food store we could provide the village with more of a service than as grocers."[271] The news story noted that such unusual items as ginger and cinnamon were now available for the more adventurous chefs.

Agnes lived and worked at the bakery until she retired in 1975. She never married or had children, and devoted herself to the bakery and the community. She was also an avid local historian and wrote a number of books collecting together the stories of people in the community, which she had gathered together from regular history sessions that she led at Westbury Library.

Throughout her life, Agnes never lived more than a mile away from the former bakery on Passage Street.[272]

271   'Health food store's success results in move to larger premises', *Bristol Evening Post*, 25 November 1970.
272   Beryl Tully, 2004, *Shoes and Ships and Sealing Wax*, Malago Press, p103-108.

EMILY SMELE
born 1856, GREENGROCER

Do you remember the first time you ate a banana? Thanks to greengrocer Emily Smele, the people of Bristol were introduced to bananas in 1901 when she became the first retailer in the city to stock the exotic fruit.

Following the abolition of slavery in the British Empire in 1833, the sugar plantations in the West Indies struggled to compete with the cost of European sugarbeet and instead found that bananas proved popular with British customers. Once refrigerated cargo ships were developed in the 1890s, unripe bananas could be shipped to the UK in bulk to be ripened on arrival. Dockers in Avonmouth unloaded the first bananas from Jamaica in 1901 and the yellow fruit instantly became a hit.

Enterprising Emily had opened her first greengrocers' shop in Bedminster's Mill Lane in 1882, which was so popular that further branches followed on Raleigh Road, Midland Road and Castle Street. In time, Emily's son George Smele would continue to expand his mother's empire by adding branches in Stapleton Road, Downend and Winterbourne.[273] George's son Jim Smele (Emily's grandson) would again pick up the reins when his own father retired in 1946 and he in turn passed the business onto his daughter (Emily's great-granddaughter). Jim remembers as a child watching the boats come in to Bristol Bridge bringing imported potatoes and soaked peas.

273 Only the Winterbourne branch remains in business at the time of going to print.

CLARA SMITH
1898-1951, OFF-LICENCE KEEPER

Clara May Smith[274] and her husband William Smith lived at 28 Firfield Street, Totterdown, above the tiny shop that they ran as an off-licence. Well, according to the 1939 Register, William ran the off-licence while Clara performed 'unpaid domestic duties' yet, according to first-hand accounts, Clara was the one doing all the work. Isn't that always the way?

Elsie wrote in her 1979 booklet *Growing Up In Totterdown*: "The main errands were to my Aunt May's shop in Firfield Street for grandfather's supper beer. I had a large quart-sized willow patterned jug, and up and over the hill I would trudge, saying to myself 'a pint of old and a half of mild' or was it 'half of mild and a pint of bitter'? I couldn't remember the combination then and I can't remember it now, but Aunt May always knew what her father wanted and I was never scolded so I suppose I got it right. The shop was tiny but Aunt was very popular and always did a roaring trade. Her shelves were tightly packed with goods and the beer was in barrels on a rack on the wall. They were draped with snowy white cloths, which were changed daily. There was also bottled beer, which was kept in the cellar for coolness. I would take my turn in the queue, and then get back and watch my grandfather prepare his beer. He had a little saucepan, which he set on a trivet by the fire. The beer would be poured in and, after a while, he would plunge in a red-hot poker. I have no idea what this did to the beer, and I haven't seen it done by anyone else in the last 45 years.[275]

---

274 Clara was the aunt of Elsie Lawrance, who has her own entry in this volume.
275 Apparently, this is called beer poking. If you plunge a red-hot poker into beer for a few seconds, it caramelises the beer's residual sugars and creates a frothy, sweet and creamy drink. However, I feel obliged to caution that playing with red-hot pokers carries an element of risk and therefore I am not suggesting you try this yourself.

"Great excitement was caused when my Uncle Bill Smith purchased a pianola and could play music with it without touching the keys.[276] On Old Year's Night, the piano would be dragged out onto the pavement and old Mrs Read (not so old then) would play for everyone to sing and dance. All of the Smith's customers would be given a glass of beer in appreciation of their continued custom, and a jolly time was had by all. At midnight the railway engines down at the sheds would blow their whistles, the bells would ring and we would bang saucepans, ash bin lids, anything to make as much noise as possible."[277]

EMILY SMITH
dates unknown, PIONEER

Emily Harriet Smith and her older sister Sophie Townsend Smith were brought up in Brighton and moved to Bristol after the deaths of their parents. They settled at Richmond House on Clifton Hill, where they lived off their inheritances. Emily seems to have been a particularly indomitable character. Following a few years of travel in Europe, she made her home in Bristol and busied herself with the women's suffrage movement where, from 1909 to 1918, she was the Honorary Secretary of the Conservative and Unionist Women's Franchise Association in Bristol. She was also a member of the Women's Patrol Committee between 1912 and 1918.

In 1921, Emily was elected to the City Council to represent

276 A pianola is a self-playing piano with a pneumatic mechanism that 'plays' the piano using performated paper or metal rolls that have been pre-punched with tunes. This meant that, before record players became widespread, people could enjoy musical entertainment at home even if nobody in the vicinity knew how to play an instrument. I recall playing on a pianola as a child in the early 1980s because a schoolfriend's family had one. Arguably, they're quite valuable now because production stopped in the 1930s, so maybe don't let little kids play on them unsupervised.
277 Elsie Lawrance, 1979, *Growing Up in Totterdown*, Redcliffe Press, p15.

Clifton South as the first female Unionist Councillor in Bristol. Later the same year, she was appointed as a Justice of the Peace, which was a rare feat for a woman at that time. Continuing her list of firsts, Emily also became the first woman to take the Chair at the Police Court, was the first woman on the Watch Committee, the first woman on the Housing and Libraries Committee and the first woman to be appointed as a Visiting Justice at HM Bristol Prison.

Her accolades don't stop there. It is such a long list that it would be tedious to go into everything, but a few more highlights include being President of the Bristol Branch of the National Council of Women: a role she held for 17 years. She was also a member of the Women's Aid Committee, 'Chairman' of the Clifton South Women's Unionist Association, a member of the Court of the University and, phew, 'Chairman' of the Bristol Branch of the Soldiers' and Sailors' Help Society.

ALICE SMYTH
1490-1546, MATRIARCH

Born to a Bristolian merchant named Lewis John, Alice John married a hooper (aka a barrel maker) named Matthew Smyth who had moved to Bristol from the Forest of Dean. Matthew became a prosperous merchant and it seems that he is the origin story for the Smyth family at Ashton Court. After his death in 1526, Alice took over the running of his business which was trading profitably in Europe. As a merchant, Alice bought wool and yarn, then exported manufactured cloth to France and Spain. She also imported wine, oil, iron, woad and alum (the latter two were used for dying fabric).

Alice and Matthew had two children, a daughter called

Elizabeth and a son called John. Their son became apprenticed to a merchant and, when the man to whom he was apprenticed died, John not only inherited his business but also married his widow, Joan White. In time, John was seen as a successful businessman and a skilled merchant, and he not only became the Sheriff of Bristol but was also twice ordained as the Mayor of Bristol. It is thanks to John's wealth that he was able to purchase the land that made up the Ashton Court estate, as well as the manor house that would ultimately become the mansion house we recognise today, although it looked very different back then.

ESME SMYTH
1863-1946, HEIRESS

Widowed Esme Smyth divided her time between her grand homes at Ashton Court, Bristol, and Ness Castle, Inverness. However, her final years were spent at Ashton Court. Esme's death in 1946 brought to an end the reign of the Smyth family at the 17th century Ashton Court.

But who was Esme? She was the illegitimate daughter of Dame Emily Smyth, who died in 1914 and had commanded respect and admiration from many in the area.[278] Esme was married to Sir Gilbert Irby and they lived at Ashton Court for 30 years; Gilbert died in 1940. Part of the stipulation for inheriting Ashton Court was that Esme and Gilbert must change their surname to Smyth, which they did in 1915.

Esme did not achieve the same level of respect as her mother Emily had. One account describes Esme as "a big awkward-looking woman, over six feet tall, and unpredictable to the point

278 Emily Smyth is profiled in Volume One of *The Women Who Built Bristol*.

of eccentricity", adding that she was known to behave erratically and once went into the snake house at Bristol Zoo where she proceeded to wrestle with a boa constrictor.[279] A descendant of the Smyth family, Igor Kennaway, said in 2016: "[Esme]was formidable. There's a story that the then-Mayor of Bristol arrived at Ashton for dinner by motorcar, and the only people allowed to drive on the estate was the family itself. And cousin Esme said, 'You've disobeyed my house rules and for that you'll miss the whole of the first course.'"

Nevertheless, Esme was recognised for her talent as a photographer as well as a hostess, welcoming guests including the Duke and Duchess of York (who would later become King George VI and Queen Elizabeth, the future Queen Mother). But, inevitably, the two world wars took their toll, land was sold off, the Smyths' coal mines were closed down and the number of servants was slashed from 30 to a paltry three.

When Esme died it was the end of the Smyth family at Ashton Court. Esme's descendant Zuleika Henry gave an interview in 2016 in which she explained how Esme's daughter Esme Francis Sylvia Smyth (known as Sylvia, and who died in 1959) was so desperate *not* to inherit Ashton Court that she converted to catholicism because "catholics were not allowed to own Ashton Court, so she was immediately free of the burden, so it went to her son"[280].

However, Sylvia's son Greville was not old enough to inherit, so everything was sold. An enormous auction of Smyth family effects was held, and the estate was parcelled up and sold off. It was broken down into 14 farms, 11 large houses, 80 cottages, two pubs, ten small holdings and endless acres of woodland. In short, pretty much all of Long Ashton went up for sale. Ultimately,

279 Bill Thomas, 'The History of Ashton Court', *Grouse*, 2021, p46.
280 ashtongatehouse.org/zuleika-henry-and-igor-kennaway

Ashton Court mansion and much of the parkland would be bought by Bristol City Council and opened to the public in 1959.

FLORENCE SMYTH
born 1608, HEIRESS

When she was 15, Florence Poulett of Hinton St George married 17-year-old Thomas Smyth, who inherited Ashton Court the following year and would later become the MP for Bridgwater. Much of the renovations of the Ashton Court estate and gardens are thanks to Florence's vision, as she embarked upon an eight-year programme of works to improve the property.

Terraces were cut into the hillside behind the house and sweet chestnut was planted. Bowling greens were installed at the bottom of the slope near the house, orchards were planted to the south of the house, and walled flower gardens were created to the south west of the mansion. At the same time, gates and estate walls were installed around the Tudor gatehouse. All of this meant that Ashton Court ended up bearing a passing resemblance to Hinton House, which was where Florence had grown up.

Unfortunately, the times of peace and home-building that Florence enjoyed in the early years of her life at Ashton Court were disrupted when Thomas went to fight in the 1642 Civil War and died of smallpox the following year. Florence was left a widow at the age of 34, with three young children at her heels and pregnant with a fourth.

She managed Thomas' business in the years that followed before marrying an Irish knight in 1647 and moving to Brockley Court near Nailsea.

FLORENCE SMYTH
1634–1692, ARISTOCRAT

In 2008, Bristol Museums acquired a painting from around 1640 of an aristocratic girl pictured with a young enslaved girl by her side. The picture by Gilbert Jackson had long been thought to depict Arabella Astry and an enslaved girl.[281]

However, detailed research by Bristol City Museum and Art Gallery concluded that the white girl in the picture was Florence Smyth of Ashton Court estate. But there is a connection between the Astry and Smyth families because Arabella's sister Elizabeth Astry *did* marry into the Smyth family, although not until 1698, but this might explain the initial confusion.

Researcher Laurence Brown notes: "The painting is particularly striking because it pre-dates the mass importation of enslaved Africans into Britain's colonies in the Americas and the increasing visibility of Black servants in English portraiture during the second half of the eighteenth century."[282]

Another researcher, Madge Dresser, adds: "If true, the presence of the young African servant strongly indicates that the connection between the Smyths, a family long noted for their mercantile interests, and the African trade might stretch as far back as the 1630s, well before Bristol's formal entry into the slave trade in 1698. This supposition ties in well with the Astry family's own associations with the Caribbean from the early 17th century."[283]

In 1653, Florence married the Bristolian MP Humphrey Hooke and they lived at King's Weston and had at least four

---

281 Arabella Astry has her own entry in this volume.
282 Dr Laurence Brown, 2010, 'The Slavery Connections of Marble Hill House', Manchester University Press.
283 Madge Dresser, Laurence Hann eds, 2013, *Slavery and the British Country House*, Historic England, p32.

children. However, as is so often the case, we know little more about her life.

MARY SOUTHCOTT
1921-2008, SECRETARY

Originally from Scotland, Mary McCallum Fyfe met her husband Merlvyn Southcott in London during World War Two and they moved to his home city of Bristol after their wedding. Theirs was a big family with five children, and Mary ensured her offspring always honoured their Scottish ancestry when it came to supporting sports teams.

A fixture of the University of Bristol's geography department, Mary joined the school in 1971 as a valued Secretary and she remained in post until reaching retirement age in 1987.

However, retirement wasn't really on the cards for Mary and she then worked at the Bristol Royal Infirmary, where a blind eye was turned to the fact that she was technically beyond the working age.

Remembering her with fondness, a tribute on the University's website says: "She was a warm, motherly, understanding figure to whom both staff and students readily related. But a Scottish education had served her well: she set meticulously high standards, and inevitably corrected our wayward spelling and grammar, even if it meant re-typing lengthy references."[284]

284 bristol.ac.uk/news/2008/12017945177.html

PAULA SPIELMAN
1927-2006, PHILANTHROPIST

Paula Spielman was born Paula Gwyn-Davies. She worked as the Bristol Old Vic Theatre School's Secretary from 1957 to 1962, becoming a major benefactor to the institution later in her life. As a resident of Dowry Square, Hotwells, Paula and her husband John Spielman quietly supported the arts and young people via the Spielman Charitable Trust. This included the Booksamazing events, a trilogy of community plays and photographic exhibitions about the history of Hotwells. The Trust mostly provided grants of up to £6,000 for charities which support young people. The studio space at the Tobacco Factory Theatre in Southville is named the Spielman Theatre in recognition of Paula and John's significant support. Additionally, one of the chapels at Arnos Vale Cemetery is named the Spielman Centre to acknowledge the contributions of Paula and John to its restoration.[285]

RITA STANLEIGH
1923-2013, PEACE ACTIVIST

Unusually, I will start this entry with a brief description of our shero's husband. John Stanleigh changed his name from Hans Schwarz during World War Two to disguise his Polish heritage. John had grown up in Brandenburg, Germany, and his Jewish family were sent to the Auschwitz concentration camp early in the war: his parents were killed at Auschwitz in 1944. John arrived in Liverpool in 1938, changed his name and joined the British Army. Despite many years of service for Britain on the frontline, John

---

285 With thanks to Shirley Brown for the nomination of Paula Spielman to this book.

was denied a military medal because of his Polish heritage and he was refused British citizenship until 1946. However, in 1944 he married Rita Alder Prebble who had grown up in London, and the two had a happy life together in Mangotsfield.

Rita and John became a force to be reckoned with and, spurred on by the horrors of the war, they were determined to campaign for peace. To this end, in 1983 they both stood as candidates for the Social Democratic Party in the local elections. Neither were elected but this didn't deter them. Also in 1983, they founded the Ex-Services Campaign for Nuclear Disarmament (CND), of which John became the President. This branch, which later merged with the larger CND, had grown to reach 1,000 members by 1989, most of whom were veterans of World War Two. In 1995, Rita was one of the three authors of a pamphlet for CND called *On Active Service for Peace*.

Rita and John returned to education in their retirement. Rita had spent the bulk of her working life in the careers service at the University of Bristol, while John had been a teacher. However, the pair attended Bristol Polytechnic (which became the University of the West of England in 1992) as mature students, and Rita graduated in 1991 with a BA in Humanities at the age of 68, something that was too expensive for her to have considered when she left school at the age of 16. Talking to the *Bristol Evening Post*, she said: "It has been the most rewarding, enjoyable thing I have done in my whole life." She went on to complete a post-graduate diploma in women's studies.[286]

The couple had two sons and four grandchildren, and Rita was Chair of the governors at St Stephen's Infant School in Kingswood.[287]

286 'You're never too old', *Bristol Evening Post*, 15 October 1991.
287 With thanks to Howard Davies for the nomination of Rita Stanleigh to this book.

JOYCE STEPHENSON
died 2019, NURSE, ACTIVIST

While she may be better known as the wife of Paul Stephenson – who was one of the activists in the Bristol Bus Boycott of 1963, which successfully challenged the colour bar to Black people working on the buses – Joyce Stephenson was also an extraordinary woman in her own right.

Born in rural Jamaica, Joyce trained and worked as a nurse. In his book *Memoirs of a Black Englishman*, Paul described her as "surprisingly militant … she was empathetic in insisting on dignity for Black people". While Lilleith Morrison, who helped Paul write his memoir, said: "Joyce was radical in her approach to politics and someone who backed Paul's political endeavours 100%."

Joyce was working in Manchester when she met Paul in May 1965. By this time, Paul had been successful with the Bristol Bus Boycott and the story had reached Joyce's ears. So when she opened her front door in Manchester to a man asking for a signature on a housing petition, Joyce was surprised to discover that this man was the activist Paul Stephenson about whom she had heard. The couple were married in October of the same year, and Joyce moved to Bristol to live with her new husband. They had two children together.

In Bristol, Joyce and Paul became well known in the community. When the Bamboo Club opened in St Pauls in 1966, the couple were regular guests. Run by Lalel and Tony Bullimore, the Bamboo Club was the first truly integrated club in Bristol's entertainment scene and became a valued space for members of Bristol's African and Caribbean community.

Joyce and Paul relocated to Coventry in 1968 when Paul was appointed as an Executive Officer to the Coventry Community

Relations Council. Paul wrote: "Joyce was very supportive of my work and our house was sometimes used as a cooling off space for young people who were having problems with their parents. We used to liaise between the parents and teenagers and help facilitate good relations between them."

Joyce had always encouraged Paul throughout his activism, attending demonstrations and events with him across the UK, and sometimes catering for large groups who were brought to their home. They were prominently involved in campaigns in Bristol asking the city to face up to its involvement in the trade in enslaved Africans, and challenged the name of 'Colston' (Edward Colston having been a prominent slave trader) that was plastered on buildings and street names all over the city.

Joyce was involved with the Bristol West Indian Parents and Friends Association, which had formed in the 1960s to tackle issues such as the slum housing offered to immigrants in areas like St Pauls and Easton. In 1991, she told the *Western Daily Press*: "We should have the same opportunities as white people. They try to keep everyone else down. Black people are just fed up with being kicked in the teeth."[288]

Following a spell in London, Joyce and Paul returned to Bristol in 1982 where they remained for the rest of their lives. They decided to extend their family by fostering, which was a natural step for Joyce who had already supported families in need with her voluntary work. Paul wrote in his memoir: "It was a rewarding experience. I had thought about fostering children but there had been difficulties; Joyce wanted to continue her nursing career and I respected that, especially as I had been commuting to London and back to Bristol which was a very stressful period ... We decided to do some emergency fostering. Our own children

288 'Preacher Scare', *Western Daily Press*, 2 May 1991.

were great about it and happy to share us with other children." Over the years, Joyce and Paul welcomed eight foster children into their family.[289]

AUDREY STUCKES
1923-2006, PHYSICIST

Born in Bedminster, Audrey Doris Stuckes was the youngest of two children. She attended Merrywood Primary School in Knowle, before earning a scholarship to Red Maids' School in Westbury-on-Trym, and finally moving to Colston's Girls' School where she achieved her Higher School Certificate in natural sciences and earned a distinction for chemistry. Science was clearly where Audrey's heart lay and she pursued a Natural Sciences Tripos degree at the University of Cambridge, followed by an MA and PhD. Audrey was also a young member of the Physical Society of London and the Institute of Physics, before becoming a member of the senate at Cambridge. Which is all extremely impressive.

Out in the world of work, Audrey took up a post at an engineering company in Trafford, Greater Manchester, called Metropolitan-Vickers, which had a good reputation for offering good opportunities to women. Through her time there, Audrey authored a number of research papers related to the thermal and electrical conductivity of semiconductors. By 1962, she had taken a teaching post at Salford's Royal College of Advanced Technology (now the University of Salford). While there, she and a colleague co-wrote a textbook on thermal conductivity in solids, which was widely declared to be a groundbreaking piece of work.

Many more academic achievements followed, and by 1982

---

289 Paul Stephenson OBE, *Memoirs of a Black Englishman*, Tangent, 2021.

Audrey was so respected in her field that she was presenting programmes on science which were aired on BBC television for the Open University. In 1986, she was awarded the status of Chartered Physicist by the Institute of Physicists and, in 1988, she retired from university work. Audrey and her husband Douglas Jones, whom she had married in Bristol in 1947, lived in Trafford during their retirement.

JANE SUMMERS
born 1852, ACTIVIST

The nautical world was, of course, largely dominated by men – and, occasionally, by women posing as men in order to be allowed to sail the seven seas.[290] But mostly by men. Nonetheless, many women were supportive of their menfolk in nautical work, and some went to extreme measures to defend these men when the situation required it. Which is how we meet Jane Summers of Pill who, with a few other sailors' wives, turned to violence when they tarred and floured a turncoat ferry Pilot called Richard Case. The claim against Case was that he represented the capitalisation of the Docks by accepting work from the larger steamship companies directly, rather than working for the independent local operators as had been the case for centuries.

The *Bristol Mercury and Daily Post* reported on 10 March 1881 how Case took a steamboat called SS Gloucester from Avonmouth to Bristol and returned to Pill in a sailing boat. When he arrived back at Pill, he and his boat were rushed by "a crowd of boys and girls" who tried to haul the boat out of the water, with some of the men challenging Case to a fight which he refused to engage in.

290 Esther McEwan, who has her own entry in this volume, helps illustrate this point.

Several people tried to throw Case overboard but failed. At this point, Jane Summers appeared and threw a large quantity of flour over Case, while others then threw mud and stones at him.

Reporting on the flour-throwing incident in the *Western Daily Press*, also on 10 March 1881, it was said: "On reaching the top of the slip, Mrs Summers threw flour on the complainant. Perhaps there was not much to complain of in that, and on some occasions it might be treated as an idle joke, but it would have been much better if it had been left undone considering all the relationships which existed in the place."

Along with a woman named Emma Dickins (at whom Case allegedly threatened to fire his gun), Jane was charged with assault, fined 40 shillings and costs, and sentenced to 14 days in prison with hard labour.[291]

ROSAMUND SUTHERLAND
1947-2019, EDUCATOR

Professor Rosamund Sutherland became a specialist in mathematics and the application of new technologies in education, and spent much of her career working at the University of Bristol.

Ros excelled at maths at school, which she went on to study at the University of Bristol. It was here that she met Ian Sutherland, whom she married in 1968 and with whom she had two children. After a career break to raise their children in their new home of Hertfordshire, Ros worked as a Tutor for the Open University's Foundation Mathematics degree, and as a Maths Lecturer at Borehamwood College, where she gained a taste for supporting young people who had not had the best educational starts in life.

291 For more information, see Rosemary Caldicott, 2019, *Nautical Women*, Bristol Radical History Group, p22–23.

Ros' time with the Open University led her to apply for research funding for what would become the Logo Mathematics Project, to study how computer programming language could be used to enhance an understanding of mathematics, and this led her to become an Academic Researcher.

In 1995, Ros came back to Bristol and worked as a Chair of Education at the University of Bristol, reconceptualising ways of teaching. She became Head of the Graduate School of Education from 2003 to 2006, and again in 2014. In Ros' obituary, a colleague wrote: "She not only generated bold and principled strategies but used her energy and drive both to motivate her colleagues and to negotiate effectively within the University. The renovation and contemporary décor of the present School of Education, funding for which she achieved almost single-handedly, symbolises her future-oriented vision."

But her passion for education didn't start and end with universities. In 2006, Ros was involved with a programme to improve the condition of schools in some of the poorer parts of Bristol. This opened her eyes to the divided state of education in this city: in the north, Bristol has one of the highest concentrations of fee-paying independent schools in the UK, while in the south, many of the state schools suffer from considerable poverty. In 2006, Ros was involved with creating a new academy in south Bristol, and she was particularly shocked to discover that the predecessor school had a failure rate of more than 80% for maths and English. With her team, Ros built strategies to tackle educational inequality, which included setting up the South Bristol Youth charity. In her obituary, it was said: "The work to which Ros committed herself towards the end of her life shows us new ways forward in times when inequalities still disfigure Britain – moving beyond mere outcome measurement to practical, formative support of learning; and beyond institutional isolation and competition to practical, evidence-informed forms of co-operation."[292]

Ros was also a Trustee of the SS Great Britain and, as a mark of respect, the ship flew its flag at half mast upon hearing of her death.

SARAH JANE TANNER
1853-1932, SUFFRAGIST, PACIFIST

Involved in the campaign for votes for women from an early stage, Sarah Jane Tanner lived at 6 Hillside, Cotham, in the 1880s. Among many other responsibilities, she was Vice Chair of the Bristol Women's Liberal Association (a role she shared with Alice Grenfell, since you ask). As early as 1888, the Association was hiring out the Victoria Rooms in Clifton for a 'soiree and public meeting' on the topic of women's liberation, which sounds fun.

In 1932, her obituary summed her up by saying: "The death of Miss Sarah Jane Tanner ... marked the close of a notable chapter of local history. For many years, she was one of the foremost leaders in Bristol of the Constitutional Movement for Women's Suffrage. Through long years of opposition and difficulty and in the face of many rebuffs, her ardent spirit and untiring energy never flagged."[293]

By 1900, Sarah had moved to Beaconsfield Place in Clifton. And by the time of the 1911 census, she was living at 46 Downs Park West, also in Clifton, with her three sisters, all of whom were unmarried. The women lived off 'private means' and employed two servants, which suggests their wholesaler father Samuel had left them a good inheritance.

292 bristol.ac.uk/news/2019/february/ros-sutherland.html
293 'Pioneer in social movements', *Western Daily Press*, 5 March 1932.

These private means allowed Sarah and several of her sisters to commit themselves fully to the suffrage cause. In 1908, alongside Mabel Cross[294], Sarah organised for the Bristol branch of the Women's Reform Union to join the National Union of Women's Suffrage Societies in London, when they marched to the Albert Hall on 13 June 1908. Alongside Mabel, Sarah was Honorary Secretary of the Bristol Suffrage Society until 1913, after which time she held the post on her own. Also in 1913, Sarah and Mabel joined the Women's Suffrage Pilgrimage, although she was attacked by anti-suffragists outside Bath while Mabel hid in a nearby house before escaping disguised as a man.

In 1916, sister Bristolian suffragists Samuella and Josephine Baretti[295] dedicated their volume of poems *Rapture of Death* to Sarah. This lyrical collection was one of a small series that the Baretti sisters published with the Carlyle Press on Park Row. Sarah herself was no stranger to writing. Her short book *How the Suffrage Movement Began in Bristol Fifty Years Ago* was published by Carlyle in 1918, and provides further evidence of the massive amount of work that the suffragists – not to be confused with the suffragettes[296] – did to secure votes for women.

During and after World War One, Sarah became a staunch pacifist and was a supporter of the peace movement. Indeed, she launched the Bristol branch of the Women's International

294 Mabel Cross is profiled in Volume Two of *The Women Who Built Bristol*.
295 Samuella and Josephine Baretti are also profiled in Volume Two of *The Women Who Built Bristol*.
296 I think it is very important that people understand the difference between the suffragists and the suffragettes. In short, the suffragists were the long-standing, peaceful women who had been publicly campaigning for votes for women, for education for women, for women to be recognised as the legal guardians of their own children and for improved career prospects for women (among many other things) since the 1860s. While the suffragettes were the short-lived organisation that is typically linked to the Pankhurst family, the Women's Social and Political Union (WSPU) and to the purple, green and white branding. The suffragettes are the group associated with headline-grabbing antics such as window smashing, arson attacks, destroying priceless artworks, getting arrested, going on hunger strike etc. Many women who had been members of the WSPU left the organisation after a few years because they wanted to distance themselves from the suffragettes' increasingly lawless behaviour. This is, of course, a very simplistic summary and I encourage you to investigate further because it's a very interesting and important distinction to make between the suffragists and the suffragettes.

League for Peace from her home in 1915, and was committed to the League right up until her death.

As an example of the influence and respect that Sarah had, organisations including the National Council of Women, the National Union of Equal Citizenship and the Women's International League all wanted to send floral wreaths to her funeral. However, Sarah had requested that no flowers be sent, so instead the organisations made donations to the Women's Aid Association.

In her obituary, the *Western Daily Press* concluded: "With a perfect genius for friendship and for entertaining, Miss Tanner was a brilliant conversationalist on any of the topics, and there were many, that evoked her interest. Literature was her chief recreation and delight but art and music also appealed to her cultivated tastes, to which only the best was ever attractive. Others have commented, and rightly, on the never-flinching courage with which Miss Tanner followed her ideals in spite of great and ever-increasing disabilities. What always attracted me, however, was the reaching forth of her spirit to that which was fresh and new."[297]

FLORENCE TAYLOR
1879-1969, ARCHITECT

Born Florence Mary Parsons, this young lady went on to become the first qualified female architect in Australia. In 1909, she also became the first woman in Australia to fly in an aircraft. And in 1926, she was the first female member of the Institute of Structural Engineers in the UK.

---

297 'Pioneer in social movements', *Western Daily Press*, 5 March 1932.

She came from humble beginnings though. Her parents John and Eliza Parsons worked in Bedminster as a quarry mason and washerwoman respectively. However, the family migrated to Sydney, Australia in 1884 when Florence was five and things began to change. John was able to get better paying work and, as a result, Florence was able to attend a good school.

By the time she was 20, both of Florence's parents had died and she became the head of the household, which also included two younger sisters. She took a clerical role at an architectural firm to bring in an income. Following evening classes, in 1904 Florence became the first woman to complete her final year studies in architecture in Australia. A number of appointments in architectural firms followed, as did an unsuccessful application in 1907 to be the first female member of the New South Wales Institute of Architects: she would later claim that the all-male membership "blackballed" her application. It would be 1923 before the Institute finally accepted Florence and, in doing so, their first female member.

In 1907, Florence married an inventor named George Taylor. One of his inventions was a 'heavier-than-air' craft and, in 1909, Florence became the first woman to fly such a craft. Between the two of them, they shared a great passion for town planning and creation and they founded the Town Planning Association of New South Wales in 1913. Florence designed around 100 houses in Sydney in the early 1900s and won a number of architectural prizes. Her influence as a town planner is undisputed and has been documented in a number of books celebrating her work. Florence was appointed an OBE in 1939 and a CBE in 1961.[298]

---

298 The suburb of Taylor in Canberra is named in Florence's honour. And a three-storey high portrait of Florence is painted on the side of an apartment building in Sydney that faces a train station.

MAGGIE TELFER
1959-2023, DRUGS CAMPAIGNER

In 1986, Maggie Telfer, who had grown up in Northumberland, co-founded the Bristol Drugs Project in a city that was struggling with a growing heroin problem and a rise in related crime alongside a lack of drugs services in Bristol. This typified her tireless campaigning for health equality in Bristol and elsewhere in the UK.

Prior to that, Maggie had attended university in Swansea and in 1980, after graduating, she managed the Swansea Accommodation for the Single Homeless, which was a night shelter for the homeless.

Bristol Drugs Project continues today and has grown from a modest team of five people in 1985 to more than 80. Maggie became the charity's Chief Executive Officer and worked hard to reduce stigma and to improve health for people, motivated by her beliefs in social justice and human rights. The charity was pioneering in its focus on harm reduction by offering practical and therapeutic support to substance users and worked in that way to try and break the cycle of addiction, crime and imprisonment. This was a groundbreaking approach when Maggie introduced it to Bristol in the mid-1980s.

Under Maggie's guidance, the Bristol Drugs Project opened one of the first needle exchanges in the UK, offered pioneering drugs services for young people, and steered heroin treatment into primary care. In the 1990s, Maggie went on to help set up the first ever needle exchange in Kenya, which still operates today.

Throughout her work, Maggie, who lived in Totterdown, helped to bring about a change in how services related to drug and alcohol misuse evolved along with ever-changing research. Indeed, she contributed to more than 50 peer-reviewed publications. Maggie was awarded an OBE in 2007 for her work in drug and alcohol services.[299]

SARAH and EMILY THOMAS
born 1802, and born 1803, TEACHERS

Despite being little more than children themselves, sisters Sarah and Emily Thomas set up a Ladies' Boarding School which they ran from 7 Portland Square. This was 1825, and Sarah was 23 and Emily was 22. In a newspaper advert in 1825, they stated: "The Misses avail themselves of this medium to convey to their Friends their grateful acknowledgements for the liberal patronage with which they have been favoured."[300] Although teaching was a very respectable business for young women, Sarah and Emily were notably young when they opened their school and it is not known what the circumstances were that led them to take this action. However, Portland Square was a fashionable area of Bristol in the early 1800s and the sisters saw a good turnover of girls at their school. They remained in business until they retired in 1860 and moved away.

IRENE THORNTON
1914-1981, WAR DIARIST

Belgian-born Irene Elizabeth Callens was the second wife to Eric Thornton, who was 22 years her senior and worked in shipping. British Eric met Irene while he was living in Belgium and they relocated to Bristol after their wedding in September 1940 and

---

299 With grateful thanks to Maggie's partner Richard Jones.
300 'Ladies' Boarding School', *Bristol Times and Mirror*, 22 January 1825.

lived here as Belgian refugees. The couple lived at Coombe Lea in Coombe Dingle for much of World War Two, but must have returned to Belgium shortly after peace was declared because Eric died in Antwerp at the end of 1945. But it's what Irene did during the war that is of most interest to us.

During the Sea Mills 100 project in 2019, a 1941 diary written in both French and English came to light, having lived on Deb Britton's bookshelf for many years and largely been overlooked. Deb's grandmother had been Irene's housekeeper at Coombe Lea and it is thought that this is how the diary came into her possession.

The first entry is for 30 December 1940, a few months after Irene's marriage to Eric, and it mentions going to see the new Charlie Chaplin film *The Dictator* at the cinema and meeting friends for dinner. Another entry, which is representative of many, gives an insight into the stress of living during wartime: "3 January 1941: At 6.30pm Air Raid warning. Poor Bristol, another Blitz attack. We spent the whole night in the shelter. The all clear was not given until 6.30am. Loads of boches[301] had come and so much gunfire! What will happen to our beautiful little town that has already been half destroyed?"[302]

But not all entries were so apparently innocuous. A researcher called Andrew Drake studied released MI5 files and Irene's diary, which both made reference to secret agents who used the names Mullet, Puppet and Hamlet. Andrew believes that Mullet was Eric's nephew Ronald Thornton. The three 'double-cross agents' worked together to pass disinformation about the British invasion plans to the Nazis, who believed that the three men were sympathetic to the Nazis... when they were really working for the British government.

301 'Boche' was a derogatory word for a German soldier.
302 seamills100.co.uk/war-stories-sea-mills-coombe-dingle/war-diaries/

In 1956, Irene, who had returned to Belgium, married again, this time to William Schultz at the British Consulate in Hamburg. She died in Antwerp in 1981 and was survived by William.

LIZ TILBERIS
1947-1999, JOURNALIST

An ambitious young woman, Elizabeth Jane Kelly (as she was originally called) from Shirehampton went on to become one of the most impressive fashion magazine editors of her generation. Following an impressive education at Malvern Girls' College and later at Leicester Polytechnic (where she met her future husband, Andrew Tilberis), Liz won an internship to work at *British Vogue* magazine in London after impressing Editor-in-Chief Beatrix Miller with her enthusiasm. This would have been a highly competitive post to have gained.

At *Vogue*, Liz paid her dues by doing everything from making the tea to picking up dress pins from the studio floor before being promoted to the role of Fashion Assistant. In 1988, her *British Vogue* editor Anna Wintour called Liz into her office and said that she was about to leave for New York and offered Liz the job of Editor. Liz gladly accepted and she delighted in watching the magazine's readership soar during her tenure.

Liz's own move to New York came in 1992 when she was offered the job of editing *Harper's Bazaar*. Shortly afterwards, she was diagnosed with ovarian cancer. She attributed this to the years of fertility treatment she had undergone in an unsuccessful attempt to have children (although she and Andrew later adopted two sons). Liz spent the next seven years battling the disease and enduring chemotherapy while continuing to edit *Harper's*. During this time, her friend Diana, the Princess of Wales, handed Liz a special award for her achievements in publishing. The girl from Shirehampton had certainly come a long way.[303]

MARY JANE TIPPETT
1858–1937, HERBALIST

There is an area in Oldland Common known as The Batch, which is between the two villages of Oldham Common and Warmley. Two main families lived here: the Iles and the Tippetts. When Mary Jane Iles married Oliver Tippett in August 1880, the two families became even more closely connected. At the time of the marriage, the Bottom Batch – the area where the Iles and Tippetts lived – consisted of seven cottages, three outside toilets, a stable, a laundry house, a workshop and some pigsties.

Like his father, Oliver manufactured boots for miners, making use of the workshop on the Bottom Batch to do this. With Mary Jane, he had seven children: four boys and three girls. When she wasn't bringing up children, Mary Jane helped her husband and son with the gardens where they grew their own food to eat.

Reportedly, Mary Jane's favourite crop was mint, for which she had a special plot. When it was ready to be picked, she sent the mint to a man called Mr Clark in Oldham Common who distilled it and used the concentrated essence in medicines.

Although Oliver died in 1924, and Mary Jane in 1937, several of their children stayed at the property in The Batch with their own families. This was until the early 1960s, when Warmley Rural District Council placed a Compulsory Purchase Order on the cottages and land for redevelopment into a new area... which is also called The Batch.[304]

303 With thanks to Eugene Byrne for the nomination of Liz Tilberis to this book.
304 Cadbury Heath History Group, 1988, *Life As It Was In Cadbury Heath & Warmley*, p11–13.

JANET TOLMAN
died 2003, ROLLS-ROYCE MANAGER

When Janet Tolman became a Senior Manager at Rolls-Royce she made history by becoming the first woman to fill any level of managerial role within the automotive company. Janet was responsible for the Design Services Department, which involved overseeing the printing, photographic and translation services offered. She was respected for her good judgement, excellent organisational skills and the way that she managed her team.

MARY TOVEY, HELEN TOVEY and ELIZABETH TOVEY
born 1819, born 1821, born 1825, SISTER SUFFRAGISTS

These three strong-willed sisters who lived at Duncan House, Clevedon, were all signatories on the 1866 mass women's suffrage petition. We know little about them except that it seems none of them married and they were funded by an inheritance from their parents. However, for the three of them to unite to sign the historical petition is definitely something worth noting.

ROSEMARY TOWERS
1918-1989, PILOT

Although born in Clifton, Rosemary Leslie Bell (as she was originally known) moved to South Africa with her parents in 1924 and they didn't return to the UK until 1936. Back in Blighty and based in Portsmouth, Rosemary took up work as a secretary and typist before marrying Flight Lieutenant Dorian Bonnett in May 1942. Dorian died in October of the same year when his aircraft crashed in England: he was 23.

By 1945, Rosemary had joined the Air Transport Auxiliary (ATA) and become a ferry pilot, after gaining her Royal Aero Club Pilot's Certificate on 3 October 1945 as part of the ATA's Wings scheme. In 1946 she remarried, this time to fellow pilot Captain Phillip Gibbs. Again, the marriage was brief after Phillip was killed in service. Rosemary married for a final time in 1949 to Richard Towers, with whom she would live in London.[305]

FANNY TOWNSEND
1864-1942, PHILANTHROPIST

Author's note – I stumbled upon 'Miss FM Townsend' while researching Knowle's Open Air School. I'd never heard of her before but something about her immediately caught my attention. I kept on digging, frustrated that it seemed impossible to unravel what those mysterious initials 'FM' stood for. There was no shortage of newspaper reports detailing 'Miss FM Townsend's numerous good works and explaining how highly she was regarded by the Bristolian community, but no hints to anything more personal about her, even when I tried guessing what

---

305 ata-ferry-pilots.org/index.php/category-blog-1944/476-bonnett-rosemary-leslie-w-155

that 'F' might stand for: Florence? Frances? No. A trawl through the Townsends who appeared on the Clifton census reports in the years that Miss FM Townsend was active in the newspapers eventually led me to a few likely candidates and, after a bit of cross referencing, I deduced that she had to be Fanny Maria(n) Townsend.[306] *It's unusual for 'Fanny' to be a first name on its own as it is usually a shortening for 'Frances' but, nonetheless, Miss FM Townsend seems to have been an unusual woman so nothing should surprise us.*

Few good causes in Bristol in the late Victorian and early Edwardian eras were untouched by Fanny Townsend's generous hand. Indeed, upon Fanny's retirement due to ill health in 1933, members of the Bristol Education Committee went so far as to call her "the modern Mary Carpenter", in reference to Bristol's famed social reformer of the Victorian era.[307] Fanny spent an impressive 41 years on the board of the Bristol Education Committee, as well as occupying board posts at many other organisations.

Her father Charles Townsend was a wholesale druggist from Edgbaston who employed a number of men, and the family lived at Cotham Park Avenue House in Westbury-on-Trym. Following Charles' death in 1888, Fanny and her mother Anna Maria lived with two servants at a house called Baycliff on Ivywell Road, Sneyd Park. Neither of them needed to work owing to the healthy sum of money they inherited. This afforded Fanny plenty of time to do good work for others. It would seem she also attended university because some news reports put the letters MA after her name, suggesting she was a Master of Arts.

Education and health were at the top of Fanny's list of priorities and she worked feverishly to do good for others.

306 I can find an almost equal number of references to her middle name being Maria or Marian, so I'm uncertain which is definitively correct.
307 'Busy Man's Summary', *Western Daily Press*, 27 October 1933. Mary Carpenter is profiled in Volume One of *The Women Who Built Bristol*.

Although newspaper reports from 1898 to 1933 frequently refer to Fanny as being in a state of poor health, she kept returning to her charitable duties and clearly she was a determined and single-minded woman.

It would be boring (and use up a ridiculous amount of paper) to list every single organisation that Fanny was involved with because there were so many. But here are a small handful of her roles: Chair of the Blind, Deaf and Special Schools' Committee (1896); President of the Bristol Working Girls Club (1897); promoting the values of evening schools and adult education (1904); Chair of the Industrial and Special Schools Committee (1906); campaigning for a trade school to be opened in Bristol (1908); Honorary Secretary of the Knowle Open Air School (1917); Chair of the Bristol Mental Deficiency Act Committee (1920); and Chair of the Bristol Infant Welfare Association (1926).

Arguably the achievement with which Fanny seemed most proud was the creation of the School for Mothers, of which she was the Chair. The School offered lessons to mothers on subjects such as childcare and nutrition, and over time employed a resident woman doctor in Dr Annie Cornall.[308] Its goal had been to combat infant mortality, and to support mothers from less privileged backgrounds to bring up their babies in clean and nourishing environments. Initially, the School had 10 mothers but this rapidly grew and, in the first five years, it extended across ten locations in Bristol and 1,400 mothers had passed through the doors. At an event in 1915 marking five years of the School, it was noted with affection that: "The chief difficulty on the Education Committee was dealing with Miss Townsend, they could not keep up with her, but after a little time for reflection they saw how wise her proposals were."[309] At this time, World War One was raging

308 Annie Cornall is profiled in Volume Two of The Women Who Built Bristol.
309 'Infant Welfare Work', Western Daily Press, 11 May 1915.

and claiming the lives of so many men that it was more important than ever to help babies grow to adulthood.

In November 1930, after the school had been open for 21 years, Fanny helped expand the school to include the Central Maternity Clinic, offering mothers excellent medical support at a time before the NHS – and free medical care – existed. A tea party celebrating the opening of the maternity clinic, saw around 300 mothers attend with their children, all of whom had benefited from the school's support.[310]

Fanny also became a Justice of the Peace (JP), a role her father Charles had also undertaken. Women had been unable to become JPs in the UK until 1919, and unsurprisingly Fanny was an early adopter when she took up the post in 1921. One report from 1922 has her presiding over a variety of traffic incidents in Bristol, and many more reports feature in the coming years showing Fanny issuing firm but fair reprimands to those who had been caught doing something they shouldn't have.

Acknowledging Fanny's retirement in 1933, which was due to a long period of poor health that saw her move into a nursing home, tributes appeared in various journals and were made by many of the organisations she supported. For instance, the Winford Orthopaedic Hospital, of which Fanny was 'chairman', said it "sustained a great loss" upon her retirement: "For many years Miss Townsend has been prominent in this city in all educational work, and in particular has been closely associated with the welfare and education of the mentally and physically defective. She founded the Knowle Open Air School, the first of its kind in the city ... She has been chairman of the committee dealing with special schools. Miss Townsend was the prime mover in the foundation of the Crippled Children's Aid Society,

310   'Central Maternity Clinic for Bristol', *Western Daily Press*, 29 November 1930.

and when it was decided to move the Orthopaedic Hospital from Grove Road into the country it was chiefly owing to her energy and organisational ability that the Winford Orthopaedic Hospital came into existence. That this was recognised by all was shown by the unanimity with which she was elected its first chairman."[311]

Fanny moved to Clevedon for the final few years of her life and died there in November 1942. The *Western Daily Press* reported that she had been "well known and loved throughout Bristol for her services to children". It continued: "Gifted with a precious personality, she never sought the limelight but went about her good work in a quiet, unassuming manner."

Writing an effusive letter to the *Western Daily Press* in praise of all Fanny had achieved, someone with the initials 'LEC' said: "No need or suffering of any child was ever made known to her in vain. To her large heart and great executive ability was due the founding of Bristol Special Schools, which were some of the first of their kind in the country. Miss Townsend had the vision and courage of a pioneer ... Hundreds of children owe very much to Miss Townsend, whose noble work must not be forgotten."[312]

Fanny's funeral was held at All Saints in Clifton and she was interred in the family's vault at Arnos Vale Cemetery.

NANCY TRICKS
1900-1973, SINGER

Frederick Tricks was a privileged young man thanks to his ancestors having been prominent estate agents in Bristol. This meant that he had ample time to pursue his passion for theatrics, and he was particularly devoted to the Prince's Theatre on Park

311   'Tribute to Miss Townsend', *Western Daily Press*, 5 May 1934.
312   'Miss Townsend: An Appreciation', *Western Daily Press*, 24 November 1942.

Row where he would become Director. This passion was shared by his daughter Nancy Tricks, although the Prince's Theatre was demolished in the Blitz while Nancy was in her prime as a leading lady. Nonetheless, her family was not to be deterred by bombs and instead turned their attention to the Theatre Royal on King Street, now the Bristol Old Vic. Nancy became a popular soprano singer and was the lead in many amateur productions.

DAPHNE TURNER
1918-2012, PHYSICAL EDUCATOR

It is believed that Daphne Turner, who taught at the University of Bristol, became the first ever Director of Physical Education at any British university when she earned that title in 1975.

Having previously worked as a PE teacher in Shropshire, Daphne moved to Bristol in 1948 and worked at the University until her retirement in 1982. She lived on Goldney Avenue in Clifton where she took great pride in her garden.

For the first 15 years of her career, Daphne had only one colleague in the physical education department, meaning that she really had her work cut out: it was only when the University installed a swimming pool in 1963 that the department began to grow in personnel. Daphne was instrumental in developing the University's PGCE course in PE and the teaching of games.

Long after her retirement, Daphne continued to be involved in university life and played badminton at the institution until she was well into her 70s.

EMILY TWIGGS
1848-1930, LADY MAYORESS

Living on Woodstock Road in Redland Green, Emily Twiggs was the Lady Mayoress of Bristol during World War One. Born Emily Gibson and then becoming Emily Barrell, she was a widow when she married a widowed carriage manufacturer called Henry Twiggs in 1899. He was appointed Lord Mayor in 1918 and Emily acted alongside him.

Reporting her death, the *Clifton & Redland Free Press* noted: "Mrs Twiggs, whose valuable work as hostess at the Mansion House during the difficult period immediately following the Great War will be recalled, was a lady of great charm and much beloved among a wide circle of friends."[313] As part of her role, on 4 June 1919 Emily was invited to plant an oak tree alongside the government minister Christopher Addison in Sea Mills when the Bristol Housing Scheme was officially launched: this was one of the first council estates in the UK and was designed to house the returning war heroes. The tree still stands and is known as Addison's Oak.

LILY UTTING and BETTY UTTING
1882-1936 and 1918-2017,
CEMETERY CARETAKERS

When Lily Homer was born in Walsall, Staffordshire, in April 1882, she could have had no idea that she would spend the bulk of her adult life living among the tombstones of a beautiful cemetery in south Bristol.

---

313 'Death of former Bristol Lady Mayoress', *Clifton & Redland Free Press*, 13 November 1930.

Lily married William Utting in Walsall in January 1909 and, by the time their first child arrived the following year, the couple had moved to the South West where they were the superintendents of Arnos Vale Cemetery, living at the cemetery's East Lodge by the main gate on Bath Road. At this time, it was a job requirement that a cemetery superintendent be married, meaning that William's wife Lily was crucial to him securing the post. Baby Alfred came along in 1910, followed by Edna in 1913, Clifford in 1914 and Margaret in 1919, and all four children grew up playing among the gravestones.

In fact, living and working at Arnos Vale became the family's business. Eldest son Alfred went on to take over as the cemetery's superintendent when his father retired, and with his wife Betty they brought up their own family there. Aged 97 in 2015, Betty told the *South Bristol Voice*: "When you live on the premises you have to live for the people who visit ... When you meet people in a cemetery they aren't happy and smiling, you meet people who are heartbroken and in shock."

When Lily and William arrived in 1909, Arnos Vale Cemetery was owned by the Bristol General Cemetery Company, a company with three directors who were solicitors on Corn Street. However, the directors took little interest in the day-to-day running of the cemetery, so William was able to maintain Arnos Vale as he saw fit: "[William] always felt it was his cemetery," said Betty of her father-in-law. In fact, it was William who had the farsighted idea of introducing cremation to Arnos Vale, recognising the need to free up burial space. Although the directors were initially opposed to the idea – they even threatened to sack him in 1927 if he didn't drop the suggestion – Arnos Vale eventually became the first cemetery outside of London to install a crematorium.

One of the rules that the directors *did* impose was that no bicycles or prams were allowed onto the cemetery grounds on a Sunday, and men were stationed on the gates to turn away any visitors who arrived with such wheeled items. Therefore, Lily and, later, Betty would often find visitors at the back door of their lodge on a Sunday, asking if they would mind looking after the baby while they visited the grave of their loved one.

Betty Edgell had grown up in Knowle where her father ran a farm. As a teenager, Betty trained as a hairdresser and loved her work. However, in 1935, Betty's father asked her how she felt about them selling up and moving to Arnos Vale where he would take the post of deputy superintendent, living at the now-derelict lodge off Cemetery Road at the top end of the cemetery. The thought of living in a cemetery didn't much appeal to Betty but she was eventually persuaded. She started working for William in the office and gradually got to know his son Alfred. His mother Lily spotted a spark between the two and invited Betty round for Christmas. Romance blossomed and Betty married Alfred in 1941 and they had two children of their own, Elaine and Howard, who also grew up playing among the gravestones.

Lily died in 1936 and William kept going as superintendent (with his second wife Ethel Weare) until he retired, and then Alfred and Betty assumed the roles of superintendents in his wake. They loved the work and Alfred kept going past the retirement age of 65 until he was 70. Alfred died in 1982 not long after he had retired, and Betty lost not only her job but also her home because the then-owners of the cemetery asked her to move out without a pension to reward her for her decades of dedication to the cemetery. All she was given was Alfred's burial plot, free of charge. Betty moved to a flat in Brislington and later to sheltered accommodation in Knowle.

But the people of south Bristol have much to thank Betty for. For instance, during the 1940s and 1950s, a baby who was stillborn was not given a burial service and instead the small coffins were interred several at a time. But Betty kept track of where the burials took place and, when she moved out of Arnos Vale, she passed this information to the new custodians of the cemetery who erected a plaque near the West Lodge. As a result, grieving parents are able to visit the graves of their children. Betty said in 2015: "I feel like I have come out on top in the end because I feel I have done my job properly and brought a bit of happiness somewhere along the way."[314]

Alfred and Betty's son Howard chose not to work at the cemetery but he was a regular volunteer at Arnos Vale until his own death in 2021, and he contributed a lovely article to *The Guardian* about his experiences of growing up in a cemetery.[315]

JANICE VIRGIN
1951–2014, ADMINISTRATOR

Janice Virgin joined the staff at the University of Bristol in January 1998 as an executive assistant in the Department of Electrical and Electronic Engineering, a department through which she was gradually promoted over the following decade. She then felt it was time for a change and transferred to the Centre for English and Language Studies at the university and then the School for Biological Sciences.

Janice had a major role in the organisation of the visit days, when prospective students could come and take a look around and decide whether to apply for a place at the university. She took on this role at a time of uncertainty in academia, with rising tuition fees and greater competition from other institutions resulting in the University of Bristol facing a 20% drop in the number of

314 Paul Breedon, 'The First Family of Arnos Vale', *South Bristol Voice*, October 2015, p30–32.
315 theguardian.com/lifeandstyle/2015/oct/30/experience-i-grew-up-in-a-cemetery

students, which they could ill afford. Thanks to Janice's ingenuity, the organisation of the visit days was completely revamped to make the school seem even more appealing to students, with guided tours and a welcome pack for visitors among other innovations.

VULCANA
1874-1946, STRONGWOMAN

Miriam Kate Williams was not a woman to be messed with. Born to a preacher in Hotwells, Kate (as she was known) was so naturally strong that she worked in a tannery after leaving school. Aged 14 in 1888, she had the natural strength to stop a runaway horse on Egerton Road, Bishopston, that had got loose and was dragging a woman and child behind it.

When she was 15, Kate met a man called William Roberts who ran the women's gymnasium she attended and she immediately fell in love with him... despite the fact he was 12 years her senior and already had a wife, Alice, and children at his home at 92 Ashley Road. Clearly William felt similarly about Kate because the two set up home together and remained inseparable for the rest of their lives. However, they never married and instead told people they were siblings. Quite how they explained their six children remains unanswered.

William was a strongman who performed in music halls under the name of Atlas. Thanks to his coaching, Kate further built her muscles, emerged as a strongwoman known as Vulcana and the couple developed a touring double act. Their first appearance as Atlas and Vulcana was in London in 1892. Two years later, they appeared together at Bristol's Colston Hall.[316] Another Bristolian appearance was at the Tivoli music hall in January 1896[317], while they performed at Bristol Zoo in August 1900 and made no fewer than six appearances at the Empire Music Hall on Old Market.

Even after Atlas' reputation became tarnished when he was revealed to be lifting weights that were lighter than he claimed, Vulcana managed to shrug off any associated damage and built on the success of her own achievements. She was respected for promoting health and fitness for women, for encouraging mothers to let their daughters climb trees, and for refusing to wear the fashionable yet restrictive corsets that she understood were physically damaging. She was a petite 5ft 4" but could lift weights of 140lbs above her head with just one arm. Photos survive of Vulcana lifting an adult woman above her head, again using only one arm. On one occasion in Bristol, she went up against a professional male wrestler at a circus and ended up throwing him all the way over her head.

Both Vulcana and Atlas retired in 1932. However, Vulcana was hit by a car in London in 1939, and was just regaining consciousness when she heard herself being declared dead. Vulcana lived for another few months after the accident.[318]

DALE WAKEFIELD
1941–2020, ACTIVIST

Born in Bishopston during World War Two and later attending Marksbury Road School, Billie Dale Wakefield became a

316   While I acknowledge the Colston Hall has now rightly been renamed and is now called the Bristol Beacon, I am referring to it by its original name in this book because that is the name it was known by when the events in the book happened.
317   Ada Mansell, who briefly owned the Tivoli, has her own entry in this volume.
318   With thanks to Eugene Byrne for the nomination of Vulcana to this book.

prominent campaigner for lesbian and women's rights in Bristol during the 1970s and 1980s. Although her professional career was in finance, education and nursing, Dale is best remembered for her activism.

Dale had married and had two children with her husband, but the marriage broke down when the youngest child was only a few months old. She then went to London where she worked as a prison officer at Holloway. It was here that Dale first fell in love with a woman. She returned to Bristol in the early 1970s, came out as a lesbian and became active in the second wave of the Women's Movement. Alongside the artist Monica Sjöö[319] and others, Dale started the Gay Women's Group and, for three years, they produced a magazine called *Move*.

While attending a Gay Women's Group meeting in Clifton, Dale noticed the phone was ringing constantly: the callers were gay men and lesbians in need of information, advice and support. This highlighted the need for a dedicated phone line for lesbians and gay men, so Dale promptly set up the Bristol Lesbian & Gay Switchboard from her home in Hill Street, Totterdown, using her own phone number. It started taking calls on 1 February 1975, only 11 months after the London Lesbian and Gay Switchboard had been started.

The Switchboard ran from Dale's house for three years, with volunteers assisting her to answer the calls during advertised hours. Outside of these times, Dale responded to calls with her friend Annie Smith, and to maintain the anonymity of their callers they would use a nearby telephone box to ring an ambulance if a caller had attempted to harm themselves.

By 1978, the Switchboard had grown so big that it moved to a new base at the Bristol Gay Centre on Gasferry Road, although

---

319 Monica Sjöö is profiled in Volume One of *The Women Who Built Bristol*.

Dale remained central to its operation until 1983 when the Centre closed. The Switchboard operated for 37 years, closing in February 2012 with any subsequent calls directed to the London Lesbian & Gay Switchboard. In 2013, the M Shed Museum included Dale's former dining room table in an exhibition in recognition of the fact that this table had been the original headquarters of the Bristol Lesbian & Gay Switchboard. Dale also helped to organise Bristol Lesbian Line, she was a founder of Bristol Pride in 1977, and she was involved with Women's Aid, which provides refuge to women escaping domestic violence.

Outstories Bristol wrote: "Dale remained a resolute advocate of women and men working together at a time when there was a lesbian-separatist trend within the movement in Bristol. A believer in collective approaches to action, she was critical of the hierarchies that characterised orthodox and male-oriented ways of organising. Her quiet authority, clear focus and belief in the power of collective action made her one of the most significant figures in the story of LGBT rights in Bristol."[320]

Her friend Tim Manning, who also worked on the Switchboard, told the BBC: "She was completely fearless, and saved lives because a lot of people who phoned were about to kill themselves. People called us and asked if we were gay, and there was a stunned silence because they'd never spoken to another gay person before. They were terrified of coming out, and we had to be careful with what we said because the police were monitoring our line in case we gave people cruising advice. There's no doubt Dale was one of the quiet heroes of Bristol's LGBT community."[321]

Dale also supported the miners' strike and opposed the Gulf War. She lived in Knowle until the end of her life.

320 outstoriesbristol.org.uk/2020/09/remembering–dale–wakefield/
321 bbc.co.uk/news/uk-england-bristol-54112171

MARTHA WAKEFIELD
1784-1878, SOUTHVILLE SCAVENGER

This Bedminster woman deserves to go down in local legend for her role as 'The Southville Scavenger'. But who was she?

Martha Paulins married John Wakefield in 1805 and the couple had seven children, including son Samuel who we will meet shortly. John died in 1835, leaving Martha to bring up the family on her own and to turn to any means necessary to do so.

She lived at Northfield in Southville and was considered the area's "most zestful early lady". Along with her son Samuel, she was appointed as the Southville Scavenger in 1851, the logic being that one man's rubbish is another woman's treasure. The census of that year lists her as having four labourers in her employment. While in the 1861 census, Martha is listed as living at 57 North Street with Samuel, as well as another son William and daughter Elizabeth.

Martha and Samuel would skim through the debris left behind by various businesses and see what they could repurpose and/or sell. It turned out to be a pretty lucrative business and the pair were also working under contract to the Board of Health as well as the Pitching & Paving Commissioners. Martha had no concerns about her reputation, although this was not a business that would be typically associated with a lady in the mid-1850s. Her name would regularly appear in the *Journals and Sanitary Complaints Minutes*. For instance, in 1851 it was recorded that there were complaints about the bad smells coming from the Wakefields' yard. The *Bristol Times & Mirror* reported on 1 February 1851: "Caution to Scavengers: Last Wednesday, Martha Wakefield and Samuel Wakefield, contractors, were fined by the Magistrates in two separate penalties of £5, and costs, for neglecting to sweep and cleanse Redcliff–hill and Temple–backs, as per contract.

The informations were laid in consequence of the numerous complaints of the inhabitants."

And a police report from 1853 explains how the Wakefields had been charged with depositing a large quantity of ash on Dean Lane. They were still at it in 1854, when a court report in the *Bristol Mercury* on 19 August 1854 states that the pair were in "violation of their contract' when they neglected to sweep up the ashes they had left behind on King Street in the city centre: "The defendants pleaded guilty and, this not being the first complaint of the kind made against them, they were fined 20s and costs." It was noted at this hearing that "many complaints" had been received about Martha and Samuel's approach to sanitation and that "in these times of imminent disease" the Wakefields' contract should be "strictly enforced". The local newspapers are actually, ahem, littered with reports of the Wakefields breaching cleanliness codes.

As time went on, the growing population of Southville made an increasing number of complaints about the sanitation and smells from the Wakefields' yard and, by the end of the 1880s, Samuel had ceased scavenging and set up what would be one of the first shops on Stackpool Road.[322]

LIZZIE WALKER
dates unknown, UNOFFICIAL MIDWIFE

As a baby, Elizabeth 'Lizzie' Walker was a foundling: an infant who had been abandoned on a doorstep. This means that nobody knew her real name or about her family of origin; she was handed in to an orphanage and given the name of Elizabeth. Lizzie stayed

322 CLASS, 2004, *Southville People and Places*, Fiducia Press, p38.

in the orphanage until she was old enough to be sent to work in service, which was the typical career path for children with no families of their own.

We know Lizzie's story in a rather second–hand way: she lived next door to Rebecca Saunders[323] and the two were good friends. So Lizzie confided her story to Rebecca, who later shared it with her own daughter, Winifred Harris, who in turn shared it with the Windmills of Time history project.

While in service, Lizzie met a young man and they married. She became Elizabeth Walker and they moved to Philip Street, Bedminster. It is thought that Lizzie must have learned a few things about delivering babies and caring for young children while she was in service, because she seemed to know about childbirth. She was in great demand in the Philip Street area and was often called upon to act as a 'handywoman' for her neighbours: 'handywoman' was the term given to a woman who acted as an unofficial midwife. Reportedly, she always had her snow-white apron at the ready and was primed to go to the house of any woman who needed her.

"For a modest sum she delivered the baby and then called twice a day for the two weeks 'laying-in' period, to care for the mother and bathe the baby," wrote Winifred. "By modern standards it seems odd, but at this time the only rest period a mother had was after the birth of a child. With a close-knit community, neighbours and relatives would rally round to care for the rest of the family. It was said that Lizzie never lost a mother and that her husband kept a book as a record of all the children she brought into the world."

The 1902 Midwives Act introduced training and supervision for midwives in England and Wales, and outlawed women such

323 Rebecca Saunders has her own entry in this volume.

as Lizzie who were uncertified and untrained. There was a small amount of money available to support some handywomen to train for the official certification, but Lizzie felt that she was too old to do this and so she stopped work. Despite no longer being allowed to deliver babies, many local women still wanted Lizzie there when they gave birth and called for her to assist them in the days after the birth. Winifred recalls how Lizzie was present when Winifred's sister gave birth in 1911 and that the doctor who helped with the birth gave Lizzie a coin in appreciation of her help. Winifred remembers: "As he left he gave her a tip and she kept exclaiming with joy: 'He gave me a shillin'!."[324]

MARY WALLBRIDGE
1898-1987, ARISTOCRAT

As the daughter of Bristol's renowned architect Sir George Oatley (the Wills Memorial Building at the University of Bristol at the top of Park Street is one of his creations), Mary Whiddon Oatley (as she was originally called) lived a privileged life. Acknowledging this, she wrote about her youth in a booklet called *A Clifton Childhood*, in which she looked back affectionately on her early years and lamented how difficult she felt it must be for children in contemporary life.

One of four children to George and his wife Edith, Mary grew up at "the enormous" Church House in Clifton. It was a massive property with around 20 rooms, of which 10 were bedrooms. As was typical for wealthy children in the Victorian and Edwardian era, Mary was brought up by a live-in nanny until she was 12, and the attic nursery was the childrens' domain in the house. "The

324 windmillsoftime.wordpress.com/2014/03/03/bedminsters-backstreets-part-3/

nursery was a thing apart. We children lived there and played there. When we went downstairs we were made tidy in a clean muslin frock – that was 5 o'clock each day, after nursery tea, for half an hour. Lunch was always in the nursery till you were old enough to behave. I remember going down to lunch, sitting on a high chair and longing to talk. Nanny stood behind me and every time I opened my mouth she shoved a spoon inside – seen and not heard was the rule."

And Nanny wasn't the only help in the house, as you might imagine for a property of that size. There were also three maids as well as a cook, parlourmaid, housekeeper and a charwoman called Brownie who worked for Edith for more than 50 years. Oh, and two coachmen. The Oatleys clearly wanted for nothing, even during the difficult war years.

But the children were not always kept at a distance from their parents. George enjoyed walking and cycling, and sometimes he would take train journeys with his family, putting their bicycles on the train and then cycling to visit churches and other notable buildings around the countryside.

When she was four in 1902, Mary was sent to Clifton High School where, in 1927, her father would be commissioned to design a new wing. Mary's headteacher was the redoubtable Eleanor Addison Phillips[325], but Mary was one pupil who wasn't a fan of her teacher. She claims that Miss Phillips preferred the "pious, good girls", of which Mary was not one – going so far as to accuse Mary of once stealing two pence: "I've never forgotten it," Mary wrote indignantly. Anaemia caused Mary to miss three terms of school, during which time she shared a governess with another girl and the two of them enjoyed lessons in the mornings and playing on the Downs all afternoon, or sliding down the

---

325 Eleanor Addison Phillips has her own entry in this volume.

rocks by the Avon Gorge.

On Sundays, Mary would help at the Sunday School at the Broad Plain Lads' Club on Anvil Street, which was attended by 150 children from less fortunate homes. The school had been started by Mary's father George and was largely attended by children from the slum housing nearby: it was quite a culture shock for Mary. In her memoirs, Mary recalls her father reprimanding her for questioning why he tipped his hat to the women they passed in the slums, which was a sharp lesson about being less judgmental.

It was a relief for Mary when, in 1913, she was sent away to boarding school in Richmond and she could form her own identity there. However the lessons in good behaviour never stopped and even at the age of 18, she was sent to bed with no supper by her father for questioning why they had invited wounded soldiers coming to tea that afternoon.

Aged 18, Mary began courting William (known as Pat) Garnett, a Lieutenant in the Royal Flying Corps, with whom she had been friends since they were children. But there were strict rules to be adhered to, especially as far as Pat's very Victorian mother was concerned. When she once saw Mary and Pat walking up Park Street arm in arm, Pat's mother ordered them never to do such a thing again: that was how servants behaved!

When the couple became engaged at the age of 18, their parents ordered them not to marry until they were 21 but, at Pat's insistence, the couple married in January 1917. Pat knew that his role in the Flying Corps was dangerous and the chances of survival for a pilot were slim. "After we were married, we had just a month together. Pat had to go to the Front. A few weeks later we had a message that he was missing, no details. Then in July 1917 I received a small parcel posted in Germany. It was in brown paper. It contained the chain Pat always wore, my last two letters, a piece of my wedding frock and a piece of the frock I wore when we became engaged. I knew the worst. He must be dead." She later found out that Pat had been shot down by the Red Baron, von Richtofen on 20 March 1917, whose habit was to go to the body of anyone he killed and retrieve personal items to send to the deceased's relatives.

Her second marriage was in July 1919, to Arthur Wallbridge, and for a time Mary and Arthur went to live in South Africa. With Arthur she had two daughters, Alice and Elizabeth. When they returned to England, the family lived in Bridgwater where Arthur worked as a town planning officer and Mary ran the home. Arthur died in 1964 and Mary survived him until 1987.[326]

IRENE TOYE WARNER–STAPLES
1882–1954, ASTRONOMER, WRITER

One of the first women to be elected as a Fellow of the Royal Astronomical Society (FRAS), Irene Warner is a fascinating character who has some interesting beliefs... particularly about the spiritual world.

Born Irene Elizabeth Toye Warner in Bristol, she was the only child to parents Amelia and Wyclif. The family lived at a house called Ardagh (previously called Poplar Cottage, 'Ardagh' is Gaelic for 'high view') on Horfield Common. The Warner family moved out in 1920, at which point Bristol Council purchased the estate of the house and five-and-a-half acres of land and redeveloped it for community use. In 1926, the *Western Daily Press* reported that the house "where Miss Irene Warner did so much of her astronomical work had "vanished", with the grounds since transformed into a series of terraces and paths leading to the tennis courts. The

---

326 Mary Wallbridge, 1987, *A Clifton Childhood*, self-published.

paper deemed it to now be "one of the most agreeable pleasure spots of the city"[327].

In the 1901 census, her former-architect father Wyclif's profession was listed as simply "thriving on own money" which indicates there was plenty of time for the Warners to indulge their various pursuits. Indeed, the census confirms the family also had a number of staff to make life even more comfortable.

Irene was one of only five women to be elected to the Royal Astronomical Society in 1916, making her one of the very first women to be given the title of FRAS. She was also listed as a 'compounded member', which meant she had life membership of the Society. Irene had been making her name in the astronomical world since 1907, when she began writing a monthly column for the *Western Daily Press* on the topic, which might explain why some sources refer to her as a journalist rather than an astronomer. She went on to publish a volume of astronomical poetry in 1912 called *In Light & Darkness: Hope!,* which was dedicated to 'WF Denning': William Frederick Denning being the well respected Bristolian amateur astronomer who had initially nominated Irene for election to the Royal Astronomical Society.

Irene was a member of a handful of other astronomical societies, too, including the Astronomical Society of Wales in 1910, which she joined soon after its formation. And her interests were varied from early on in her career: for instance, in January 1910 she wrote an article called 'Ancient History and Worship of the Planet Venus' for *The Cambrian Natural Observer*, and in September 1912 she wrote another entitled 'The Religion of Ancient India'. The articles are detailed and full of meticulous research, showing Irene's absolute passion for her subjects.

She was also a member of the Women's Social and Political

327 'A transformation scene', *Western Daily Press*, 24 April 1926.

309

Union, which was the militant organisation led by the Pankhurst family that campaigned for votes for women.

In 1920, Irene married her cousin Albert Staples who was 25 years her senior, becoming Irene Toye Warner–Staples in the process. Albert lived in South Africa but had been visiting the UK and they stayed in Bristol for the first ten years of their marriage. The death date of Irene's father Wyclif is not known, but it seems safe to presume that his death would have been around 1930 and this prompted Irene and Albert's decision to set sail for Cape Town with Irene's mother Amelia.

In an article looking back at the early women of the Royal Astronomical Society, Sue Bowler wrote in 2016: "Warner's popular writing gave astronomical observations a strong cultural context; she told her readers about historical references to astronomical events such as apparitions of Halley's Comet. Warner's wide interests meant that, alongside classical ideas about the constellations, she also discussed Indian and Australian Aboriginal interpretations of the sky."[328]

In Cape Town, Irene continued to write about and study astronomy for a variety of journals both in South Africa and the UK. She also published a number of books about the occult and magic, which was very fashionable at the time, and had papers published in the *Occult Review* in Africa, America and Australia. But this was not a new subject for her: in 1928, Irene had written a book entitled *Critics of the Christ Answered by Spiritualism*. Equally, on 27 October 1928, the publication *Light: A Journal of Psychic, Occult and Mystical Research* was describing Irene as "a valued contributor to our pages ... as a writer on physical matters of which she has an intimate knowledge".

In 1929, following Albert's death two years before, Irene

328 Sue Bowler, 'Observers, writers, teachers...' in *A&G*, August 2016.

returned to the UK. She visited Cardiff where she contributed to a three-part BBC radio travelogue called 'Trekking by Caravan in South Africa', which was also published as a book entitled *Through the Cape by Caravan and Car*. This followed a journey she had undertaken with her mother Amelia and aunt Ada in a caravan driven alternately by oxen and horses. She then stayed in Bristol for a number of years, settling at Shortgrove House, 62 Worrall Road, Clifton, where she lived with Amelia and Ada. It is for this reason that she again returns to the pages of the Bristol newspapers, where she writes articles about the occult and spiritualism, and patiently pens letters explaining why readers who have written in to doubt her are wrong: "There is no conflict between Christianity and Spiritualism, and never has there been through the ages; nor is there between those two and modern science."[329] And again, years later: "Let me warn 'Agnostic' [who had written a letter refuting her claims about psychic mediums] not to frivol over it, but to conduct experiments in a serious, scientific manner. Many people have mediumistic power which could be cultivated and scientifically tested."[330]

Irene returned to Cape Town for a final time in 1936, presumably after the death of her mother Amelia, and she continued writing and publishing up until her death in South Africa in 1954.[331]

329 Irene Toye Warner–Staples, 'Objections to Spiritualism answered', *Western Daily Press*, 9 February 1920.
330 Irene Toye Warner–Staples, 'Many have the power', *Western Daily Press*, 28 February 1934.
331 With thanks to Eugene Byrne for the nomination of Irene Toye Warner-Staples to this book.

HELEN WATTS
1881-1972, SUFFRAGETTE, NURSE

Granted, Helen Kirkpatrick Watts is really a woman who built Nottingham but… the Bristol Docks played an important role in us learning more about this extraordinary suffragette's story. So here she is. She's one of us.

In the early 1980s, around ten years after Helen's death, a dockworker in Avonmouth unearthed a crate that had been received at the Docks several years earlier and never claimed. Inside, were Helen's letters, speeches and a range of suffrage memorabilia including her Women's Social and Political Union (WSPU) hunger strike medal. Thankfully, this treasure trove was not thrown in a skip but handed over to a schoolgirl who had placed an advert in a local newspaper asking for information about the women's suffrage campaign for a history project at school. A man from the Docks contacted the girl to let her know about Helen's unclaimed crate, which had originally been sent from an address in Canada (Helen had emigrated to Canada in 1965, although she returned to the UK shortly before her death in Somerset in 1972). With the help of a teacher, the girl arranged for the contents of the crate to be given to the Nottinghamshire Archives and, as a result, the city of Nottingham came to understand so much more about Helen than they would have done otherwise.

Even aside from her astonishing life after death, Helen's suffrage story is extraordinary. Born to a religious family in County Durham, Helen was the eldest of eight children and the family moved to Nottingham when she was 12. As a girl, Helen had an interest in helping young women to better themselves, as demonstrated by an essay she wrote for the *Girls' Realm* magazine in favour of education for women. Her parents were in support of women's suffrage and were early members of the East Midlands

Federation of the National Union of Women's Suffrage Societies and offered up the church hall for several suffrage meetings, some of which Helen attended.

She joined the WSPU in 1907 after hearing Christabel Pankhurst speak in Nottingham, and her sister Alice Watts also worked for the WSPU in the city. But 1909 was Helen's year of suffrage activism. She took part in a number of protests, was arrested three times, imprisoned for the cause twice and underwent a 90-hour hunger strike for which she received the WSPU medal found in her crate. Helen was much in demand as a public speaker for the cause because of her balanced views, despite having a hearing impairment and a strong accent. After her release from prison, Helen said: "We must come down from the various little pedestals on which we have been mounted by birth and education and forget everything but the fact that we are part of humanity, fighting for a human right, on absolutely simple and straightforward principles."[332]

Becoming alarmed by the WSPU's increasing militancy and lawlessness, Helen left that organisation and instead joined the Women's Freedom League. A photograph survives from 1911, showing Helen planting a juniper tree at the Suffragette Arboretum in Batheaston.[333] In May 1962, she made a return visit to Batheaston; out of the 60 women who planted a tree or bush in the Suffrage Arboretum, Helen is the only one who is known to have revisited the garden after the vote was won in 1928.[334] While the arboretum was overgrown and on the verge of being bulldozed,

332 goldstarguides.com/blog/?post=helen-kirkpatrick-watts
333 For more information about the Suffrage Arboretum, please see the entry for Emily and Mary Blathwayt in Volume One of *The Women Who Built Bristol*.
334 This is mere conjecture, but I don't think it was necessarily a lack of interest that stopped most women from returning to the Suffrage Arboretum in Batheaston. Instead, mother Emily Blathwayt died in 1940 and daughter Mary Blathwayt died in 1962 and, from the war years, both lived a quiet and unassuming life of relative poverty in only a small number of rooms at Eagle House. It is likely they had withdrawn from public life and simply lost contact with most of their former comrades.

Helen was pleased to see that her juniper was still alive. The local paper noted: "Her plaque is missing, all attempts to find it have been unsuccessful, but her tree is still there, easily identified from the photographs she has of the original planting."[335]

By 1911, Helen had left Nottingham and was living in Somerset with her married brother and his family. During World War One, suffrage activities were largely paused and during this time Helen trained as a nurse and worked as such in Bath. She later became a civil servant at the Ministry of Pensions. The Nottingham Women's History Group planted a juniper tree in Helen's honour in 2017, adding a commemorative plaque in 2019.

EMILY WEBB
1859-1935, MAGISTRATE

Women were not eligible to become magistrates until 1919 when the House of Commons passed the Second Reading of the Sex Disqualification (Removal) Bill, so Emily Ann Webb was certainly breaking new ground in her actions when she became Bristol's first female JP. Until this point, there was a great deal of resistance from men to women joining their profession. For instance, Lord Walshingham, himself a magistrate, complained: "Women have not the judicial mind. Their more sensitive souls are always hampered by some sentimental consideration to the doom of justice."[336]

Unlike many of her contemporaries who came from comfortable backgrounds and families which afforded them the luxury to spend their time contributing to the community, Emily

335 Quoted in Cynthia Hammond, 2012, *Architects, Angels, Activists and the City of Bath 1765-1965*, Routledge, p185.
336 lawgazette.co.uk/women-in-the-law/the-indomitable-100-years-of-women-magistrates/5102575.article

came from a more humble home. She lived at 14 Carlton Park, Whitehall, with her husband Alfred, who worked as a railway signalman, and their sons Arthur and Reginald, who also worked on the railways. Emily did not take paid employment but she certainly was not idle: there were a great number of good causes in Bristol that benefited from her patronage.

One such organisation was the Women's Guardians' Society, founded in 1881, which was concerned with the poor state of working-class housing and saw Emily work alongside such notable figures as Mary Clifford and Elizabeth Sturge.[337] However, while women such as Mary and Elizabeth were early Guardians, Emily was one of the new generation to join the organisation when she did so around the early 1900s. The Guardians were generally middle-class women with good connections, although they came from a range of backgrounds in terms of age, faith and politics. The one thing all these women had in common was a desire to make a significant improvement to civic culture.

Other organisations that benefitted from Emily's support were the Public Assistance Committee (which provided paid work for the unemployed), the Blind Asylum Committee (promoting the welfare of visually impaired people), the Civic League (an early form of social work), and she was one of the founders of the Railway Women's Guild (supporting the widows and orphans of railway workers). Additionally, in 1929 Emily became a City Councillor for St George West, and at the time of her death she was the Chair for the St George Ward Labour Women's Section.

By the time Emily died in July 1935, she was a widow who had also buried both of her sons; the heartbreak she must have felt is unimaginable. She is buried at Avon View Cemetery, St George. Her funeral was held on what would have been her 78th birthday

337 Mary Clifford and Elizabeth Sturge are both profiled in Volume One of *The Women Who Built Bristol*.

and was attended by dignitaries including the Lord Mayor Alderman HJ Maggs and many of Emily's fellow City Councillors and Magistrates. In his address, Alderman Frank Sheppard said that he thought no one who had met Emily could have failed to love her: "It has been my privilege to have known Mrs Webb for about 40 years. I have never found her wanting in her willingness to render service to her fellow creatures in one way or another. There was nothing of lip-service about her work, she got down to it and did it with the greatest possible sincerity. Whatever there is great in our race at the present time is largely attributable to women of the type of Mrs Webb. She was a truly fine type of English motherhood."[338]

FLORENCE WEEKS
1909-1993, COTTON FACTORY WORKER

Barton Hill is an area that was developed to house the many people working at the nearby Great Western Cotton Works, which opened in 1838. Florence Weeks was one of the last surviving women to have worked in the factory.

Florence Louisa Ackerman (as she was born) grew up with her parents and four siblings at 44 Barton Street, Barton Hill. Her father William worked as a stoker for the Royal Navy and was often away from home, and her mother, also called Florence, kept things running in his absence. Young Flo started work at the Great Western Cotton Works in 1922 when she was 13.

Looking back on her experiences there, she told the Voices of the Past project: "I started work in what was known as the winding room. This was winding bobbins from the larger spools

---

338 'Striking tributes to city's first woman JP', *Western Daily Press and Bristol Mirror*, 9 July 1935.

316

of cotton. I was in charge of 16 to 20 winding machines. I didn't like this work so I applied for a job in the weaving shed. I had to earn my money by piece work. The wage amounted to about 15 shillings to £1 10d. I started at 7am until 6pm and 7am till 12pm on Saturdays.

"The noise of the machines was deafening so you could not hold a conversation with another worker. You just had to shout as loud as possible. It was hard and tiring work as you had to stand up all day long with just a short walk from one loom to another. Steam pipes ran the whole length of the sheds, so there was a damp atmosphere. At the end of the week there was three to four inches of cotton fluff on the looms.

"I didn't go home in my dinner hour but my mother would send my sister to me with either a 2d lot of fish and chips or faggots and peas in a basin. I used to eat them as quickly as possible, then I would clean the older women's machines. Sometimes I would get 2 shillings for cleaning eight machines."[339]

In 1932, when she was 23, Flo married Joseph Weeks, who was known as John.

ENID WETHERED
1907-2005, ACTIVIST

The daughter of Judge Wethered, Enid Mary Wethered strived to achieve social change on her own account. She grew up at Fort Lodge, 11 The Avenue, Clifton (the property is now called Wethered House) as an only child and, thanks to her father's work as a Solicitor and Magistrate, they were comfortable and had a number of servants. Judge Wethered was so respected that he was

339 voicesofthepast.org.uk/women–that–made–barton–hill/j6tujc4u1lezgs446llefv0c54gl1s

entrusted to host members of the royal family when they visited the city.

Taking inspiration from her mother Jessie, Enid was also involved in good works. For instance, she was involved with the Guiding in Bristol organisation, which was a forerunner of the Girl Guides. Enid and Jessie also had strong links to the Folk House in Bristol, which had been set up in 1887 to provide education and support to the more deprived people in Bristol. On the same lines, Enid and Jessie took an active interest in social work in Bristol, particularly concerning infant welfare. In August 1937, Enid was one of four women to be appointed as Magistrates in Bristol, bringing the total of women acting as Justice of the Peace in the city up to 12. In 1942, Enid married an Office Manager called Rodney Motson. They lived with her parents at Fort Lodge but later moved to Surrey.

EDITH WHEELWRIGHT
1868-1949, SUFFRAGIST

Rejecting the militancy of the Women's Social and Political Union (WSPU), of which she had been a member, Edith Grey Wheelwright instead aligned with the peaceful campaigning organisation of the National Union of Women's Suffrage Societies while lobbying for votes for women. Between 1910 and 1912, Edith was the Secretary of the Bath branch and lived at 52 Sydney Buildings. She became a regular and prominent speaker for the suffrage movement around this time.

Born in Surrey, Edith studied botany and geology at the University of Oxford before moving to Bath with her mother Caroline following the death of her father. In 1890, she won a competition with an essay entitled 'The Intellect of Women'.

Developing her skill for writing, Edith spent the late Victorian era as a novelist, with three books to her name: *The Vengeance of Medea* (1894), *Anthony Graeme* (1895) and *A Slow Awakening* (1902).

However, Edith's strong desire to help secure votes for women led her to put writing to one side for the next few decades and focus on campaign work. In 1910, she planted a bush at the Suffragette Arboretum in nearby Batheaston. Unusually for a suffragist, Edith did not boycott the 1911 census however she does list her occupation on the document as: "Voluntary work in women's suffrage and educational movement", making her position quite clear.

After the outbreak of World War One and the cessation of suffrage campaigning, Edith returned to botany. She lived for a while in Buckingham and worked at a medical herb farm. Her enthusiasm for botany led her to strike up a friendship with the children's author and illustrator Beatrix Potter, to whom she dedicated her 1939 book *The Physick Garden*; a tome which was republished in 1974 and remains available today.

However, Edith's life after she left the suffrage movement was not without trouble. In October 1912, there is a newspaper report detailing how Edith was attacked while walking to visit a friend, chloroform was used to knock her unconscious and a pearl and emerald ring (in WSPU colours) was stolen from her finger. No other jewellery was taken and her handbag and purse remained untouched, leading me to wonder if this was a threat made towards Edith's suffrage views. Edith employed a "lady detective" to look into the case after her suspicions were raised by an Irish woman, Emily Manning, who had sent Edith some libellous letters. Emily eventually admitted to the attack but she died before any sentence could be passed. Edith was reunited with her stolen ring.[340]

A few months later, another report covers how a passer-by found Edith unconscious beside the canal in Bath where she had been studying the weeds before she slipped and fell into the water.

In the early 1930s, Edith moved to Clevedon, where she lived for the final two decades of her life, before being found dead in front of the gas cooker in her kitchen. The inquest recorded an accidental death from coal gas poisoning that was sadly attributed to the forgetfulness for which Edith had become known in her later years.[341]

MAY WHITBY
born c1910, CINEMA READER

Growing up near the Malago in Bedminster, May Whitby had two older siblings but they were orphaned after their mother died following a backstreet abortion.[342] Their father was a veteran from World War One and didn't feel able to look after the children himself so, with the support of an allowance from the government, the children were placed in the care of a local widow, Maimee, who was a friend of the family.

Going to the cinema was a treat for young May but, with little money to spare, she was used to making do with the hard wooden seats in the gallery, until a trip with her older friend Flossie who was on a date. Flossie's date paid for them all to sit on the comfortable plush seats in the stalls: "It was a revelation," May later wrote during a Broadsides' writers' workshop.

340 'Chloroformed on roadside', *Evening Despatch*, 9 January 1913.
341 With thanks to the research of Helen Hobbs: docs.google.com/document/d/1-Att6xrc9EQbPxSld FJ4QCZrLPF3ac4cFxv_32hEzpE/edit
342 Abortion was not legal in England until April 1968. The avoidable deaths of thousands of women such as May's mother demonstrates why the change in law was so essential.

The cinema would become a regular part of May's life after two women who lived on her street and who were illiterate asked her to accompany them to the cinema and read out the title cards that appeared between the scenes in the silent movies. The women were Mrs Brown and Mrs Derrick and, as compensation, they paid for May's ticket. Sometimes they also gave her sweets afterwards – but never during the film, as sucking a sweetie might interfere with her ability to read outloud and then they might lose track of what was happening.

Mrs Brown was May's favourite of the two because she didn't notice if May skipped a few lines from the cards and she didn't mind if May ignored the credits and cast list. If May ever became tearful by a sad story, Mrs Brown would simply wait until May had composed herself before asking her to keep reading.

But Mrs Derrick was more demanding. Wanting to get her money's worth from May, Mrs Derrick wanted all of the credits to be read aloud, and somehow she seemed to know if May ever tried to miss a line.

However, not everyone was a fan of having a reader in the cinema. Some people, who could read the cards for themselves, found it annoying having everything narrated for them and would shout out: "Aw shut up, put a sock in it!" While others, who were also illiterate, quickly grew to recognise May as 'the reader' and, when they saw she was in the cinema, would flock to sit nearby so that they could also benefit from having the cards read outloud, sometimes demanding that she speak up.

Looking back on her time as a cinema reader, May said: "If the film was funny there was no need for me to read, the laughter around would have drowned out my voice. I loved to see the audience rocking backward and forward on the wooden benches, helpless with laughter. I always tried to get a glimpse of them. To see them all absorbed so completely and forgetting for a while their own cares and surroundings immensely intrigued me."

After leaving school in 1922, May went to work at the Will's tobacco factory in Ashton, which was considered the best employer around and therefore one of the most difficult to get in with. When she was called for her job interview, May was asked to bring a needlework sampler with her to demonstrate her neatless and her ability to focus. And, when she was offered the job on a month's trial, it was on the condition that she agreed to be vaccinated. May worked in the packing department, feeding cigarettes into a machine for them to be boxed up for sale. As a small and slight young girl, May found the physical labour hard going, and her hands were too small to gather up enough cigarettes to keep the machine fed.

When your monthly wage depended on how much work you accomplished, there was no room for May to make errors. But she found one way to compensate her colleagues for helping with any slippages she might have made in her work was to keep them entertained with the stories from the novels she read each night: yet again, finding that reading helped her to make her way in the world. Soon, word spread through the factory that May could tell these wonderful stories to her co–workers and different departments started asking for her to be loaned to their floor for an hour or two so that they could also hear the stories. "I was obliged to always be ready with three or four chapters, sometimes of different books, and I never let the girls down. The repetition was boring but I revelled in my popularity and the acceptance of my inadequacy as a machinist."[343]

343 May Whitby, 1988, 'A Sort of Childhood' in *More Bristol Lives*, Bristol Broadsides, p7-25.

ALICE WHITE
dates unknown, BEDMINSTER BARROW GIRL

Referring to Alice White as the Bedminster Barrow Girl feels like doing her an injustice. Because yes, that was what she was known as, but she was so much more. Alice's children Nelly and James White shared the story of their mother with the Windmills of Time local history project. They say that Alice worked hard every day until she was 70, humping hundredweight sacks of potatoes and coal from one place to another, hence her nickname as the Bedminster Barrow Girl.

"She never had a holiday and yet she always had time for others," Nelly and James said, revealing that Alice thought nothing of opening up her house at 76 Philip Street, Bedminster, to women who were fleeing abusive husbands and needed a place to stay. "Battered wives with black eyes and bruises, thrown out by their husbands, could always find a refuge at 76 Philip Street. They were always put in my bed," remembers Nelly.[344]

EDITH ROBINSON WHITE
born 1878, PHILANTHROPIST

In Victorian England there was no shortage of educated, middle-class ladies doing good work for the benefit of others, or that's how it seemed anyway. And Edith Sara Robinson White falls into this category. Born in Surbiton, Surrey, she trained to be a teacher after leaving school, but following her marriage to widowed schoolmaster Christopher Robinson in 1902, who was 14 years her senior, she moved to Bristol with him and his children from his

---

344 windmillsoftime.wordpress.com/2014/03/03/bedminsters-backstreets-part-3/

first marriage. The family settled at 44 Victoria Park, Fishponds. Following Christopher's death, Edith married again in 1927, this time to Mr H White.

Among Edith's many posts, she served on the Bristol Board of Guardians, she was a City Councillor for Stapleton, she became a Justice of the Peace in 1927, and was 'Chairman' of Bristol North Women's Conservative Association. During World War One, Edith worked tirelessly for the Red Cross Society as a fundraiser. At the risk of writing a long list, I've only included a small selection of Edith's good works to give you a taste, but in essence she was particularly concerned with causes that benefited women and children.

LYDIA ROGERS WHITE
1760–1827, LITERARY HOSTESS

Born in Bristol, Lydia Rogers White was the youngest surviving daughter to an heiress mother and, when her father died in 1797, she was left very comfortable. As such, Lydia was never troubled financially. However, while Lydia's two sisters both married, Lydia's single status seemed to bother her, and the Bristolian writer Fanny Burney noted in 1780 that Lydia was threatening to take her own life because she was lonely.[345] Prior to her father's death, Lydia had devoted two years to caring for him. They lived in Bath where Lydia had become a popular character at the Bath Pump Rooms and was admired for her great wit. She set up a literary salon in Bath, where her guests included the poet Lord Byron and his admirer Caroline Lamb. Lydia later moved to London and set up a salon at her home in Grosvenor Square,

345 B Rizzo (ed), 2003, *The Early Journals and Letters of Fanny Burney*, McGill Queen's University Press. Fanny Burney is profiled in Volume One of *The Women Who Built Bristol*.

before embarking on a grand tour of Europe before ill health forced her to return home to England.

MAUD WHITE
1916-2003, PUB LANDLADY

When Maud White died in 2003, she had the honour of being the oldest pub landlady working in the Bristol area. Maud had run the Cross Keys in Hanham since 1956, pulling pints for 47 years. Speaking at a party in 1996, celebrating 40 years behind the bar and her 80th birthday, Maud said: "I've got to know all my customers over the years and watched their children grow up. It's hard work but I enjoy it and I've got no plans to retire."[346]

Prior to coming to the Cross Keys, Maud and her husband Joseph had first run the Sandy Bank Inn in Batheaston in 1944 and then the White Lion in Redfield. Following Joseph's death in 1966, Maud kept going solo. A portrait of Maud with her two dogs still hangs proudly on the Cross Keys' wall. Indeed, Maud was so well liked that, more than 20 years after her death, some locals still refer to the Cross Key not by its official name but simply as 'Maud's'.[347]

MARGARET WHITEHEAD
1936-2018, HISTORIAN, ARCHIVIST

For decades, Margaret Whitehead was easily recognisable as she cycled around Keynsham, a town she knew inside out and for which she was an admired historian.

346 'My 40 years behind bars', *Bristol Evening Post*, 3 December 1996.
347 With thanks to Annabel Marshall for the nomination of Maud White to this book.

Born Margaret Patricia Down in Dublin, she married Trevor Whitehead in that city in 1962. They moved to Keynsham in 1968 where their son was born a few years later. Coming to Keynsham was not a random decision, though, because Margaret was able to trace a family link to the town back to the 1860s.

A lifelong history lover, Margaret extended this passion to archaeology and, between 1977 and 1991, she was involved with the maintenance of the former site of Keynsham Abbey.

In 2009, Margaret received the Good Citizen Award in recognition of her work. In 1987, she became the Archivist for the former abbey and joined the committee. This was the perfect outlet for her passion for local history, which included recording the memories of some of Keynsham's older residents so that their stories would always be remembered.

When the Keynsham Heritage Trust was established in 1987, Margaret was the clear choice to be the director. And, alongside Barbara Lowe, Margaret assumed joint responsibility for the archives of the Keynsham Collection. As you might imagine, with this wealth of local knowledge, Margaret was instrumental in the creation of a number of local history books.[348]

SARAH WILKINS
1849-1917, MATRIARCH

There is a property in Bradley Stoke called Woodland Grange, which was once a fine house that stood in well maintained grounds. The house was built in 1908 by a Bristolian builder called George Wilkins to accommodate both himself and his wife Sarah, who had retired to Bradley Stoke after living on Cromwell Street,

348 With thanks to a tribute by Sue Tatford in the Keynsham and Saltford Local History Society's 2019 book *Around Keynsham and Saltford Past and Present*.

Montpelier. George designed the house to have a dining room that was 61 feet long so that it could fit a table long enough to seat Sarah and himself, their 16 children, plus their 31 grandchildren. In the summer months, Sarah and George would invite local children to a tea party and games afternoon in their gardens. And at Christmas, they would give a silver sixpence to the children who came to sing carols.[349]

ANNIE WILLIAMS
1860-1943, SUFFRAGETTE

Hailing from a humble Cornish family where her father was a carpenter, Annie Williams was afforded the best possible education and qualified to become a teacher before rapidly becoming a headteacher before she was 40. However, Annie gave up her career in education in 1908 in order to commit herself fully to the suffrage cause. She became a paid Organiser for the Women's Social and Political Union (WSPU) in Bristol, working alongside Annie Kenney, one of the Pankhursts' most trusted soldiers in the cause of votes for women.[350] Like many suffragists, Annie is missing from the 1911 census in protest at not having political representation.

Although Annie W later returned to Cornwall, she remained in close communication with Annie K and continued her work for the WSPU as an Organiser, travelling around the UK to help facilitate meetings and events for the cause.

On one occasion, she spoke in Batheaston in support of the WSPU's self-denial week, where people were encouraged to give something up for a week and donate the money they would have

349 The building remains but has been repurposed for business use.
350 Annie Kenney is profiled in Volume One of *The Women Who Built Bristol*.

spent on that luxury to the cause.

A local newspaper report stated: "Miss Williams said they had to remember that while they were enjoying themselves in that delightful sunshine, there were other women shut up in the cells of English prisons for deeds of militancy. Those women in the cells saw the same vision which had ever been seen by reformers, by people that stepped out of the ordinary way of life, where all seemed safe to tread the unknown, a *via dolorosa*[351] ending very often in martyrdom and a crown of thorns. Their critics regarded them as fanatics who were giving up the real things of life for shadows."[352]

Annie was arrested three times during her fight for the vote and later returned to teaching. She never married or had her own family.

EMMA WILLIAMS
born c1830, COTTON FACTORY WORKER

The manager of the Great Western Cotton Factory in Barton Hill was John Ashworth who, unfortunately, had a reputation for unkindness towards his largely female workforce. He was known to prowl around the factory, closely watching the workers and monitoring for any mistakes they made. For instance, the women would be fined every time a thread broke during their work, so to get around this the women started hiding their mistakes and taking broken bundles of thread home to dispose of in secret. However, Ashworth soon rumbled this scheme and introduced a policy of searching staff at the end of each day. As a result, the

351 A '*via dolorosa*' is a religious processional route, representing the route that Jesus was forced to take by the Romans on his way to the crucifixion.
352 'The women's war', *Bath Chronicle and Weekly Gazette*, 18 July 1914.

factory gates were kept closed at the end of each working day and the slow process of searching the women would begin. It didn't take long before the workforce took matters into their own hands. And they weren't just protesting about the fines and locked gates, they were also pursuing a long-running complaint against Ashworth for their low wages.

On 26 February 1852, some 600 factory workers stopped work at 6.10pm and attempted to leave but of course the gates were locked. The women demanded that the gates be opened but the gates remained closed. On the other side of the gates, a crowd gathered which included angry people who had recently been dismissed from the factory by Ashworth for petty reasons. Stones were thrown at the factory and 148 window panes were broken by the time the affray was resolved. The situation was becoming dangerous with almost 2,000 people eventually involved on both sides of the gate.

Ashworth arrived with two guard dogs and a sword which hit one of the workers when he swung it around. Emma Williams was knocked to the ground where she hit her head. Another factory worker, Sarah Leonard, confirmed in court that Ashworth had then picked Emma up and shaken her several times. Ashworth proceeded to kick Emma three times, he then struck her again with the sword and ordered that the factory's fire hoses be set upon Emma and the other trapped women claiming that "it would be a nice lark". The women were hosed down for more than an hour. The ensuing panic caused a mass surge of women against the locked gates and many women were trampled in their rush to escape.

Emma, who had worked at the factory for six years, promptly led a group of women workers to raise a complaint of assault against Ashworth, which was taken up by the Magistrates Court. Ashworth claimed that "he was not only justified in what he did, but deserved applause for it, inasmuch as he had taken a very lenient mode of quelling a riot". He also denied the severity of his assault of Emma and the other women, and claimed that the use of the hose had been overstated. Clearly, the magistrate saw through him and Ashworth was fined £5: a result that "was received with the loudest demonstrations of joy" from the women when they heard the news.[353]

ALICE WILLS
1827–1881, SOCIAL REFORMER

We hear a lot about the Wills family in Bristol, chiefly for the men's involvement in the tobacco industry. But we don't hear so much about the women in the Wills family, which is a shame because there were plenty of interesting women behind those men. One was Alice Wills, previously Hodgkinson, who was married to Henry Overton Wills III (the same HO Wills who is honoured by the University of Bristol's tower at the top of Park Street). Alice was born at Redland Knoll and the couple married in 1853 in Plymouth and had seven children. She is buried in the family tomb at Arnos Vale Cemetery and, reporting on her death, *The Times* wrote on 7 December 1881: "On Sunday, the 4th Dec, at Redland Knoll, Bristol, after a very short illness, Alice, the beloved wife of Henry Overton Wills."

353 'X', *Wells Journal*, 6 March 1852.

GWENDOLEN WILLS
1872-1949, SOCIAL WORKER, NURSE

If your grandfather was Henry Overton Wills, the man who had founded one of the biggest tobacco companies in the world, then your family had so much money that you didn't need to work if you didn't want to. But Anne Victoria Gwendolen Wills, known as Annie as a child and Gwendolen as an adult, *did* want to work and she devoted her life to doing good for others.

Gwendolen's father was Stephen Wills, who was the eldest son of Henry Wills, a man who had 18 children. As a child, she grew up in Abbey Park, Keynsham and in 1928, after the deaths of her parents, she moved to Longreach House on the Bath Road.

Gwendolen always chose to work. In the 1890s, she had trained as a Nurse at University College Hospital in London and worked there after qualifying. By the time of the 1911 census, Gwendolen was the Matron of Her Majesty's Hospital for Sick Children in Stepney, London, which had been set up by Dr Barnardo. She continued to work as a Nurse in London until 1923 when she retired and began to focus on her other interests.

She had attended a number of Dr Barnardo's fundraising events, and had supported the Young Helpers' League by giving talks and helping to raise funds for them to support sick children. In January 1918, women in Keynsham formed a branch of the Women's Institute (WI) and invited Gwendolen to be their President: this was a role she gladly accepted and she remained in post until her death in 1949. The WI would become a significant part of Gwendolen's life.

The Keynsham WI rapidly grew from 43 members in 1918 to an impressive 233 by 1921, which seems extraordinary to imagine now. The group quickly outgrew the church schoolroom where they had initially met and bought their own premises near the

Public Hall (now the Drill Hall), which boasted not only a meeting hall but also a kitchen, cloakroom and electric lights.

As well as supporting her local branch, Gwendolen was a popular speaker at other WI branches to which she was often invited to give talks sharing details of her travels to places as far flung as Australia (she didn't rate the Sydney Harbour Bridge, declaring it to be "a monstrosity"), Canada, Fiji and the US. And her talks weren't confined to her travels, because she also spoke to WI groups about issues including home nursing, the psychology of childhood and whether or not married women should remain at work.

Alongside the WI, Gwendolen was an active member of the Frome Division of the Conservative and Unionist Party, attending meetings and giving campaign speeches throughout the 1920s when she stood for election to the local council. In April 1924, Gwendolen was elected to the local council, beating her next placed rival by more than 150 votes. As a Councillor, Gwendolen concerned herself with issues such as providing recreation grounds for children, securing good housing for those on lower incomes, and improving the conditions of slum housing.

She was repeatedly re-elected until she stood down in 1943. She also became chair of the Keynsham Division of the Conservative and Unionist Party in 1930 and, just as she did for the WI, she opened up her home at Longreach for the Party to use for social events. In 1930, she was sworn in as a County Magistrate for Somerset and served in that role until her death.

Clearly a sharp mind, Gwendolen kept pace with the rapidly changing technology of the age. As well as owning a car, she was also one of the very first people in Keynsham to have a telephone line installed in her home: her number was Saltford 36, which is an indication of how rare phone numbers were back then.

As well as her political roles, Gwendolen held a number of prominent posts locally, which included being: Chair of the Keynsham Hospital Management Board, Vice Chair of Keynsham Out-Relief Union, Vice Chair of Keynsham Board of Guardians, 'Chairman' of the Frome Area Guardians committee, and President of the Keynsham Branch of Soldiers, Sailors and Airmen's Families Association.

In addition, Gwendolen was Secretary to the Keynsham and Saltford Nursing Association for 25 years; in 1934 she was C of the Bath & West Club (which had started in 1931 as the Bath Nurses' Club), and she was involved with the Bristol Maternity Hospital and Temporary Home, which welcomed unmarried mothers.

All of this is only the tip of the iceberg, if I carried on this entry would degenerate into a long list of all the good causes that Gwendolen worked for. She truly was a generous-hearted woman who cared deeply about the community, and particularly the fortunes of women and children.[354]

MONA WILSON
1872–1954, SOCIAL REFORMER

Mona Wilson devoted her life to trying to improve the conditions of working women in industrial areas of the UK. After joining the civil service in 1911, she became one of the first women to earn the same pay as a man doing the same role.

Her father, Rev James Wilson, was the headmaster of Clifton College, so Mona was educated at Clifton High School before attending Newnham College at the University of Cambridge.

---

354 The work of Jane Bambury was very helpful in writing this entry, particularly her article about Gwendolen Wills in *The Journal of the Keynsham & Saltford Local History Society*, Series 3, No 3, 2022, p5-14.

With a strong interest in social and industrial issues, Mona joined the Women's Trade Union League where she met many like-minded women and would later become the Secretary. When Mona's work started catching people's attention, she was commissioned to write a handbook concerning the legal regulations affecting women working in factories, workshops, retail and laundries.

As a result of this, in 1902 she investigated the social conditions of an area of East London, later leading an enquiry into housing, income and employment in Dundee: *The Times* called this one of the most exhaustive social studies ever undertaken.[355]

The work kept coming. In 1909, Mona joined the board of the Trade Boards Act, enforcing minimum wages and working conditions in some of the most exploitative industries, such as chain-making and paper-box making. She also worked for the Home Office on a committee looking into industrial accidents. When she joined the National Insurance Commission in 1911, her annual salary of £1,000 made her the highest-paid female civil servant of the time and one of the first women to receive equal pay to a man in the same role.

Later in her life, Mona became a researcher and writer, publishing biographies of a great number of female writers from the 18th and 19th centuries. Additionally, she wrote a number of short stories under the name Monica Moore, which were generally tales of working women.

355 'Obituary: Miss Mona Wilson', *The Times*, 30 October 1954.

GERTRUDE WINCHESTER
1888–1934, SINGER

Bristol's very own Dame Vera Lynn was Gertrude Rose Winchester from Effingham Road, St Andrew's. By 1911, Gertrude was working as a professional singer. Her first listed performance was at the Colston Hall[356] in 1902 when she was just 14 with a rendition of 'Abide With Me'. Gertrude later studied music at Trinity College, London, and became a member of the choir at City Road Baptist Chapel as well as the Bristol Royal Orpheus Glee Society. During World War One, Gertrude used her talents to try and keep the public's morale up and she performed in more than 180 concerts between 1914 and 1918. When the war ended, Gertrude formed the Bristol Ladies' Choir. She lived in Redland and sang at concerts all over the UK. "She will be long remembered for her singing to wounded soldiers," lamented the *Western Daily Press*.[357]

REBECCA WOLFSON
1879–1961, TEACHER

Rebecca Wolfson was the middle of seven children to Pase and Sophia Wolfson. Her father Pase was a picture frame maker and glazier, and the family lived on Woodwell Crescent close to the city centre. The Wolfsons were members of Bristol's Jewish community and in the Victorian era it seems the city was not always welcoming to Jews.

Rebecca was a pupil at Hotwell Girls' School and hoped to

---

356 While I acknowledge the Colston Hall has now rightly been renamed and is now called the Bristol Beacon, I am referring to it by its original name in this book because that is the name it was known by when the events in the book happened.
357 'Bristol Vocalist's Death', *Western Daily Press*, 19 June 1934.

become a teacher there. However, the school was troubled by the fact that, in the Jewish faith, Saturday is the sabbath and no work must be done on that day. But school examinations were held on a Saturday and Rebecca was therefore unable to sit them: the school seemed to be considering excluding her on this basis. The case made the pages of several local newspapers. Letters were sent on Rebecca's behalf from her father Pase as well as their rabbi, Rev L Mendelsohn. The school complained that Rebecca had missed several lessons that had been held on Saturdays because they had coincided with religious festivals. The upshot of the case, as heard by the Bristol School Board, was that Rebecca was allowed to stay at the school but that she would not be promised employment with them as she had hoped. It's worth saying that some members of the Board did express the view that the attitude of the school was very out of date. The Board made it clear that it was not happy about the precedent that they felt Rebecca's case had set.

By the time of the 1911 census, the Wolfson family had relocated to London (perhaps believing it to be a more welcoming city) and Rebecca was indeed working as a teacher. By 1939, she was living in Northampton and still teaching.

CHARLOTTE WOOKERJEE
1852-1914, MUSIC TEACHER

Charlotte Pergam (as she was originally called) led a fascinating life of intrigue and deception: a music teacher with no real qualifications; a widow who likely never actually married the man with whom she had a son.

Born in Cheshire to lawyer Edward and Mary Pergam, Charlotte was the eldest of three daughters to a respectable Victorian couple. Yet despite this veneer of respectability,

Edward declared himself bankrupt and young Charlotte was sent to Devon to live with her widowed grandmother Mary and unmarried aunt Ann, who both ostensibly brought her up from this point. By virtue of being away from her parents, Charlotte also missed growing up with her younger sisters Julia and Laura. Charlotte's mother Mary left Edward around 1860 and moved to Plymouth with daughters Julia and Laura, so the women in the family may have had more contact after this time.

When grandmother Mary died in 1864, aunt Ann assumed full responsibility for Charlotte and the pair moved to Plymouth where they boarded in the home of another family until 1879 when they moved to London. In the capital, when she was about 20, Charlotte met an Indian merchant called Cowasjee Wookerjee who imported goods from India via his business in London's Leadenhall Market.

Charlotte and Cowasjee lived together as man and wife, although no record of any formal marriage exists and it is likely they may never have actually married at all. Two sons were born in London: Pheroze in 1879 (who died the following year) and Khoosow in 1880. But it seems the relationship didn't last more than a few years, because by 1885 Cowasjee was back in India and Charlotte and Khoosow were living in Ealing, London, with aunt Ann. Charlotte disguised the fact she was a single mother by calling herself a widow. By this time, Charlotte was earning a living as a music teacher and a singer: she performed as Madame Elcho.

Branding herself a Professor of Music, Charlotte claimed to be a Fellow of the Society of Science, Letters and Art. This was a Society run out of a house in Kensington which asked students to sit for exams, although these were never marked, and which handed out diplomas, although these were purchased. Charlotte traded off this qualification for a number of years until the

Society was outed as being fraudulent in 1892 and those behind the Society were imprisoned. It is quite possible that she didn't realise she had been scammed.

After a few years in Ealing, Charlotte, Khoosow and Ann moved to Southall where she continued to teach piano, organ, singing and music theory, while performing regularly as part of a musical group. By the end of the 1890s, the trio relocated to Chippenham where Charlotte shrugged off her Madame Elcho persona and instead used the more exotic teaching name of Mrs Cowasjee Wookerjee. By 1895, the family had moved again, this time to Keynsham. Charlotte taught music and was the Musical Director for concerts in Bath and Bristol, specifically on Park Street and in Staple Hill, and at the Bristol Workhouse Infirmary in what is now Castle Park. In 1902, Charlotte applied for a licence to turn a property at 11 Dighton Street, Kingsdown, into a singing, dancing and music venue.

The 1901 census shows Charlotte, Khoosow and Ann living in Cumberland Street, St Pauls, which was a fashionable address at the time. Khoosow, now 20, was working as a clerk for the post office. He went on to marry in 1907 and remained in Bristol, living in St Phillips and becoming a father of four. Although Charlotte is missing from the 1911 census, newspaper reports suggest she was in Frampton Cotterell by this time running a market garden before her death in 1914 and subsequent burial at Coalpit Heath.[358]

358 Huge thanks to Lucy Whitfield of The Women Who Made Me project: thewomenwhomademe. wordpress.com/2022/03/05/charlotte-c-ws-story/

ELIZABETH WOOLNOUGH
1742–1825, LANDOWNER

On 1 September 1757, 15-year-old Elizabeth Woolnough married Sir John Smyth of the Ashton Court Estate at St Augustine The Lesser in Bristol, and this marriage cemented the union of two wealthy landowning families.

Elizabeth was an heiress who brought with her a marriage settlement of £40,000 made up of properties in England and Jamaica. Her ancestors on both her mother and her father's sides had been very successful merchants, and only-child Elizabeth inherited all of their collected income. This was a massive boost to the Smyth family's estate: one estimate puts the income from the sale of sugar from one plantation in Jamaica alone at £17,000 amassed over several decades. This is a staggering amount of money: it is equivalent to just over £2.5 million in contemporary money and would have been a vast fortune in Elizabeth's time.

The Smyth family had long been known for their mercantile interests. Jarit Smyth (John's father) was a member of the Bristol Society of Merchant Venturers, an organisation which lobbied on behalf of Bristol participants in the African, American and West Indian trades.

This suggests that their links to the trade in enslaved Africans could date back to the 1630s, which would predate Bristol's first formal entry into the slave trade which has been noted as 1698.[359]

Already wealthy, the cash injection that Elizabeth brought to the Smyth family led them to make substantial renovations to Ashton Court. It is thought that it was Elizabeth who had the idea of inviting renowned landscape gardener Humphry Repton to remodel the grounds at Ashton Court.

359 Madge Dresser, Laurence Hann eds, 2013, *Slavery and the British Country House*, Historic England, p32.

Following the death of John in 1802, Elizabeth moved to live at Clift House in Bedminster, which has since been demolished and is now the site of a large garden centre. On 23 April 1822, there was a grand ceremony to mark the opening of Coronation Road which was led by the Dowager Lady Smyth in a coach with four horses, in front of a procession that included Captain Smyth's troop of Yeomary. At this time, the new area of Southville was popular with artisans, seafaring men and people trying to make their way in the world and was seen as a step up from the labouring classes who lived in nearby Bedminster.[360]

LURLEEN WYNTER
1917–2022, COMMUNITY STALWART

Known to the people of St Pauls as 'Mother Wynter', Lurleen Wynter lived an astonishing life during her 105 years.

Born in Jamaica, Lurleen travelled on the HMT Empire Windrush and arrived in Bristol in 1950. In common with many families at the time, she left her children behind until she could afford to send for them to join her in the UK. As other families began to arrive in Bristol from Jamaica, Lurleen let people stay with her until they could find homes of their own. Her family remember regularly finding strangers sitting in her home eating soup, as Lurleen offered them a warm welcome here in Bristol.

Lurleen's grandson Nicholas Feurtado posted on social media after his grandmother's death and said: "During my 20s, I can remember seeing chaps who worked on doors as bouncers, who scared the life out of most, suddenly turn into little boys and gush when they met her as she had looked after many of them when

360 CLASS, 2004, *Southville People & Places*, Fiducia Press, p20.

they were children."

The church was a key part of Lurleen's life and she was involved with the City Road Baptist Church as well as the wider community in St Pauls. She was an integral part of what would become the St Pauls Carnival, which played to her love for the arts. Lurleen threw herself into community work and charity fundraising, including raising money to buy cows for families in Africa to enable them to become self-sufficient, and fundraising to help research for sickle-cell anaemia. In 1999, Lurleen was selected to receive Maundy Money from Queen Elizabeth II, in recognition of her charity work over the decades.

There was even a story that Lurleen wrote a letter to the disgraced Tory MP Jonathan Aitken when he was sent to prison for perjury in 1999, in which she sent him a £5 note and suggested he buy himself something from the prison shop. She told him that she would be praying for him and that she hoped he would take time to reflect on his actions.

When she was in her late 90s, Lurleen auditioned for a TV advert for the soft drink Lilt, which had put a call out for "a charming Caribbean lady of senior years who exudes warmth, charm, fun, wit and welcoming friendliness". While Lurleen certainly met that brief, unfortunately she was not selected to take part.[361]

LILIAN YEATES
c1890-1967, PUB LANDLADY

Born to a Bristolian railway family, Lilian Young married a railway man when she wed Charles Yeates. But, unlike the men in

---

361 bristol247.com/news-and-features/news/tributes-paid-much-loved-st-pauls-community-elder

her family, Lilian became a pub landlady.

Lilian's father was a railway platelayer, which meant that he checked the conditions of the tracks to ensure they were safe for use. He worked on the harbour railway in Bristol, of which a few historical reminders can still be seen close to the M Shed Museum, and therefore the family lived close to the Harbourside.

After school, Lilian worked as a waiter in a railway restaurant and helped her mother to look after the boarders who lodged at their home. She then moved to Chippenham in 1912 to work at the station restaurant there, and by 1915 she had married train guard Charles Yeates. The couple had two sons.

However, in 1932 Lilian decided to move away from railway work and with Charles she bought the Old Road Inn in Chippenham, which was a popular drinking haunt for railway workers.

Lilian had worked for the previous landlord running the inn's kitchens, so her move to become manager made good sense. Charles was named as the inn's landlord, although he kept his job as a train guard.

In reality, then, Lilian did the grunt work in keeping the pub running, assisted by her two sons in breaks from their official jobs. Astonishingly, despite being the main worker at the inn, the 1939 Register lists Lilian's role as "unpaid domestic duties at home", which is pretty rude.

Charles died early in World War Two and her son Ewart was also killed in service. Lilian suffered these two close bereavements within a year.

The Old Road Inn was a central part of Chippenham life, and a key meeting place for railway workers, so Lilian was well known to everyone.

Lilian remained as landlady of the Old Road Inn until she retired in 1957, although even during retirement Lilian kept up her central role in the community, as well as enjoying time with her grandchildren.[362]

FLORENCE YOUNG
born 1920, LAUNDRY WORKER

Florence Young grew up in Hanham. As a ten-year-old, she remembers playing with her friends in a large field known as Thirty Acres which was off Hanham High Street, and would later become a part of the Kleen-E-Zee factory site. With only a bottle of water and some bread and jam to sustain them, the children would make a den out of the hay and play house there until it grew dark. When haymaking season was over, the field's owners let the field to Cobham's Aerial Display, and the kids would switch from playing house with the hay to doing acrobatics on the wings of the aeroplanes.

Florence left school in 1934 at the age of 14 and started work at Willways Laundry, which was known as the "white slave factory" and was staffed almost exclusively by women. She recalled: "I was working in the starch house and I wore clogs up to my knees and a rubber apron down to my ankles ... The pay was 10 shillings a week, and I remember working on Christmas Eve until 9 o'clock." She worked at Willways Dye & Laundry Company for two years, leaving this gruelling labour when she suffered a ruptured appendix caused by lifting the heavy buckets of starch.

However, handing in her notice was no picnic for Florence. "We had a devil of a forewoman," she remembered. And after telling the forewoman that her father had said she could no longer lift the buckets, the forewoman told Florence: "Your father

362 Huge thanks to Lucy Whitfield of The Women Who Made Me project: thewomenwhomademe. wordpress.com/2017/11/28/lilian-ys-story

doesn't run this factory." At the age of 16, Florence moved to work at Langridges corset factory on Two Mile Hill, and stayed there for two and a half years until she got married. Her husband had been injured in a work accident and received £500 compensation which, as Florence notes, was "a fortune back then."[363]

LILY YOUNG
born 1879, COTTON FACTORY WORKER

Having been born in St Philips Marsh, Lily Young went to work at the Great Western Cotton Factory as a cotton winder. She was married to an ironworks labourer from Barton Hill, with whom she had a son, Reginald, in 1909. Their family life in Whitehall was shaken up in 1914 when her husband George was called up to serve during World War One. In October 1917, Lily received word that George was missing and, despite its best efforts, the Bristol Inquiry Bureau was unable to ever find out what happened to him, writing to Lily in February 1919 to say: "We have not succeeded in hearing anything." Lily was one of thousands of women in Bristol who were widowed during the war.

---

363 Florence Young, 1988, in *Hanham Our Home*, p15, 29–30.

ACKNOWLEDGEMENTS

That there is a third volume of this book is no small thing. As ever, a work such as this cannot be done in isolation although, obviously, I take full responsibility for any accidental errors that may have crept into the book despite my best intentions. If you do spot a howling factual error, please let me know and I will endeavour to correct it in any reprints. My enormous thanks go to the many people, credited throughout, who have nominated women for inclusion in this book.

Volume Three has been a slow burn, in large part due to the many distractions offered by researching and writing other books, which is definitely not a complaint. But it's been a big job and I would like to express my very heartfelt thanks to the following people for their various contributions in a variety of forms, many of which they perhaps didn't even realise they were doing.

Those thanks are particularly due to: Tina Altwegg (for her stunning cover illustration), Clive Burlton, Joe Burt (for yet again designing a beautiful book), Eugene Byrne (who patiently endured an endless stream of emails that began, "Hello Eugene, just a quick question…"), Paul Duffus (who has to live with me), Dawn Dyer, Helen Holland, Richard Jones, Andrew Kelly (who prompted me to stop talking about writing Volume Three and to, perhaps, just get on and do it), Michael 'Mike' Manson, Naomi Paxton, Kate Spreadbury and Lori Streich (proofreaders *par excellence*), Philippa Walker, Evelyn Welch, Lucy Whitfield and Rosie Wilby. A special thank-you to Amanda Adams, Ryan Garvey and the team at Bristol Old Vic for all their help with the book launch: I adore this incredible theatre.

My thanks also to the staff at Bristol Archives and to the wonderful people who keep the many libraries in the Bristol and South Gloucestershire areas going, and who patiently tolerated me asking them to find the dustiest books from the back of the stacks. Our libraries are a phenomenal resource and we must use and enjoy them while we can.

ABOUT THE AUTHOR

Jane Duffus qualified as a journalist in 2001 and has worked as a journalist and editor for numerous best-selling national magazines and publishers. *The Women Who Built Bristol: Volume Three* is her seventh book, and Jane has edited several books for other authors. After relocating from London to Bristol in 2008, Jane founded the award-winning What The Frock! Comedy project in 2012 to challenge an industry that knowingly overlooks women's talent. In addition, she continues to work as a freelance writer, editor and public speaker, and has spoken at events ranging from the Edinburgh Fringe Festival to a Berlin arts centre and everything in between. Jane takes a break from all of the above by running ridiculously long distances for fun.

BY THE SAME AUTHOR

Yeovil Cinemas Through Time (Amberley, 2012)
The What The Frock! Book of Funny Women (BCF Books, 2015)
The Women Who Built Bristol: Volume One (Tangent, 2018)
The Women Who Built Bristol: Volume Two (Tangent, 2019)
Elegantly Understated: 175 Years of the Fears Watch Company (Bristol Books, 2021)
These Things Happen: The Sarah Records Story (Tangent, 2023)